GO AB31457

THE ECONOMICS OF INTERNATIONAL TRADE

THE ECONOMICS OF
INTERNATIONAL
TRADE

An Independent View

David Z. Rich

Q

Quorum Books

New York · Westport, Connecticut · London

3 8 2

R 4 9 8

Library of Congress Cataloging-in-Publication Data

Rich, David Z.
  The economics of international trade : an independent view / David
Z. Rich.
        p.   cm.
  Includes bibliographical references (p.   ) and index.
  ISBN 0-89930-753-1 (alk. paper)
  1. International trade.   I. Title.
HF1379.R53   1992
382—dc20   91-33600

British Library Cataloguing in Publication Data is available.

Copyright © 1992 by David Z. Rich

All rights reserved. No portion of this book may be
reproduced, by any process or technique, without the
express written consent of the publisher.

Library of Congress Catalog Card Number: 91-33600
ISBN: 0-89930-753-1

First published in 1992

Quorum Books, One Madison Avenue, New York, NY 10010
An imprint of Greenwood Publishing Group, Inc.

Printed in the United States of America

The paper used in this book complies with the
Permanent Paper Standard issued by the National
Information Standards Organization (Z39.48-1984).

10 9 8 7 6 5 4 3 2 1

This work is dedicated to my mother, Vanessa, to the memory of my father, to my sisters, family, and friends, and especially to Diana Lerner, for the everyday dynamic disequilibrium.

CONTENTS

Part I

THE PROBLEM SITUATION

Chapter 1

ON THE NATURE OF THIS WORK

Twentieth-century economists have formulated competing and often conflicting theories about the economic and political mechanisms underlying the dynamics of international trade. One economist, Jacob Viner, asserted in his *Studies in the Theory of International Trade* that the classical theory of trade developed by David Hume and John Stuart Mill prevails as the predominant theory, inasmuch as "no strikingly different mechanism has yet been convincingly suggested." [1]

In retrospect, however, it would seem that Viner's opinion was stated somewhat hastily. At the time he expressed his view, John Maynard Keynes's *General Theory* [2] had appeared and significant contributions of many Keynesian disciples were already incorporated into the lexicon of international economics. Such terms as *international multiplier, marginal propensities to save, consume, import, accelerator,* and *marginal efficiency of capital* were then and are now conceptual tools of the international trade economist. Moreover, as the world's business leaders meet in international commerce using post-Keynesian theory, economists are certainly justified in adapting concepts originally developed for the national economy to meet the requirements of the international arena. These are the concepts that economists have been taught and have learned to master.

Regardless of the lapse of decades since Viner made his statement, considering the manifold changes in the world's economies with respect to economic trade theory, much of Viner's sentiment is perhaps justified. The general theory of international economics remains fairly close to the theories of Hume and

Mill, rendering international economics the dubious honor of being that branch of economic reasoning most in need of repair and restatement.

The reasons for this state of affairs are twofold, and both are historical. The first reason is due to the almost total rejection of mercantilism after the publication of Adam Smith's *Wealth of Nations,* a work that had placed the focus primarily on the national economy, demonstrating how the division of labor can increase efficiency while maintaining a competitive product. Indeed, the era of the Industrial Revolution that had begun when Smith's book was published resulted in classical and neoclassical economists following Smith's tradition in their discussions on the causes and origins of national wealth and relegating international economics to a mere extension of domestic economic activity.

Mercantilism was strictly a British approach to economic wealth and differed radically and indeed contrasted with its French counterpart of physiocracy. In the cool rationalism for which French thinking is traditionally famous, physiocracy was a philosophical-cum-economic theory that maintained that a country's wealth stems from the productivity of its soil. Agriculture was the most important industry, for it provided the food necessary for feeding the population. On the basis of surplus foodstuffs, trade would enable these surpluses to be exported for goods and services not obtainable—either in sufficient quantities or at all—from the domestic markets. The greater the crop yield, therefore, the hardier the livestock yields, the healthier the population, and the stronger the economic position.

The mercantilist school both differed from and rejected the logical physiocracy of the French. In the tradition of empiricism and experimentation that had developed in Great Britain, the British approach maintained that a nation's wealth is based solely on its trading prowess. For this, it was of no significance whether the goods traded were domestic in origin or acquired from other lands. Wealth was proclaimed in coin obtained by trading more than was received in goods and services with surpluses made up in coin, thereby possessing a claim on the trading partner's economy. This situation was termed the favorable balance of trade and this was sought on the part of the British exporters to acquire surplus foreign coin.

The difference between the mercantilist and physiocratic approaches to trade was also manifested in their respective approaches to exploration. Both the British and the French engaged in the expansion of their countries' power by encouraging military conquests of lands. The British, as subjects of an island country, were very aware of the burden of markets placed on them by their geographical separation, and while they did not neglect the fertile lands of their agricultural sectors, they did recognize their limited space and the lack of resources. By obtaining the natural resources of other lands and by mobilizing the peoples in these lands into cheap labor, they could direct their activities to foreign commerce and obtain foreign currencies to continue their activities.

The French approach to exploration was not so much as to conquer other peoples, but to obtain new agricultural lands so that their produce could be traded under French rule and in French coin. The French enslaved conquered peoples to till the soils and increase agricultural yields, so that surplus crops and agricultural by-products could be traded for finished goods and services.

These two different philosophical and practical approaches found common ground in the reasoning of Adam Smith. His French was sufficient to allow him to engage in deep philosophical and economic discussions with Dr. Francois Quesnay, the main spokesman for the physiocratic school; he also debated with Quesnay's followers. With Smith's background in the mercantilistic tradition, and his participation in the debates with Quesnay and his school, the ideas were formulated into the theory stated in the *Wealth of Nations*.

Smith recognized that the degree and kinds of enterprise existing in Great Britain and France were not, in themselves, adequate for economic expansion. Guilds and other forms of unions that protected their members' status and the qualities of their trades were limiting both economic expansion and growth. Instead, he argued for private and free enterprise in which individuals take the risks and reap the profits or bear the losses, as the case may be. While Smith considered agriculture to be of prime importance, he nevertheless deflated its physiocratic significance and placed it soundly within the economic function of feeding the populace. Surplus agricultural produce could most certainly be exported and goods and services not provided by the domestic economy imported. Hence, for Smith, international commerce should not be neglected, as it is important for stimulating production and earning foreign coin. However, emphasis should be placed on individual initiative and enterprise as the means of building national wealth because enterprise brings standard and new products into the markets and stimulates new demand and competition. Therefore, both agricultural development and the establishment of domestic and foreign markets should be both the consequences and the supportive factors of private enterprise.[3]

Historically, the impact of the *Wealth of Nations* is that it pointed inward to the development of the national economy, based on individual initiative and enterprise. Smith's analysis of the division of labor was of such importance for the Industrial Revolution that had just begun when his book appeared that the readers of the *Wealth of Nations* paid little or no attention to his comments on international trade. The focus of Smith's followers was mainly internal, on the domestic economy and the establishment of entrepreneurship and the division of labor as the factors of economic growth and development.

Smith's followers concentrated on various aspects of his work. J.-B. Say, for example, posited a theory of market regulation based on Smith's concept of the "invisible hand" for clearing the markets.[4] In his *Treatise on Political Economy* (1803) Say developed the concept of the entrepreneur as the person who establishes the markets, which are then cleared for production and consumption. His argument is that supply creates its own demand, so that as supply increases so does demand and as supply decreases a corresponding decrease in demand occurs. A product is presented in the market and brought to the attention of consumers, who allocate a part of their purchasing power to its consumption; the supply has generated demand and the greater the demand the greater the increase in production until no increase in supply or demand is warranted. Should there be a radical shift in one or both sides of the transaction, then as the product is phased out, demand shifts toward other products and the supply-demand relationship is reinstated.

Following Smith's argument—and in part responding to the physiocratic influences that still remained on the Continent—T. R. Malthus pointed to agriculture, but not as the source of wealth in the physiocratic sense, but as the source of nourishment with respect to the expansion of industrial output. Malthus's argument was also based on the principles stated by Adam Smith, but with the paradox of closed reasoning inherent but overlooked in the new economic thinking that had become so powerful in the early stages of the new era of the Industrial Revolution. With the expansion of output and industry, population would expand accordingly due to the greater ease of life. Agriculture may also expand, but certainly not sufficiently so to keep up with the population expansion, so that eventually hunger would result, the population would decline, with a corresponding decline of the labor force. This would be maintained until population and agricultural output were in equilibrium, and the process would be renewed. Even for Malthus, a business cycle of sorts existed, based on the population-cum-agricultural ratio over time, with population increasing exponentially and agriculture, while subject to the elements of nature, increasing arithmetically, except for famine reducing the population accordingly.[5]

Another economist who certainly appreciated the value of land was David Ricardo. A contemporary of both Malthus and Say, Ricardo posited that land's value is determined by the demand for the land. As industry expanded, land would appreciate in value according to its scarcity and location, with respect to industrial demand. There was also the demand for dwelling space as well as for agricultural output; as land became exhausted or of marginal use, its value would depreciate accordingly. Ricardo also emphasized output, internal efficiency in industrial output, as well as entrepreneurship in the mustering of capital and resources for production. The Malthusian problem was certainly known to Ricardo, as Malthus and Ricardo engaged in extensive correspondence. But Ricardo maintained that the Malthusian situation could be offset by the value of land for agriculture fluctuating with respect to its supply and demand conditions. When agricultural land becomes scarce and its value increases, more people will be attracted to that profession; efficiency in agriculture would lead to greater crop yields, corresponding to the demand for foodstuffs, thereby preventing the Malthusian famine situation.

With respect to Ricardo, Viner was somewhat hasty in his statement, for he neglected Ricardo's significant contribution to the body of international economic theory. Ricardo considered foreign economies as extensions of the domestic economy, so that foreign commerce could be treated from a perspective similar to domestic commerce. This enabled him to formulate his theory of trade on the basis of comparative production costs, so that if product x costs more to produce in country A than in country B, and similarly, if product y costs more to produce in country B than in A, and if each country requires both products, then A would produce y more cheaply than x and B would produce x more cheaply than y. The countries would export to each other the surplus of their products not consumed by their domestic populations. This is how the various sectors are developed within an economy, and in the same manner they are developed internationally. This concept of comparative costs provided the basis for Mill's theory of comparative advantage in trade.[6]

Hume's argument with respect to trade is significant for two reasons. One reason is that he wrote prior to Smith's work and indeed Smith referred to it several times. Hume thus wrote during the period of mercantilism, when the desired coinage to compensate for goods and services traded was gold with the favorable balance of trade being held by that country which received gold instead of a complete barter for the transaction. Hume's Law, or the specie-flow mechanism, takes the mechanism in which an excess of merchandise imported leads to short-run gold exports. This gold loss reduces the country's money supply, since either gold or coinage pegged to gold is kept by the country's banking system. A decrease in the country's money supply leads to a decline in that country's prices for its goods, because with less money available people spend less and less spending with constant output results in lower prices to move the goods.

Lower domestic prices will encourage foreigners to purchase from that country, so that more foreign exchange is brought into the country at every foreign exchange rate. Moreover, lower prices also reduce imports since domestic consumers will purchase less expensive goods from their countries rather than the relatively expensive goods of foreign countries. In this way, the flow of coin or gold was considered to bring about an adjustment in the international position of a country.[7]

Hume's argument helped weaken the mercantilist view that an increase in exports was desirable on the grounds that it resulted in gold or specie imports, and that specie and gold per se provided the value of the economy. Hume argued that the mercantilist position was invalid as the inflows of gold or specie would be reversed as prices would rise, induced by the increase in the money supply due to the initially lower prices in the domestic economy, leading to a preference of imports over exports over time. Gold and specie would then flow out and weaken the domestic economy, with respect to the mercantilist argument. The domestic economy in the international arena operated, according to Hume, in regulatory manner of markets being cleared, in a manner similar to that described later by Smith with the "invisible hand" in the domestic markets, and still later with the more sophisticated and enduring Law of Markets posited by Say.

Hume's Law was primarily based on production and consumption, with money

serving to regulate the supply and demand for goods. As industrialization progressed during the Industrial Revolution, banking systems increased in sophistication and tariffs were levied in international trade to protect fledgling industries as well as vested interests. Each country established its own financial
systems and laws within the systems to cope with the dynamics of industrialization; the smooth world described by Hume, and later by Smith and Say, was
never to be. In this sense, the concept of comparative costs posited by Ricardo
was certainly more adequate and provided a better description of economic
reality. Costs are prices, and greater economic efficiency in production is achieved
if the intended product can be manufactured at lower comparative costs. Similarly, for the consumer, if the desired product can be purchased at lower consumer costs as the selection is made among the merchants stocking the product,
consumer efficiency is achieved, thereby releasing greater purchasing power
for other purposes, either in consumption or for saving.[8]

Ricardo's theory also had the clearing mechanism of the markets. When
costs become too high, alternatives are found at lower costs, thereby bringing
these alternatives into economic use. The demand for these alternatives eventually leads to the rise in their use costs due to scarcity, and they will rise,
with the resultant decline of the previous costs. Even land that has become
uneconomic due to its overuse will become economic over time as other land
that substituted at lower costs becomes increasingly expensive due to continuous demand.

Comparative costs were important in international trade as the costs of goods
imported declined and then rose over time with respect to domestic goods. The
"invisible hand" and Say's Law were prevalent in Ricardo's theory, and this,
indeed, was another expression of Hume's Law.

However, Ricardo's consideration of foreign markets within the same theoretical context as domestic markets was invalid, in spite of the significant contribution he made to economic theory. This could be attributed to the fact that
when he wrote, the Industrial Revolution had not developed to the extent that
it had during John Stuart Mill's time, so that tariffs and banking systems had
not developed to the extent that they had during Mill's time. David Ricardo
was certainly one of the pillars of economics on which Mill and other great
economists have stood to expand their vision.

Mills' contribution to international economics lies primarily in what is called
the Law of Reciprocal Demand. Each country seeks to be self-sufficient, providing all the goods and services that its population consumes. But this is usually unobtainable, especially for small countries with limited resources that have
to import goods from the larger countries. In international commerce there is
very rarely a one-to-one correspondence in the exchange of goods, so that in
most instances a ratio of exchange exists. Country A, for example, seeks to
trade wheat for cloth with country B. A's cost for processing a bushel of wheat
is $1.00, while the price of manufacturing a yard of cloth in B is $1.05. Costs
are considered in the transaction, but so are profits and these are determined

with respect to demand. A wants to import 14 yards of cloth and is willing to exchange five bushels of wheat, while B is willing to exchange 10 yards of cloth for seven bushels of wheat. If each country is willing to engage the other in this exchange, the Law of Reciprocal Demand will result in bargaining between the trading partners until a price is reached for the final transaction, according to each country's domestic needs. The intensity of this demand will determine the ratio agreed upon, with whatever differences still existing made up in specie. Should no agreement be reached, each country will then look for another partner. The Law of Reciprocal Demand takes into account production costs when the bargaining prices are established, but it also points out that the selling prices are determined by what the market will yield according to the pressures of domestic demand and alternative markets to compensate for the absence of the deal being finalized. Should the agreement be reached, money enters into the transaction to cover differences in positions.[9]

Common to the theories of Hume and Mill, as well as Ricardo before him and the neoclassical trade theorists and the neo-Keynesian post–World War II theorists, is the sentiment expressed by W. Arthur Lewis, ''The extent to which a country participates in international trade depends partly on its resources, partly on the barriers it places in the way of trade, and partly on its stage of development.''[10] A country's resources, and the manner in which they are allocated, determine the type and quality of goods and services it produces. These are consumed domestically and exported for other countries' consumption. The barriers it places in the way of trade are twofold. They are tariffs and import quotas to protect domestic industry, generating retaliation and hence limiting their exports to other countries, and this is strictly economic with the domestic economy being hindered because of the diseconomies resulting from lower production due to the limited exports. They are also political, as when sanctions are levied against countries due to their domestic and/or international policies, unacceptable to part or most of the other countries.[11] With respect to the third point, the stage of a country's development, this is a limiting factor on the country's ability to trade in the case of the underdeveloped economies. It is also a limiting factor on countries who become too involved in the politics of international relations to the extent of financing other countries' development and growth, so that the balance of trade becomes too negative and to some extent irreversible. These points will be discussed further in the last part of this book.

What is also common to these positions is the lack of consideration of the domestic economy's position within its business cycle dynamics with respect to its position in international commerce. In spite of the increasing international commerce due to industrialization and the sophistication of the banking systems, as well as the influence that trade was having on the domestic economies, economists still maintained their vision inward in the tradition of the classical theories of Smith, Ricardo, and Mill, concentrating on the international aspects of their theories only as sidelines. The attitude was that should the domestic economy be looked after, the consequences for international commerce would be beneficial, for such commerce is an extension of the domestic ability to produce and manufacture. With a healthy domestic economy, viable trade will result.

It is somewhat of a historical paradox, therefore, that Keynes, who was so influential in restructuring economic theory during the Great Depression and made a significant contribution in the establishment of the postwar International Monetary Fund and recognized the necessity for international trade for revitalizing domestic economies, exerted little influence on his followers in this area, the majority of whom continued to maintain their interest mainly in domestic economics. The consequence is that there has been a serious bifurcation in this branch of economic theory, with business people going in the direction that fortune and their fortunes would take them, entering into foreign markets and establishing multinational companies, and engaging in trade without comprehending the dynamics of economics and being concerned only with finance, while economists tend to neglect the aspects of international commerce in a world that is now undergoing tremendous and unpredictable changes.

The emphasis on domestic economics, important as this may be, has certainly given credence to Viner's sentiment, as international economics remains relegated to a secondary status in the discipline of economic thought. Even though our era is one in which tremendous international changes are occurring, the main body of international economics remains very much the same as the theories of Hume, Ricardo, Mill, and Keynes. This demonstrates a serious fault in economic thought, while the international arena is confronted with tremendous problems. The United States is experiencing a huge balance of payments deficit, while countries in Eastern Europe, the Middle East, and Latin and South America turn to the United States for assistance in their economic development. The European Community is forming into a central economic unit, and such a union is being considered by the Comecon, the Eastern European community formed by the Warsaw Pact countries. Multinational companies are special cases as they gain in sophistication in the changing international arena, existing in countries trading among themselves.

Moreover, there is the problem of the emerging and developing countries who confront the advanced countries with the disadvantage of lacking sufficient industry and infrastructure to compete, yet competition is the means by which they can develop their industrial basis and gain the technology for raising their standards of living. The contributions made by the economists from Hume through the Keynesian revolution are not invalid. Their theories provided the basis for economic growth and development. But they dealt with issues that are no longer relevant to our era. The emerging and developing countries cannot undergo an industrial revolution, for they can acquire the technology of our era and apply it to their economies. The banking systems do not have to undergo the conditions for trading that existed during the Industrial Revolution, because communications have vastly improved and gold is no longer the monetary unit of measure. The Japanese yen competes with the dollar and with sterling as a currency for trade, as the Japanese have become a serious contender in the world's markets. Comparative advantages in trade are depending increasingly on knowledge, which has become a major natural resource.

Still, a country's ability to engage in trade depends on its internal economic position, and this must be taken into account within the contemporary context when discussing trade. Hence, there is also the problem of emerging countries trading with the developed countries, so that because of their relatively weak economies they will not be exploited in the exchange.

In light of our contemporary era, a theory of trade must be developed that takes these new circumstances into account. Such a theory will be stated in this book. It will treat the dynamics of trade in a manner that will allow commerce to be conducted among the advanced economies and the advanced economies with the emerging and developing economies. It will provide a basis for analysis of the multinational companies, and will develop criteria for the less advanced economies to move into a cyclical pattern of growth to be able to compete successfully with the advanced economies. The ultimate objective of economic theory is the elimination of poverty and the establishment of a system of thought that can provide wealth. No single country can control the dynamics of the international marketplace, and it is here that the dynamics of competition are the most rigorous. Competition stimulates economic efficiency, and efficiency results in growth and an increment in the wealth of nations. This is an economic fact finally being realized in our changing era, and for this reason, international economics must be elevated to the status of domestic economics, for in our era, one depends directly on the other. This is the subject matter of this book.

Chapter 2

TRADE IN AN UNCERTAIN WORLD

Because the exchange rate is changed infrequently and only to meet substantial difficulties a change tends to come well after the onset of difficulty,
to be postponed as long as possible, and to be made only after substantial
pressure on the exchange rate has accumulated.

—Milton Friedman,
"The Case for Flexible Exchange Rates" [1]

BEGGAR THY NEIGHBOR

Earlier in the same essay, Milton Friedman wrote:

Because money imparts general purchasing power and is used for such a wide variety
of purposes abroad as well as at home, the demand for and the supply of any one
country's currency is widely spread and comes from many sources. In consequence,
broad, active, and nearly perfect markets have developed in foreign exchange whenever
they have been permitted—and usually even when they have not been. [2]

He stated further that changes in the rate of exchange occur rapidly because
the rate is an extremely volatile price. These changes occur automatically and
continuously, tending to produce corrective movements before tensions can ac-
cumulate and a crisis develops.

This may be the current situation, because of the lessons learned during the

Great Depression. Governments are now actively involved in shoring up currencies that are under attack. In quieter times exchange rates tend to be stable, fluctuating within upper and lower limits set by the governments, usually with the tacit agreement of other countries.

This was not always so. Prior to the Great Depression the gold standard was used as the measure for determining the value of a country's currency in the international markets. This was a throwback to mercantilism, when gold was the most sought after means of exchange. The gold standard was used because the processes of industrialization were new in world history, while the value and desirability of gold was as ancient as the history of civilization. Gold was the symbol of royalty, of great wealth, of the immutable metal on which paper money can be based. Moreover, during the volatile period of industrialization, the gold standard provided international stability in foreign trade. Countries maintained the value of their currencies in a fixed relationship to the precious metal. Currencies with a fixed ratio to gold thereby maintained a fixed relationship to one another, and on the basis of these fixed currency relationships, foreign trade was conducted.

The difficulty with the gold standard was that it did not reflect the countries' internal dynamics and economic strength. Mercantilism considered national wealth to be measured in the holding of foreign coin, and preferably another country's gold. The ancient metal had no real bearing on output, and its use as the measure of currencies in trade reflected only a country's gold holdings and not its actual or potential for generating real wealth in the production and consumption of goods and services.

During the business cycles that occurred in the process of industrialization, aggregate production and employment varied according to the cycle's phase. The role of the government was uncertain with respect to the economy, and with respect to economic management, the governments of the industrializing countries tended to adhere to the Jeffersonian dictum that the government that governs best, governs least. Even though development did not adhere to the teachings of the great economists in the sense that there was no Law of Markets to clear the markets to allow for the reordering of inventories, that no invisible hand–type of regulator kept the economies of the industrializing countries operating within equilibrium, the classical doctrines still held sway over governing officials. This was because Smith's teaching of the division of labor was paying dividends in production, especially with the increasing use of technology in production resulting in the adaptation of the labor force—albeit, after a time-lag for acquiring the necessary skills—to the new technologies. Moreover, industrialization was expanding and as economics was considered the science that explains and analyzes such expansion, its theories held and were taught by the academicians and preached as political economy by the politicians.

Trade continued, based on surplus production and foreign demand for domestic products. Tariffs were established to protect industries against competition from other countries manufacturing similar goods, thereby limiting domestic consumption for the foreign goods over domestic product. As the gold standard maintained the prices of currencies, and the goods and services that were traded, these prices bore little relation to the cost and price of these goods domestically. This practice continued, as it was acceptable by all sides in foreign transactions. Currencies fluctuated in value in the domestic markets, but gold did not tarnish and maintained its intrinsic chemical value. The gold standard seemed immutable, permanent, and even necessary in the era of industrial development.

Necessary, perhaps, but the gold standard was not immutable nor permanent. The standard, which has been so much a factor of foreign transactions and a symbol of wealth from the period of mercantilism and into the twentieth century, crumbled during the period of the Great Depression.

The relationship between currency and output had become clear during this period, and the mystique of gold as the standard for measuring the value of a country's currency gave way to other methods. Great Britain left the gold standard and went over to sterling. The United States and other countries devalued their currencies with respect to gold. Gold was still accepted as the measure of currencies, but the ease of devaluation demonstrated the arbitrariness of gold, for this metal had lost much of its mystique as the measure of currency, and as Keynes pointed out, it was the economy's ability to produce and provide employment that determined the currency's value on the international markets. There were echoes of Hume's theory in the writings of Keynes, for Hume was an economist who stressed production over currency as the means for generating national wealth, even though Hume's Law demonstrated the importance of currency in foreign exchange.

Still, during the difficult times of the Great Depression, there was somewhat of a regression in thinking in the financial circles of the various governments. A form of quasi-mercantilism was reinstated in devaluations as a means for stimulating domestic activity. As the depression deepened, countries would devalue with respect to other countries' currencies, so that its currency would be cheaper with respect to other countries' currencies, thereby making the exportable goods of the devaluating country cheaper on the international markets. This would generate demand for that country's commodities, offering serious competition with the industries of the importing countries. Because of this generated demand, employment would be revived as production continued. There would be expected retaliation by way of devaluations in other countries, but the time lag in response would be sufficient to get the domestic economy of the devaluating country back into production. Hence, through devaluation, the depression would be alleviated domestically and exported to other countries, with the time lag considered to be of sufficient duration to set the production processes on the path of revival, rectifying the temporary setback to full employment.

This was a beggar-thy-neighbor policy, exporting the depression from one economy to another. It was conducted with the assumption that when retaliation in the form of devaluations came from other countries, the damage of receiving their imports would be minimized, due to the resurgence of domestic economic growth. This, however, was based on two misconceptions. One misconception was that a country's currency is a source of that country's pride, with the value of its currency being a symbol of national economic strength. During the period of the Industrial Revolution, depressions also existed, yet they were of relatively short duration and the cyclical downswings were rectified over time, giving credence to the classical and—after Karl Marx's *Capital*—the neoclassical theories of economics, in which a Say-like regulator always brought the economy to a resumed growth position. A country's currency rate remained stable with respect to other currencies as a matter of pride and because there was no great necessity to vary the ratios. It was assumed that devaluation, being a drastic step, would not be met with extreme retaliation because of the national pride in other countries' currencies.

The second misconception was that should devaluations take place, as they were expected to, they would be undertaken only as a means of realignment, to maintain a ratio fairly close to the original ratio prior to the country's devaluation. With the depression being so deep, a country's devaluation with the intent to export its difficulties to other countries would not be met in kind, because of the fragile global economic situation and the repercussions such a response would generate. Hence, it was thought that the beggar-thy-neighbor policy of exporting the depression in order to strengthen the domestic economy would not be met in kind.

Both misconceptions proved to be erroneous. Devaluations were met swiftly with retaliation and even with steeper devaluations. National pride as expressed in a country's currency went to the winds as the realization that the domestic economies had to be protected by retaliation in kind and swiftly eliminated all the expected benefits of devaluation. The revitalization of domestic economies due to devaluation was not realized and the world's industrialized economies remained depressed until World War II. Keynesian economics were applied domestically to revive the economies, with the concentration of international economic theory taking a back place. Devaluations not only failed to provide a solution to the Great Depression by seeking to export the depression to other countries by way of the devaluation process, international suspicion and hostility were generated and intensified. Hence, the beggar-thy-neighbor policy failed to stimulate both the domestic economies and international commerce to any significant extent.

How long the Great Depression would have lasted had there not been another world war, is mere speculation. There were fears over signs of upward cyclical movement, fear because the political and economic leaders did not understand the business cycle sufficiently to comprehend the movement. The cycle had been depressed for so long and so completely, that when the movement upward did set in, it was consciously reversed by the countries' leaders. The cost of living index was allowed to rise, resulting in second thoughts by consumers;

inventories were repressed as new demand tapered off, and the uncertainty over the countries' financial institutions prevented the establishing of an atmosphere for personal investment on the part of those people who were employed and earning more than a marginal salary. The cycle turned back downward, with all subsequent movement regulated by the governments. A deliberate motion of the cycle, brought about by the intentional activities of the governments, was preferable to the natural motion of the cycle discussed by the neoclassical economists. Trade suffered, with the beggar-thy-neighbor policy being shown in its true light as a complete failure for domestic recovery. It may very well be that the recovery programs instituted by the various governments would have brought the cycle into its upward motion. These Keynesian policies did, after all, provide employment to the multitudes of people who would have otherwise most likely remained unemployed. Whether they were employed efficiently so that their contributions to the economies were more than the money spent from their earnings, is better left to the historians to consider. The Great Depression was indeed terminated, however, by World War II.

HELP THY NEIGHBOR

Prior to the cessation of World War II, the Allies realized that for global economic growth to be achieved, there must be stability in the international markets; that foreign trade is necessary for domestic economic growth; and that local populations needed foreign goods and trade to achieve prosperity. There was the real fear that after the war the world would slip back into depression after the adjustment to peacetime production, and that those countries on whose soil the war was waged would take too long to recover, if at all.

This situation was approached from two different points. One was the Bretton Woods Monetary Conference, held in July 1944, which led to the Articles of Agreement of the International Monetary Fund and the International Bank for Reconstruction and Development being drawn up and adapted by the United Nations. The objective of the IMF is the reconciliation of the expansion and the balance of growth in international trade, eliminating the disruptions to trade by unstable exchange rates and the removal of foreign exchange restrictions, while maintaining the high levels of employment and real income within each country. Thus, international rates of exchange were not to be set arbitrarily by each country, but became the concern of all countries, so that the par value of a member's currency would be expressed either in terms of gold, or to the United States dollar. Equally important is the condition that a country could not change the value of its currency internationally except to correct a fundamental balance of payments difficulty that could not be corrected unless devaluation or revaluation, as the case may be, is undertaken.

The IMF's resources consist of currencies and gold that can be drawn upon by member countries by purchasing these currencies with their own currency. Interest is charged, depending on the IMF's position at the time of the loan, and the borrowing country's ability to repay. Even though the IMF was founded at the dawning of a new historical era,[3] it is rooted firmly in the Great Depression. Its purpose is not only to provide international economic stability, but also to prevent serious and structural unemployment from developing and remaining in a country's economic system.[4]

The International Bank for Reconstruction and Development was also founded during the Bretton Woods conference to provide short-term capital for postwar reconstruction and long-term policies for providing a larger flow of international private investments. The World Bank was established to operate together with the IMF, with each member subscribing to the World Bank's stocks and each member having 250 votes and an additional vote for each stock held. The World Bank is to promote international private investments by providing guarantees or by participating in loans when there is a need and private capital is not forthcoming. However, to protect the World Bank's funds, loans must be made for specific projects. Furthermore, borrowers must be in a position to repay the loans according to the terms stipulated. The loans must be used only for the purpose specified, and loans are provided in foreign currencies required directly for financing the specific projects.

To facilitate the workings of the IMF and the World Bank, the General Agreement on Tariffs and Trade (GATT) was concluded in Geneva in 1947 to assure the reduction of tariffs and to make trade more competitive. This was also a postwar response to the depression years, when tariffs were erected to reduce the imports of goods that competed in the domestic markets and to restrict the allocation of domestic spending on foreign goods at the expense of domestic production. Tariffs were also erected to protect domestic industries after the war to insure domestic growth and provide sufficient employment of demilitarized personnel to prevent domestic recessions.[5]

The IMF, the World Bank, and the GATT are international organizations, whose purpose is to stimulate trade and to lower restrictions on the flow of international commerce. The other point from which the new situation was approached was the U.S. effort at postwar reconstruction. This was the Marshall Plan, also known as the European Recovery Program established by Secretary of State George C. Marshall in 1947. Its objectives were twofold: One was to provide financial assistance to a Europe devastated by the war, in order to facilitate growth in production, leaning to the financial institutions to provide income, markets, and international trade. The other objective was political, to ensure the establishment and stability of European democracy, in light of Europe's immediate past and the threat of Soviet influence as the Cold War set in. The impact that the Marshall Plan had on European economic development and trade revitalization was that of an economic renaissance. Not only did the Marshall Plan provide funding for the reconstruction of industrial bases; it also insured that the latest techniques in manufacturing and marketing, developed in the United States for coping with aggregate demand accumulated by demobilized service personnel, were incorporated into the European conceptualizations of manufacturing and marketing, to provide the mutual relationship of marketing and production.

Economic assistance on a large scale was also extended to the countries in the Far East, both friend and previous foe alike. As with Europe, U.S. economic influence was certainly great, but each country receiving assistance was allowed to rebuild its economy according to its traditional conceptualizations. Two conditions were imposed, however. One condition was that each country would be democratic in its political processes; the other condition was that the economies would be modern, within the traditional concepts, exploiting the latest available technologies and marketing procedures.

The first condition was not stressed, however, as the Cold War persisted and intensified. Allies were important, not only for their resources and support in the United Nations, but also because an ally is not an enemy and at the height of the Cold War, this attitude was of the greatest importance. The second condition was readily adapted and pursued by the receiving countries, because it was to their advantage to obtain the funding for industrialization and to modernize as quickly as possible. People were to be employed, profits were to be made, and national and personal wealth was to be acquired.

HELP THYSELF

Trade was to be important in these receiving countries, both European and Asian. Markets were sought to sell domestic products, and while domestic consumption became adequate, foreign currency was sought by both governments and industries within the countries. This was not only to boost these countries' standings in the world economic organizations, but to strengthen these countries' abilities to acquire natural resources at prices advantageous to their economies. Often, these resources could be acquired through trading, and strong foreign currency holdings allowed for leverage in international transactions. The British pound sterling, the German deutsche mark, the French franc, and eventually the Japanese yen became currencies sought after in the international markets for facilitating the flow of goods and services across international borders. Yet the dollar, during the reconstruction period and at present, is still the most sought after world currency. Indeed, these currencies have been traded as commodities, fluctuating between points set by market conditions and the various world organizations, with central banks acting as regulators, buying and selling currencies if their prices are too high or low, as the case may be. This also provides stability in international commerce, as currencies are not allowed to fluctuate too wildly and disrupt trading because of the preference of one currency over others during a specific time period.

By 1973, there was sufficient economic stability in the world's markets to abolish the Bretton Woods agreement on fixed but flexible exchange rates. Although in the 1950s and 1960s the majority of international trade economists advocated the abolishment of the Bretton Woods agreement, its abolition was due in fact to its failure to deal effectively with the countries' current accounts imbalances. The year 1973 began as a year of optimism; the developed countries were experiencing growth and the developing and emerging countries were benefiting from the developed countries' ability and willingness to provide assistance through aid and trade. Moreover, they were more concerned with their own macroeconomic situations, and international commerce was still considered to be an offshoot of their macroeconomic strength.

The end of 1973, however, provided a different situation, one that set the world in a state of confusion and turmoil, in which the developed countries relinquished their political independence to a large degree and submitted themselves to those emerging countries which controlled the great oil wells. The reason for this situation was the Yom Kippur war and the Arab control of the oil wells in its aftermath. The only gold that counted then was the "black gold" of oil. The price of gold rose from $35 an ounce to over $800 an ounce in the aftermath of the price rises for oil. Currencies fluctuated widely, even to the point that it was cheaper for Americans to fly to London and purchase goods from the prestigious store, Harrod's, than to purchase these same goods or similar products on the home markets.

Foreign trade experienced then instability such as was not witnessed since the Great Depression. However, there was a difference, one that proved to be of great significance. The Great Depression was an economic adjustment, brought about by the de facto conclusion of the Industrial Revolution.[6] The understanding of that situation was lacking, because of the neoclassical concepts on which business and governments were operating. Keynes pointed out the errors of these concepts, especially that of full employment.[7] The lessons of the Great Depression were learned, the full-employment condition of neoclassical thinking was certainly not part of the thinking of the Keynesian revolution that governed thinking and policy making during this period, and macroeconomic considerations held preference over all other aspects for the decision makers.

As this was not a cyclical condition, but one brought about by external circumstances, the Keynesian theoreticians did not seek to revise their theory, but sought to expand it to take into account the unemployment and the industrial slowdown brought about by high energy prices. Governments sought to bring alternative energy sources on line, and they accomplished this, but only after serious readjustments in the economy. Moreover, there was the additional factor of the recycling of the profits of the oil industries into the developed economies. Some of the money was used in the Arab countries to improve the industrial infrastructure, the education systems, and, of course, for defense and for the sponsoring of various international adventures in the military sphere.

With respect to international trade, the cooperation that had existed during the Bretton Woods period was no longer to be. The disruptions in domestic economies due to the high energy prices and the unemployment resulted in the economic introspection and in measures to be taken that would eventually lead to economic recovery. The necessity for trade and the complexities of the international commercial situation were established beforehand, and the continuance of the Cold War could not allow for changes in international commerce that would be drastic in nature. The beggar-thy-neighbor policies of the previous historical era were unthinkable and tariffs were used to the extent to protect domestic industry and employment within limits that were tolerable in the various international markets. The beggar-thy-neighbor policies employed in the era of the Great Depression would not have been tolerated. The international markets had achieved a stability due to the Bretton Woods agreement that could not be reversed. The recession that was occurring was not cyclical and hence not within the framework of being a consequence of the natural path of economic processes. It was due to the external force of the rapid rise in energy and the consequences that ensued. But foreign commerce also includes foreign investments in the various domestic markets, and as the profits acquired from oil could be maintained only through their being invested, the best markets were those that had the most advanced economic infrastructures. This meant that the money was invested in the developed countries, and this eventually stimulated production, especially as other and cheaper energy sources became on-line. The emerging countries were hurt the worst, because they lacked foreign currency at levels necessary to maintain their purchases of oil. They were not substantial exporters in any case and were in need of foreign aid and assistance. The single-product exporters suffered as the global demand for their products declined due to the slowing down of importing economies and the price rises for these products in the various domestic markets. But they too would be hurting even when the extent of trade increased, because of their subjugation to the elements, and to domestic instability that often affects the production of the single-export product.

The attitude that prevailed during this period was, therefore, not of beggar-thy-neighbor, but of help thyself. The domestic economic problems were certainly pressing. The recession hit as suddenly as the rises in energy prices. There were no cyclical warnings, no indicators that had shown an imminent slowdown, no signs of high unemployment in the near future. Thus, when the energy prices were raised and businesses slowed down due to the unexpectedly higher costs of production, the recession phase of the cycle was initiated, resulting in high unemployment and reduced output.

There was another consequence, one unique to this situation: prices being raised without output increasing significantly. This was the stagnation and inflation which typified that period. Foreign trade fluctuated as the prices of currencies fluctuated. Domestic prices of exported goods and services rose to keep their prices competitive and profitable in the international markets. Tariffs were imposed to maintain domestic competition due to the low prices of foreign goods on the domestic markets. Again, these tariffs were not to pass on to the foreign markets the unemployment and inflation that each domestic market was experiencing. The futility of that maneuver was learned during the Great Depression, when such policies were countered by reciprocal tariffs. The cooperation that had benefited trade since then had become part of the established behavior, and all measures undertaken were to protect the domestic markets.

Another situation had gained considerable momentum during this period. As the industrialized countries were recovering from World War II, they began to allow the nations that had emerged from the war to produce goods for their industries. Production costs, including labor, were lower in terms of the hard currencies of the industrialized countries, and this also provided skills, training, and education in the emerging countries. This was manifested in two ways. First, there were the government-to-government investments and the back-up services to enable these countries to exploit the assistance. This was done with great skill, so that while traditional customs and rituals were preserved, the most modern technology was provided and clashes between tradition and technology were kept at levels tolerable for both economic progress and cultural development. The help-thyself attitude was realized in this situation because of the personal and political contacts that helped heal the deep wounds of the war and establish economic relationships. Trade was encouraged, with the neoclassical notion of developing domestic specialization for domestic production and export. The war-emerging countries would manufacture goods on several technical levels, leaving the developed countries to specialize in higher technological output.

The second way this was manifested was the continuation on a much more intensive level of a procedure that had begun prior to the Great Depression: the establishment of multinational companies. Originally the concept of the multinational company was of a company with subsidiaries in several countries. These countries would most likely be on similar levels of industrial development as the home country, so that the products in question would have appeal to target groups with similar incomes and styles of living. This form of production was not very developed, however, due to the concentration on domestic development leaving the establishment of branches in foreign countries a lower priority. International travel was not developed to any significant extent, and foreign trade increased at the rate of increase of domestic industrial growth.

After the war, however, businesses established branches in the war-emerging countries. Resources were available, but production costs were lower than in the developed countries. Also, it was to the advantage of the war-emerging countries to have these businesses, for they provided employment, as well as assisting in the rebuilding of these countries. Not only was infrastructure reestablished, it was also developed in order to handle new concepts of industrialization that were being formulated in the developed countries. Computers, the origin of which is prewar with the concepts of the British mathematician Alan Turing, became important tools, both in science and in industrialization. They were introduced and developed in the war-emerging countries. Originally it was components, the elements of both soft and hard systems. The auto industries, developed prior to the war, had to be redeveloped as these industries were converted to the war effort and in many instances were destroyed because of bombing and because the lack of manpower sufficient to maintain their operation. By investing in these industries and by opening plants in these countries, the developed economies gained footholds into markets that were largely, prior to the war, the sole property of the host countries. The market potential certainly existed, and the opportunity for sales was great.

The theoretical basis for these policies is rooted in the works of Ricardo and Mill. Comparative costs provided the incentive to assist the war-emerging economies; comparative advantages provided the terms of trade and the establishment of infrastructure necessary to maintain trade. Comparative costs took on a meaning broader than the initial definition that Ricardo offered. Granted that internal efficiency in industry was important then as it always is, but on the government-to-government level, the concept of comparative costs took on a dimension that Ricardo had not considered. There were political costs, as calculated with respect to the Cold War. Assistance, whether in the form of loans and investments or in outright aid, became necessary, therefore, not only as a means of rebuilding the economies of the war-emerging countries, but also to gain influence in these countries and to limit or eliminate the influences of the Cold War adversaries. The political costs were weighed against the pure economic costs, and the governments made their decisions on how to approach these countries and assist their rebuilding.

Governments also influenced private industries to invest in these countries. Tax incentives were used to encourage investments because industries were initially wary of the abilities of the labor force in the war-emerging economies to be able to produce and compete effectively. After the initial doubt was overcome, however, such investments continued and were encouraged to a degree by the host countries. The need for economic recovery was urgent. Those political leaders with foresight realized that the new era dawning on the world would be different qualitatively from the era that had just closed. The technology of waging war had demonstrated this, and the pent-up civilian aggregate demand was being unleashed on economies unprepared to cope with it. They needed foreign capital and technology, they needed the education of the developed economies, and they needed the ability to exploit new concepts that made the industrialized countries strong and flexible.

Mill's concept of comparative advantage was exploited by the developed countries and the war-emerging countries alike. For the developed economies, this was exploited by exporting the middle and high technology, the education, and, in the case of construction, the infrastructure necessary for the war-emerging countries to enter into the new era and become productive in a meaningful and economical manner. In exchange, the war-emerging economies would sell to the developed countries those goods that could be manufactured at costs lower than in the developed economies, so much so that it was cheaper to import them and allocate resources for other more profitable ends. The concepts of comparative costs and comparative advantages resulted in the reconstruction of the war-emerging economies, to the benefit of all involved. It seemed that the sentiment expressed by Jacob Viner held during this period.

Eventually, however, there was an alteration in trade patterns. In the war-emerging countries, especially West Germany and Japan, the growth patterns that had been established by the Allies had set in with growth increasing at rates faster than in the United States, their main ally and supporter. Germany had, of course, a tradition of industrialization and a skilled work force to exploit it. Prior to the war, Germany was industrialized; indeed, the country had been a part of the Industrial Revolution, and its war machine had been so capable because of its industrial infrastructure. Japan, however, sought industry not by the natural growth of the revolution set off by Adam Smith's work and the forces of science and manufacturing that had merged at that opportune moment in history. The Japanese achieved industrialization mainly through the processes of copying and learning from other countries that had already achieved industrialization. Japan, like Germany, had a disciplined work force, industrious and after acquiring the concepts of industrialization, certainly capable of competing again, as its military had so aptly demonstrated.[8]

While the growth rates of the industrialized countries were increasing, the growth rates of the war-emerging countries were increasing at a faster rate. This did not, however, affect the comparative cost ratios among the countries to a significant extent, so that the war-emerging countries still maintained their cost advantages over the industrialized countries. However, with the absorption of high technologies and the abilities of the labor forces to convert this knowledge into production, the competitive edge in the high technology fields enjoyed by the industrialized countries began to shrink, so that eventually competition among the war-emerging and the industrialized countries was for similar markets. As well as the quality and serviceability of the competitive products, advertising emphasized emotional appeal for the countries' products over foreign competition. In the United States, legislation against cartels and monopolies affected the shape of the nation's industries, while foreign competition did not have laws as stringent, so that the concept of competition in the domestic markets, so essential for the development of industry in that country, meant, in fact, that resources were being allocated among competing companies, while in the foreign competitive countries monopolies and cartels were tolerated to the extent that resources were not divided to the same extent. This, together with protective tariffs in the foreign countries, as well as the continuing contributions made by the United States to other economies, set the U.S. economy at a disadvantage in the trading situation that had little to do with competition in trade.

This situation persisted after the Yom Kippur war of 1973, when countries were vying for oil at prices that would keep their economies from undergoing too severe of a recession, and for offering the best terms to the oil producing countries for recycling their money to gain the highest profits. This was a period of great uncertainty. There was the recession, intensifying and causing great disruptions in the delicate economic balances within the economies and among the countries that had achieved postwar stability because of the Bretton Woods agreement. Production patterns were being reviewed as aggregate demand shifted due to unemployment and to the international instability that prevailed. Countries that had achieved a degree of economic independence had to realign their policies to cooperate with the Organization of Petroleum Exporting Countries (OPEC) in their attempt to condemn Israel in the international forums that occurred; they did this to obtain oil at rates that would not afflict their economies too severely.[9] There was, in spite of this, confidence that alternative energy sources would go on-line, to compete with OPEC oil. There were the North Sea oil wells, but the British and Norwegians controlling this source had, to some extent, already borrowed on their output to pay for their other financial needs. They also wanted to use their reserves as a hedge against OPEC sources, to have oil available to sell in the future if OPEC prices brought about too much damage to the industrialized countries. The United States had reserves in Alaska, Texas, Oklahoma, and Louisiana that were untapped, but environmental concerns restricted their uses, and they were also being held, to a certain extent, in case OPEC applied excessive pressure. Atomic energy was exploited, brought on-line, providing knowledge of its benefits and dangers. Solar ponds were formed, converting solar energy to electric energy. Automobile motors were manufactured to consume gasoline more efficiently. Car pools were formed, reducing the number of automobiles on the roads, and by 1980 the OPEC hold on the industrialized world, at least, was broken.

The OPEC countries with their single product for export, had to reinvest some of their profits into building the infrastructures of their countries. They lacked the technology and the expertise to accomplish what they had neglected for so long. Therefore, as well as recycling their profits into the economic systems of the industrialized countries, they had to import foreign know-how and the ability to make this know-how work in their countries. This provided them with a unique opportunity of bring their societies into the present era, and to abolish the backwardness that left their countries fundamentally unchanged for many centuries.

Countries that were traditionally poor, lacking in industrial wealth, were able to exploit their oil effectively. Mexico, for example, has good quality oil and the profits from the sales of crude were ploughed back into the Mexican economy. But the concentration on this single product—the allocation of resources into oil production over the establishment of an industrial base for handling the economic growth processes—proved to be unsound. Of course, there was the rationale that now they had a money-making product that would be of substantial benefit to the economy, and that it should be exploited as much as possible. Competition among the OPEC members, for example, resulted in their negating their treaties individually in order to exploit the demand and to monitor their supplies to their advantages. OPEC maintained its unity, but became a de facto organization for establishing guidelines, without real enforcement power to impose them.

In a sense, then, the Ricardian-Mill considerations held during this period. Comparative costs of energy did not have validity at first, and became relevant only when alternative sources were available. However, given the energy restraint, comparative production costs did enter into calculations, with the consequences of production cutbacks and unemployment. Comparative advantages also were significant, as the initial monopoly of the oil producing countries prevailed over all forms of production; this too was loosened considerably after alternative energy sources were utilized effectively in production.

The Yom Kippur war had, therefore, been the watershed in international commerce. Prior to that war trade progressed according to the Ricardian-Mill considerations. While Say's Law functioned to some extent as postwar trade became stabilized, and while Malthus' theory on population and food was relevant only in the very poor emerging countries, this was changed suddenly due to the rapid rise of oil as the prime energy source. Comparative costs and international advantages still held, but these were due not to conditions inherent in the business cycles, but because of the political use of oil as a weapon in international commerce.

Only when oil lost its power as a political weapon and the relationship between the oil producing and consuming countries had stabilized once again, with the oil producing countries recognizing their dependence on the industrial countries for recycling their profits and for supplying them with goods and services, did international trade resume along economic lines. But the laws of international trade had changed. The concepts of comparative costs and comparative advantage took on nuances certainly not intended by their originators. Creditor countries were held in check by debtor countries which were unable to repay their commitments, yet required further assistance and investments in order to enter the new era. Multinational corporations gained in number and in strength, with their operations often conflicting in the various countries. A new dynamism entered the international commercial environment, one in which both the self-assertedness of the countries operated together with the requirement of stability.

To update Viner's comment, no new economic theory for international trade has been formulated since Hume, Ricardo, Mill, and Keynes. Their theories, forming the body of neoclassical and post-Keynesian international economics, are inadequate for our contemporary era. A new theory will be posited in Part II, one that redefines comparative advantages and costs, and reconsiders Keynesian theory in light of our era, one that treats both customs unions and multinational corporations. The emphasis on the domestic economy should not render international commerce as a consequence of domestic economics, as a means of transferring goods and services not sold in the domestic markets to export markets. For a theory to be valid, it must clarify the situation for which it pertains and allow consequences to be drawn from it. This will be attempted in the chapters to follow. International economics must relate to the current situation and allow ramifications from both the theory and the system it delineates. International commerce is too important in our era to be relegated as an extension of domestic macroeconomics; it requires its own theory if such commerce is to be conducted efficiently and effectively. This will be treated in the Part III of this work.

Chapter 3

TRADE THEORY: COMMENTS AND CRITIQUE

International economics, in both its real and monetary aspects, has advanced substantially during the past twenty-five years. Major theoretical innovations, refinements, and modifications have been made. Extensive empirical work has been undertaken and has opened up fruitful new lines of inquiry. If a common trend in international economic theory can be discerned, it is the systematic elaboration of simple general equilibrium models as frameworks for the expression, extension, and testing of the basic ideas.

> —Arthur I. Bloomfield and Wilfred Ethier,
> "Developments in International Economics"[1]

If a common trend in the history of the theories of international economics can be discerned, it is that Viner's sentiment has held consistent, that from Hume to Mill, and indeed including the modern international economists, no strikingly different mechanisms have yet to be suggested. Consider the statement above by Bloomfield and Ethier. Their opinion is that the common trend in international economics is the elaboration of simple general equilibrium models as frameworks for the expression, extension, and the testing of the basic ideas. Can it be that simple general equilibrium models have provided the foundation for the empirical work that has been undertaken, opening up new and fruitful lines of inquiry?

One example of a general equilibrium model that has been adapted is the

Monetary Approach to the Balance of Payments (MABP). A basic proposition to this approach is that a change in the domestic money supply will lead to the broadly offsetting change in foreign reserves. The argument runs as follows: Let M be the money supply, D the domestic money, and R the foreign reserves held by the central bank. Then for aggregate money supply M, $M = R + D$. The argument continues, that $\Delta M = \Delta R + \Delta D$. Furthermore, $\Delta R = CA + CAP$, with CA being the current account, and CAP the capital account of claims of residents of one country on another, or the national foreign debt or assets, as the case may be. The current account is described by $CA = T + i*SF$, with T being the trade balance, and $i*SF$ being the foreign interest rate with respect to the home currency price of a unit of foreign exchange and the foreign assets held by domestic residents, so that $i*SF$ signifies the interest earnings from foreign assets.

This model represents a flow concept, with foreign reserves being increased or diminished as the case may be. Hence, $CA = -CAP$, when the change of R is zero, that is, under equilibrium conditions. However, this equilibrium situation becomes disturbed when a change in M will lead to a change in R. The domestic money supply will also change as agents acting for firms engaged in international commerce use their increased liquidity to purchase further foreign assets, either monetary or in goods and services.

Given this situation, a country's trade balance can be expressed by the following equation: $T = -a_0y + a_1y* + a_2s$, with T as the trade balance, $-a_0y$ the negative affect on domestic income, a_1y* the positive affect on foreign income, and a_2s the positive affect on the exchange rate.

Now, given the equilibrium situation between two trading countries, $E_1 \equiv T_{E_1, E_2} \equiv E_2$, with E_1 and E_2 being the trading partners. Indeed, for equilibrium to exist, the Marshall-Lerner condition must hold, the assumptions of which are that only one export and one import good exists, there exists an infinite elasticity between exports and imports, that trade is in balance, and that full employment exists. Given a single import and export between two countries with an equilibrium relationship, trade will indeed be in balance, for a certain period. However, other conditions exist that destabilize this situation. The domestic aspects of the economy, for example, have to be considered. A slight downturn of the cycle will certainly disrupt the full-employment assumption, even for the single export-import item. Equilibrium will be disrupted to the decline of employment, for even though the export sector will not be immediately affected, the decline of M in the economy reduces purchases and imports are among the first items eliminated in the consumption patterns, so that the trading equilibrium situation will be disrupted.

As for the assumption of infinite elasticity between exports and imports, this, again, places demands on the economies' internal conditions. Given full employment as a constant, there can be no changes in the export-import elasticities, and they will indeed be infinite. But the discussion has focused only on the trade situation in equilibrium, and not on the internal economic conditions.

Even in an equilibrium model of an economy, there are fluctuations introduced to demonstrate how the economy adjusts to conditions of inflation, recession, growth, and prosperity. Given these adjustments, the value of the country's capital depreciates or appreciates accordingly, and this brings the basic equilibrium model into a contradiction.

The Marshall-Lerner condition states, in effect, that depreciation of the value of a country's capital will improve its balance of payments situation, while an appreciation of the value of capital will worsen the position. Of course, in a totally static model, demand for exports and imports is of infinite elasticity, but given the dynamic inputs mentioned above, both demand and supply fluctuate, with the balance of payments so affected. The contradiction is that it is not the value of capital that determines the country's balance of payments position, but its ability to meet its export-import obligations, and this, ultimately, depends on the liquidity position in the macro economy, which is a function of employment. This contradiction is sharpened further by the conflict between static and dynamic equilibrium, for in order to understand even the simple two-country model, it is necessary to introduce the time element and to include more than a single export and import. This eliminates the infinite elasticity condition, thereby limiting the Marshall-Lerner condition to a variation of Tobin's point that the currency account balance in domestic currency varies directly with exchange rates/prices, so that if the exchange rates are fixed—as with the stable equilibrium situation—prices remain fixed and the model represents a moment in time.[2] Given internal dynamics, prices and the exchange rates have little in common, unless devaluations or revaluations are undertaken. Exchange rates determine the markets of international currencies as commodities for arbitrage, or for holding against other countries as debts or as reserves. Prices determine both domestic consumption and production for both domestic and foreign produced goods and services. Domestic production and consumption depend on the supply and demand for these goods and services, and these depend on the aggregate liquidity position and on close substitutes and lower prices. Foreign production for domestic markets depends on the ability to market these products, to exploit the benefits and appeal of these products for the domestic markets; this ability depends on the comparative prices for the foreign goods and services against those produced domestically. Where no viable substitutes exist, the elasticies of these products tend to 1 and not to infinity according to the Marshall-Lerner condition for the two-country two-product stable equilibrium model.[3]

The reason for the contradiction is due to the point made by Bloomfield and Ethier, that the discernable common trend in international economic theory is the systematic elaboration of the simple general equilibrium model as the framework for the expression, extension, and testing of the basic ideas. Simple general equilibrium models are necessary for holding dynamic factors constant while the basic factors of economics are analyzed. But such models must be expanded upon, developed, and brought as close as possible to the real economies, with all their political and economic complexities. Econometric models have been constructed for macro economies, and the construction of such models for trading blocs, for commonwealth relationships, and indeed for the world economy, although of great complexity, are necessary for really understanding the dynamics of trade. Simple general economic models result in simple situations being derived, situations that throw no real light, provide no substantial understanding, of how the world's economies operate in relation to one another. The emphasis on such models, even though some dynamics have, out of necessity, been introduced, gives credence today to the sentiment expressed by Viner, that from the early classical economists and from Hume to the modern economic thinkers, no real significant contributions have been made to trade theory. This does not mean that no useful models of trade have been established to serve the basis of understanding of this most complicated of situations. Several useful models will be discussed here, after which a theory of international economics will be stated, one hopefully that will provide a better understanding of the complexities of the international commercial dynamics.

COMMENTS ON THE $2 \times 2 \times 2$ MODEL

One of the important general equilibrium models is the $2 \times 2 \times 2$ model. This model has a significant advantage over the single-product model discussed above because it contains not only two countries, but also two products and two factors of labor and capital. These countries differ only in their fixed endowments of capital and labor, and the differences account for the different products and their production costs. This also allows for each country to have a comparative advantage in the goods it produces, thereby maintaining its production patterns over its trading partner and preventing competition for the same markets. This is a concept based on the Hecksher-Ohlin model of the equation of factor endowments with respect to production and advantages in trade.

The usefulness of this model can be seen from the three theorems relating to it, and its possible expansion to a $n \times n \times n$ model ($n > 2$), providing a greater sense of realism and a closer proximity to the real world.

One theorem is Paul Samuelson's factor-price equalization argument. Should both countries maintain production of both goods under free trade conditions, common commodity prices mean common costs of production in both countries.[4] Increased wages relative to fixed costs raise the cost of the labor-intensive good relative to the capital-intensive good. As relative costs are directly related to relative factor prices, the equalization of costs implies the equalization of the factor prices. Absolute factor prices and costs must also tend to equality, for if not, there would be no serious comparative advantage in the trade situation and hence no basis for trade. Specialization into production areas other than those established originally by the terms of trade will lead to diseconomies because of the endowment of resources. However, if the two countries' resources differ sufficiently so that production in one country is capital-intensive while being labor-intensive in the other, free trade may lead to incomplete specialization because of the unused resources in the employment of labor and capital to meet the conditions of trade. In this case, the Heckscher-Ohlin model is a limit case of the trade situation, a model of the specialization model. Specialization may result in the international transfer of factors—such as labor mobility and the establishment of productive plants in the other country—and if this transfer brings about an equalization of prices, then free trade is again established in equilibrium, with no further gain from transfer of international factors, even if this were possible again.

Another theorem is that posed by Samuelson and Wolfgang F. Stopler, pertaining to the impact of relative commodity price changes on real factor prices. A price change of x percent would affect production costs by less than the change. Competition insures that price can be no greater nor less than costs, so that a rise (or fall) of one factor price must result in a fall (or rise) of the other factor prices. The consequence of this approach is that it links factor price changes to the dynamics of the domestic economy; it does so, however, while maintaining the entire trade process in an equilibrium position.[5]

Still another consequence of this model is T. M. Rybczynski's contribution. If one of the factors of production, say capital, increases by x percent, and if the production of both goods increased by less than x percent, all the additional capital could not be employed resulting in the output of one of these goods to rise by the x percent rate. With a fixed labor supply, the output or both goods cannot be increased, so that of the second good falls accordingly. As the countrywide capital/labor ratio has increased, the capital-intensive industrial output increases and the labor-intensive output decreases at the same rate of the increase.[6]

Both of Samuelson's arguments and the argument of Rybczynski include the dynamics of the internal economy in the processes of international trade. They are, however, based on the Mill position of comparative advantage, and basically on dynamic equilibrium, on Hume's argument. In Samuelson's first argument the absolute prices of the production factors must equal costs, to establish the comparative advantage which forms the basis for trade. Equilibrium is established and maintained by the international transfer of production factors, moving to the country with the lowest costs and highest profits. As these are reduced due to restrictions or greater increases in consumption, the factors will move back again, thus maintaining the system in equilibrium.

Samuelson's second argument and Rybczynski's position of the internal economy's influence of factor prices on output demonstrate the comparative advantage of one factor over another. Factor price increases result in one of the factors to decline in output, thereby altering the comparative advantage established previously and redefining the terms of trade. In this model, the shift from one source of trade leads to a responding shift in the other country's resource allocation, with the new trade situation being in equilibrium. This new situation may not be static, because a result of the shift may lead to reduced (increased) costs and a reorientation in the production makeup. If so, this new dynamic—it makes no difference from which country it is initiated—will result in a further orientation of production factors and costs, but again, the system will reach a Humean equilibrium position, dynamic as it may be.

An interesting consequence of the $2 \times 2 \times 2$ model is the paradox brought into the open by Wassily Leontief.[7] He posited that an average basket of U.S. exports required less capital per worker than did a close import substitute. The paradox is that the United States is an extremely capital-intensive country, even compared to other developed countries from which close substitutes would be imported. Prior to 1966, U.S. exports had a relatively higher labor content than did its imports, so that for an increase in exports more jobs would be created while imports would have minimal effect on the labor situation. But, after the 1960s, this was no longer so. One explanation for this change is posited by Richard Barnet and Ronald Müller, who state that:

The reason, we strongly suspect, was the rise of the "export platform." Between 1966 and 1970, there was a rise of 63 percent in exports produced in U.S. factories of global corporations (with a labor component) and a spectacular 92-percent rise in exports from their foreign subsidiaries (more labor-intensive). . . . By the end of 1970, more than 25 percent of all their workers were outside the territory of the United States. (At the same time, the capacity of the U.S. manufacturing sector as a whole to provide jobs for Americans was declining at a rate of six times that of the 1950's.) When more than a quarter of worker and managerial energies of the leading industrial firms are outside the country, it is questionable whether the Federal Government will be able to develop an effective employment policy.[8]

Whether the federal government should be involved in developing employment policy is a question that cannot be treated here. The central governing bodies of nations must play a part in economic regulation, but providing employment should be best left to the business sectors. The economics of multinational corporations will be discussed in the last part of this work. But, indeed, this may be a reason for the Leontief paradox. There is, however, another explanation, theoretically based, for this paradox. This will be discussed further in Part II, but it suffices here to mention that the utility of capital in production, and not merely the presence of capital intensivity, is the solution to this paradox.

COMMENTS ON THE MUNDELL-FLEMING MODEL

The Mundell-Fleming model provides an approach to international trade on the basis of a small economy's internal dynamics. However, the constraints placed on this model tend to deflate its realism. For example, the economy is open, subject to the world interest rates, and a perfectly elastic supply of imports at a given supply price. This model is further constrained by its assets, being a domestic and foreign bond, each having the same maturity, and a domestic and foreign currency in which trade is conducted. Expectations of change are held static, with arbitrage maintaining an equilibrium between the currencies and the bonds.

The world economy is thus composed of two separate economies whose industries are interlocked through trade. Their interest rates, both for their internal dynamics and their mutual commerce are equal, so that $i_A = i_B$, or $i = i^*$. The money market equilibrium for our economy is stated by $M/P = L$, with L being a function of i and Y, interest and income. L is thus real money demand which depends on the interest rate, M is money, and P is the price of domestic output which is assumed to be constant in the model. Y is domestic output, and this depends on real money demand for the goods produced, as well as the interest rate charged for the money.

The country's balance of payments equilibrium position, K, is thus stated: $K = T(S, Y, n) - C(i)$. T is the trade balance, Y domestic output, n, the variation in export according to the goods being exported, and $C(i)$, the change in the capital market as reflected by the interest rate. These variations in exports and the interest rate reflect changes in the original equilibrium in the goods market. But this equilibrium position is formulated to reflect changes, making the Mundell-Fleming model dynamic internally. This can be seen by its formula for equilibrium in the goods market. Hence, $Y = D = A(i, Y) + T(S, Y, n) + G$, with Y as domestic output, and D the components of demand being determined by the consumption of the goods domestically or by spending money for other purposes. T is the trade balance of goods with the other partner and depends on personal income, the exchange rate for a fixed-period pricing, and n being the domestic output. Changes in n, due to better technology, or increased labor efficiency, alter the entire balance of the equilibrium equations. These changes are not external in the sense that they are demand-oriented, but are internal, relating to the conditions that determine output Y. As n changes, so does Y, with the other elements following suit, reflecting the new economic situation. This will also be registered with the trading partner, who will alter its conditions accordingly.

The G element is, of course, the government, and its policies bear directly on equilibrium in the goods market and hence on the trade balance. The reasons for government action are that either demand is too high for the money supply, so that inflation sets in and upsets the trade equilibrium, or that demand is too low and the money supply increased in order to stimulate a positive atmosphere and generate confidence that can be translated into economic action, or to adjust the interest rate to maintain a balance of interest rates with the trading partner, whose rate has been raised (lowered) to attract (detract) investors.

Hence, the government sets both monetary and fiscal policy with respect to the economy's internal conditions, but also with concern as to how these policies affect international commerce. Given that equilibrium is maintained even though fluctuations occur, given imperfect capital mobility due to the inability for its absorption or because of economic pressures to keep foreign capital to a minimum acceptable to all parties concerned, an increase in savings will result in a decrease of money in the economy for consumption, with the consequence of the foreign monetary relationship being affected. If trade is in balance, then less liquidity will result in a corresponding decline in consumption, so that foreign goods are not consumed at the previous level (remembering that this is a limited market model). The result is that the trading partner now has a balance of payments deficit, which will be translated into reduced commercial exchanges. This reduction will be rectified by lowering interest rates, increasing liquidity and hence production at reduced costs, and exporting again. Both economies will have reached an equilibrium position with respect to one another as the distortion in the trade balance is eliminated. In this condition the increased domestic demand will not influence prices as production increases correspond to the demand increase and the flow of goods from the trading partner, as their relationship is reestablished in equilibrium.

As for changes in fiscal policy, should the economy be in recession, an increase in budgetary expenditures will lead to a rise in employment and consumption, but with greater imports than exports in the short-run period. This is because imports will be available in the markets, while exports have declined together with domestic production during the recession. Given a fixed exchange rate, this will result in a deterioration in the current balance of payments account, until industry can begin producing and exporting again.

Should the economy be in a period of prosperity, reduced budgetary expenditures to cool off the economy result in unemployment and reduced consumption, with the consequence of greater imports than exports. Then, depending on the stage of the cycle and the monetary policies that will be enacted to curtail the fiscal policies, a balance of payments deficit will exist, with the consequences being a situation prolonged only by industry's inability to produce exports to reduce the deficit. Given fixed exchange rates, fiscal and monetary policies often clash with one another, eliminating the objectives that each policy seeks to achieve.

In the above example, the fixed exchange rates distort the economy's ability to compete. Only through production alterations can equilibrium be restored. However, given flexible exchange rates, fiscal and monetary policies need not necessarily clash. For example, with a recession under way, interest rates can be lowered for production and raised for investment, bringing foreign currency into the country. This will affect the exchange rate in a manner that will offset the deficit accordingly, as investment is a purchase over time. This will encourage production, without extreme monetary policies that counter or distort budgetary policies, so that export production is stimulated and equilibrium is achieved again. Even in the two-country model, flexible prices favor trade and equilibrium.

Bringing into the model speculation on the exchange rate, two points have to be considered. One is speculation against devaluation of one currency with respect to the other, and this often results in the self-fulfilling-prophecy effect, when the pressure of speculation results in its objective of devaluation. Likewise, speculative activity for a currency against the other results, ceteris paribus, in that currency's revaluation. Whatever the policy is, devaluation and revaluation have both monetary and fiscal repercussions on the domestic economy, given fixed exchange rates. The monetary impact is that the devalued currency, turning more toward domestic than imported goods, tends to increase employment as more domestic goods are manufactured compared with imported goods. This also leads to a reduction in imported goods prices, making them more competitive. The benefits of increased domestic employment depend on the rate of price reductions on the imported goods, for if elasticity is diminished for these goods, the price reduction need not be so great to remain competitive, and employment will revert to unemployment as more domestic income is spent on the imported goods.

Revaluation, given a fixed exchange rate, has the monetary impact of stimulating employment in the other economy as the import prices are reduced with respect to the domestic economy. Whether this has an impact on employment, however, depends on the ability of labor to maintain or increase production at lower costs and hence lower domestic prices.

For devaluation, given a fixed exchange rate, fiscal policies are required to increase domestic output so that at least these prices remain stable or are lowered. Taxation, as a government tool, must be applied with great caution in order to maintain employment and allow for increased production, so that imports do not redirect both resources and investment liquidity.

For revaluation, taxation must be implemented with respect to maintaining employment so that the reduced import prices, while attracting consumption, do not affect domestic output and hence bring about unemployment. Business taxes should be reduced to increase employment and domestic production, generated by increased liquidity for investment as a result of lowered business taxation.

Should monetary and fiscal policies which are ineffective be introduced, the lower-priced goods will draw consumption to the point that manufacturing will not be able to keep up the rate of output. Prices will then rise, and demand will shift to the other products as their costs are lowered to become more competitive and eventually come into price-line with the other products. In either way, equilibrium is eventually achieved, even though a new exchange rate is fixed. Speculation with fixed exchange rates is profitable only temporarily because the diseconomies resulting lowers the value of the other currency—a process with rapid impact but one that can be rectified only over time.

What about the Mundell-Fleming model given flexible exchange rates? The influence of exchange speculation depends on if it is equilibrating or disequilibrating. If this speculation is equilibrating, it will tend to decrease the exchange variations resulting from internal fiscal or monetary policies. Fleming states that the greater relative effectiveness that a flexible rate gives to monetary policy, compared to fiscal policy, is attributed to the stronger influence exerted by monetary policy. He states, however, that

since the greater relative effectiveness which a floating [that is flexible] rate gives to monetary policy, compared with budgetary policy, is attributed to the stronger influence that the former exercizes on exchange rates, it is to be expected that equilibrating speculation, by damping down exchange rate effects, tends to reduce the difference in effectiveness between the two kinds of policy.[9]

Moreover, Fleming maintains that disequilibrating speculation, by exaggerating exchange rate variations, tends to accentuate this difference in effectiveness. Indeed, for fixed exchange rates speculation would be absent, but should there be a decline in confidence in the fixed exchange rates, fear of bringing about disequilibrating movements of capital tends to limit the duration and magnitude of expansionary fiscal policies, especially of money policy, the effect of which would be more adverse on the balance of payments than of the budgetary policy.

The difficulty with this model is that it tends to two differing goals. It seeks equilibrium between the trading partners, which at the same time contains a dynamic that brings the economies into disequilibrium. The n factor of domestic output, for instance, is certainly destabilizing, as improvements in labor efficiency and technology lead to reduced costs which are passed on in reduced prices. Once prices are reduced, the equilibrium is eliminated, bringing about disequilibrium in the balance of payments and in the quantity traded. This is a two-way affair, as each country undergoes such changes and the exchange rates have to bend. The n factor is neither due to monetary nor fiscal policy, but with production and improvements in the state of the arts. Indeed, both fiscal and monetary policy have to take this into account, and the n factor can generate conditions not established in the model, such as other products for internal and international commerce. Moreover, both fiscal and monetary policies are instituted with respect to the business cycle, and to neglect the impact of the cycle on international trade is to leave undiscussed a very important part of the economic process. Certainly more work in this type of model is required concerning business fluctuations. Maintaining equilibrium eliminates change and expectations. Keeping change and expectations within the framework of floating exchange rates does not show their effects on the n factor. The Mundell-Fleming model is certainly instructive, as it attempts to deal with economic forces acting within an equilibrium situation, although allowing for some disequilibrium to demonstrate how changes can come about in the model. This disequilibrium, however, is to show movement that will eventually bring the countries back to an equilibrium position. This is surely in the tradition of the classical and neoclassical economists, thereby vindicating Viner's sentiment.

COMMENTS ON PARITY PRICING POLICY

The parity pricing policy is one of the persistent concepts in international economics. It rises to be considered a viable approach when existing exchange rates are considered unrealistic and a search is undertaken for equilibrium rates. According to B. Balassa, it was first invoked, in somewhat ambiguous terms, during the Napoleonic wars, and received its statement by Gustav Cassel during World War I, to be resurrected after World War II.[10]

Balassa discusses two forms of this policy. One form, the absolute, states that purchasing power parities, when calculated as a ratio of consumer goods for any two countries, would tend to approximate the equilibrium rate of exchange. The other form, the relative interpretation, asserts that in comparison to a period when equilibrium prices prevailed, changes in relative prices indicate the necessary exchange rate adjustments.

Consider, for example, a good g produced in the United States and the United Kingdom. Let us say g is suitable for both countries and hence is freely tradable, so that no tariffs exist and transportation costs are equaled out and hence negated. If $P_{g\ U.S.}$ denotes the price of g in the United States, then for sterling, the price must be $P_{g\ U.S.} = P_{g\ U.K.S.}$ For the absolute price parity to hold, this relationship must exist for all products traded between the two countries. In this situation, there is no hoarding nor speculation, no restricting the flow of the goods in order to influence their prices. This is the absolute price parity and exists in this type of situation for the duration of stability between the two countries.

Consider, however, the relative form, when prices are determined by a base period over time. For such parity to hold, weights have to be assigned to the two economies for a specified time period, and prices and the exchange rates are measured with respect to this period. With $S_{t,b}$ (equal to S_t/S_b, t and b being time period and based period), then for all the products traded between the United States and the United Kingdom,

There are, however, well-known difficulties with this approach. While the relative form offers greater flexibility, taking into account the indices of the countries involved, it is relevant only for international trade, so that nontraded goods and services used in the economy also enter that country's index, and this exerts an influence on the basing of parity price policy, even though these products are irrelevant in international commerce. Moreover, retail price lists have to be included in this calculation, as well as the gross domestic product deflator and the year on which this is based. Alternatively, using those goods and services that are directed to export markets as well as domestic markets brings up the issue of determining which products fall solely into this category. This is also a time-bound concept, for products directed for only domestic consumption during one time period may be exported to a certain extent during another period. One possible method is to use the base only for strictly non-traded goods, but together with the time-period situation, this does not account for production differences, market orientations, and the differences in cyclic positions.

Moreover, such a position would require the restructuring of the exchange rates as frequently as there are changes within one of the economies. This will lead to a breakdown of the pricing system and move the situation into a flexible exchange rate. A partial parity policy offers stability in the international markets, and thus can be employed to provide a bottom price for the exchange rate. But there must be sufficient price flexibility to allow for international capital mobility, especially when multinational corporations are concerned. This problem must also be considered with respect to investing in the emerging and developing economies, those most in need of foreign financing and technology.

The difficulty with the policy of parity pricing is that it too is founded on the classical concept of equilibrium. In a two-country model, parity pricing allows for the mobility of the goods and services traded, providing that they are sufficiently different and in demand to generate and maintain trade. A model can be constructed in which countries of similar infrastructure and productive capacity base their pricing on an agreed upon basket of goods and services, which is an extension of the two-country model. However, the two-country model operates only when equilibrium is maintained; as was shown above with the Mundell-Fleming model, however, equilibrium tends to break down when cyclical fluctuations and growth take place. The currency basket pegged to goods and services can serve as a form of parity pricing, but only among countries with similar industries and infrastructures. This may be appropriate for customs unions, but it also eliminates much of the world's markets. Moreover, when countries involved with this parity pricing policy trade in earnest with those countries with differing infrastructures and industrial bases, the parity pricing system tends to collapse because it cannot apply in this situation. Having one policy for one set of countries and another for the other sets not only results in administrative difficulties as with the case of multinational corporations, but also flounders when other countries in the parity pricing system also trade with these same countries. Seeking better terms of trade influences the exchange rate, eventually disrupting the parity pricing system. It must be said that customs unions present a special situation in international economics and this will be discussed in the last part of this work.

Balassa states that the parity pricing policy could still find application if productivity increases and wage adjustments were identical in every country,

and if we also assumed neutral production and consumption effects. Under these, admittedly restrictive, assumptions, parallel changes in the general price level will take place and the doctrine will give the correct answer: there is no need for adjusting the rates of exchange.[11]

These assumptions are, indeed, restrictive, and should the conditions hold, there would be no need for adjusting exchange rates. But this is a model of static equilibrium in which trade is conducted for the same products in each economy. There is no cyclical fluctuation, no monetary nor fiscal policy that would alter the economic circumstances in any of the countries involved. It is a model without real life, without the dynamics of the business cycle. Hence, it is a model that may be of interest academically, but fails to make a real contribution to the dynamics of foreign commerce.

FURTHER COMMENTS

The emphasis on equilibrium in economic reasoning stems from perhaps two sources. One source may be the desire on the part of economic theoreticians to portray the discipline of economics as a science. The construction of models that work mathematically reenforces the scientific aspect of economics, and economists can point to the uncertainty in the physical sciences and in mathematics itself and claim that even in these fields exactness is elusive and uncertainty prevailing.[12]

The second source may be a desire to view the world with the same clarity and understanding as did the classical and neoclassical giants of the discipline. Hume and Smith, for example, posited equilibrium systems and their contributions were outstanding. Say expounded on this and refined Smith's "invisible hand" concept into a working economic law that bears Say's name. Arthur C. Pigou had a version of economic equilibrium, manifested in his doctrine of full employment, certainly not true during the Great Depression. However, even with the knowledge that neoclassical economics, with its prevailing concept of equilibrium, was no longer adequate, Keynes, who gave a brilliant critique of Pigou's work, stated his *General Theory* in such a way that Say's Law is derivable from that theory.[13]

Equilibrium persists in economic reasoning, even though it has little significance in the real world. Granted, that trade is conducted usually in a two-way stream among two countries, the terms of trade vary with the very disequilibrium conditions in each country. Exchange rates may be fixed or flexible, according to a country's policies, but this has nothing to do with equilibrium. The concept of equilibrium is one that is necessary in explaining models, constrained by certain conditions to demonstrate how other conditions perform, given specific dynamics. However, while this is necessary for understanding, it must also be considered that the real world operates differently, that the constraints are few, the dynamics overlapping, and uncertainty prevailing.

There are other aspects of exchange rate theory that could have been discussed here. The sticky-price model and the monetary currency substitution and portfolio balance models are just two examples. What is required, however, is a theory of international trade that provides a concept of exchange rate determination based on dynamic disequilibrium, portraying the dynamics of the economies. Moreover, countries do not trade only among others with similar infrastructures and industries, but also both emerging and developing economies, so the exchange rates must take this into consideration. Also, there is the aspect of multinational corporations who place their businesses into countries on the basis of resource availability at acceptable costs, and on the governments of these countries to manage the foreign exchange rate.

In the chapters to follow, a theory of international trade will be attempted that will be based on dynamic disequilibrium, and a concept of exchange rates based on this theory will be stated. After which, the theory will be applied to the conditions of customs unions, multinational corporations, and to the most vulnerable participants in trade, the emerging and developing countries.

Part II

THE THEORY OF INTERNATIONAL TRADE

Chapter 4

INTRODUCTORY COMMENTS

But the significant changes, in the economic as in the political context, are precisely those brought about by large numbers of people changing their behaviour in the same way at the same time.

It is plain that in an economic system with these characteristics, almost anything can happen. Alternations of feverish activity and langour will no longer take us by surprise but will be regarded as normal: we should be very surprised if they did not take place.

—Guy Routh,
The Origin of Economic Ideas[1]

While the significant changes in economics and politics are brought about by large numbers of people changing their behavior in the same way at the same time, there is no nonscientific reason why such mass behavior should not surprise us. Each of us is different from the other—different in appearance, in genetic composition, in the degree of our sensitivity and ability to comprehend and contribute. Our responses to the same stimuli differ, and this accounts for the wide diversification in tastes, interests, hobbies, and professions. Personal psychology is the only scientific field that deals with the individual and his or her likes, dislikes, tastes.

To say that for politics and economics there is such a phenomenon as mass psychology, is an incorrect combination of terms. Mass behavior occurs when people react—either responsibly or irrationally—to the general circumstances that confront them. Their actions are based on their understanding of the available information. This is a crucial point for politicians, for those who control the media also control the quality and quantity of information on which people base their daily lives. Those in control tend to think that they have the peoples' best interests in mind when they deliberately change the contents of the media to present a specific point of view. Of course, the subjective element in reporting cannot be eliminated, nor can the personal comprehension in understanding the news be prevented.

Economists deal with information and usually understand the information regarding their own countries better than the information from other countries; for international commerce, this can present difficulties in the decision-making process. Indeed, with the world so integrated, it is now necessary that finance ministers, secretaries of the treasury, and exchequers make the information of their countries' economic policies as clear as possible to the decision makers of other countries in order to uphold whatever economic confidence exists in the international marketplace and to support the exports of their industries.

Since the end of World War II, we have entered a new era, an era of knowledge in which technology, together with knowledge industries, have joined with industry to increase production, diversify industrial output, and, as we are now witnessing, break down political barriers.[2] We are establishing new trading partners, hence new markets; we are investing in economies with different infrastructures and political systems, not out of altruism, but because these economies are opening up to trade and profits are to be made.

Still, two vestiges of the early period of our new era exist and exert great influence on our time. There is, for example, the issue of foreign aid, primarily from the United States, to those countries which are in various stages of emergence and development, and now to those countries that are undergoing the changes of political and economic reorientation after being released from the constraints of political dictatorship and economic planning. The significance of the Marshall Plan in the aftermath of World War II has not been forgotten and such a plan may be formulated to reconstruct Eastern Europe and to some extent the Soviet Union, in light of the new economic dawning coming upon them.

Since great strides have been made in science, technology, and industrial orientation and output in our new era, another approach is being utilized for building these economies. Education is being provided to peoples of these countries, and trade, in order to bring their economies into the new era, is also being undertaken. Indeed, the issue of trade and aid for these economies is one of great importance for their economies and for the donor economies as well. This has increased the interest in international economies among world leaders as they have to understand how trade can affect their economies and comprehend the economics that is the basis for trade. As aid is also important, the economic utility of the monies received for the domestic economy has to be understood, especially the relationship between the domestic economy and its business cycles, and trade that depends on the economies of other countries. Aid used for the development of the domestic economy, without consideration toward building up a viable trade industry, is money limited in its potential. This issue will be discussed further in Part III.

The other vestige is that of trade theory itself, and to this point Viner's sentiment relates. While the models discussed in the previous chapter are certainly far from exhaustive, they nevertheless represent the direction that trade theory has taken. It is equilibrium-oriented, with models ranging from static to dynamic equilibrium in presentation. The real world, both for domestic and international economics, operates under a different assumption, that of dynamic disequilibrium, with the three components of the domestic economy—government, industry, and labor—often in conflict in direction and purpose. As trade is an extension of the domestic economy, these components have to be considered in a theory if it is to be both comprehensible and viable. For example, the value of a country's currency depends on its ability to produce and sell. As a country's currency is valued relative to other countries' currencies, its value is determined by its productive capacity compared with other countries. A country's productive capacity depends on its industrial management and its labor force for developing products and markets, as well as manufacturing the products and distributing them to their markets efficiently. This productive capacity also depends on the government's ability to reduce the deleterious consequences of the business cycle inherent in the economy. During recessions unemployment reduces output and hence the liquidity in the economy; the government must know how to act to reduce unemployment, stimulate the conditions for economic growth, and to move the cycle upward from the recession phase. A theory of international trade must take these components into account as they pertain to a country's productive capacity and the value of its currency in the international marketplace.

Moreover, countries with similar economic infrastructures and productive capacity tend to produce similar and competing goods and services. These countries maintain trading relations and because of their economic similarities, comparative advantage as a concept is no longer viable. The emphasis must be placed on comparative utilities in production, in product quality and service, and on price—which depend on the economy's productive capacities and are consequences of its cyclical position.

Still, there is a basis for trade, and this is the competitiveness of products, their advantages as explained to their potential and actual consumers. While this is certainly valid for competing industries within a domestic economy, its validity holds for the international marketplace, where similar industries compete among each other for consumers' purchases.

This holds even more so for trading partners with different infrastructures and industrial bases. For in this trading situation, commerce is not conducted among competing goods, but for different goods and services, usually lacking between the trading countries. Tourism in Morocco has attractions that tourism in France lacks, and France certainly has tourist attractions lacking in Morocco. Morocco imports high technology goods and services from France, while France imports foods and consumer items from Morocco. The United States and France, countries with similar infrastructures and industrial bases, trade in foods, culture, and tourism, but compete in automobiles, computers, and aerospace technologies, to the extent that national pride often enters into the bargaining process. As these countries undergo their business cycles, the terms of trade are altered, either to encourage imports or discourage them, as the finance ministers, pressured by the industrialists, comprehend the situation. Hence, a theory of trade must consider a country's cyclic position and dynamic disequilibrium when treating the trade situation. While the tendency is that countries with similar economies are influenced by each other and are thus on the same cyclic position, this tendency is not absolute nor consistent. Each country's position in fact depends on the skills of its financial and labor leaders in dealing with the circumstances at hand.

There is another set of circumstances existing among the emerging and developing countries with respect to trade. As their businesses and industries engage in international commerce, the monies are brought back to their own countries and invested, resulting in increased infrastructure, better social services, better living conditions. The extent of these conditions, of course, depends on the moral statures of their governments. But countries engaging in trade among their similar countries' economies will benefit from these additional markets. As they trade with developed countries, they will tend to be brought into similar growth patterns, and their lower living standards raised accordingly; these foreign markets supplement the deficiencies in their own markets. Continuing trade with the developed countries will, if left unhampered, bring their economies into similar cyclical patterns as the developed countries, but this must wait until the last part of this book.

Finally, with respect to Routh's point that significant changes in economics are precisely those brought about by large numbers of people acting the same way at the same time, this behavior is due to information presented to the people as consumers, manufacturers, tax payers and employees, engaged in the economic processes. These people act upon the information available to them and behave rationally with response to the business cycle's phases. On the basis of this behavior, government policy is formulated in its directing the economy; indeed, it forms the basis of predicting and forecasting behavior patterns with respect to economic policies. Because of these behavior patterns, economic policies can be formulated and control exerted over the economy; without these behavior patterns there could be no economic activity and a government's attempt to establish an infrastructure and basis for economic activity would only meet with failure.

The point is, however, that Routh's sentiment does not take into account a factor of economic activity which is not very responsive to government policies or to a lesser degree, the phase of the business cycle. This factor is entrepreneurial activity, or managerial activity in planning and executing new product manufacturing, or in the case of imitators, entering into already established markets and earning profits and providing employment. This is not the behavior of large numbers of people, predictable and on the basis of which government planning is formulated. It is the basis of economic activity, however, and itself, to be successful and profitable, depends on large numbers of people being persuaded to purchase the products. This is not to say that entrepreneurs and managers (these terms are interchangeable, depending on the size of the business and the scope of activity) are outside the pattern of the general economic situation. But as they are the generators of economic activity, the very people who muster the capital and build the plant, who employ workers to produce the goods and services to be consumed, these entrepreneurs and managers establish the very patterns in which the economy takes in its growth processes.

Certainly, entrepreneurs and managers, innovators and imitators in the dynamics of economic activity, have been the subjects of discussion since Adam Smith formulized his "invisible hand" concept, and J.-B. Say brought this concept into the economic Law of Markets. This has set the format for the discussion of entrepreneurial and managerial activity, which have been the subjects of the classical economists, such as Ricardo, J.-C.-L. Simonde de Sismondi, James Mill, and the neoclassical economists such as J. S. Mill, J. A. Schumpeter, Vilfredo Pareto, Alfred Marshall, and even into the watershed period of J. M. Keynes.[3]

However, the economic roles of entrepreneurs and managers in the development of foreign markets has not enjoyed the same attention as for domestic economies. This is certainly a deficiency in this branch of economic theory, for exchange rates, important for government regulation of foreign currencies, are also significant in the agreements reached among trading businesses. The very conditions to which managers agree to trade depend, in part, on the rate of exchanges and hence the profits made from the trade. With profits to be made, more labor is contracted and the greater the impact trade has on the economy. Moreover, government policies regarding the terms of trade, such as with customs unions, also affect the types of trade and its extent.

Still, trade is an extension of the domestic economy, and while governments regulate trade through the exchange rates, managers and entrepreneurs act on the basis of their information concerning foreign marketability of their products, and the political and economic climates in which they intend to trade, both in their own countries and their target countries.

With this having been stated, it is the class of managers and entrepreneurs that generates economic activity, both within the domestic economy and in foreign commerce. While there is risk in every economic venture, the psychological risks are greater when dealing with foreign markets, because of the unfamiliarity with the traditions, cultures, and procedures of foreign countries. This is one reason for multinational companies. However, as with the domestic economy, risks can be minimized in foreign trading if the procedures for trading are comprehended.

Consumers are the same everywhere in the sense that they allocate a specific portion of their incomes to purchasing the goods and services available. In this sense, Routh's sentiment is correct, for people act en masse in their consumption. People have different tastes, however, and this accounts for the differing products, the variations in product quality as they are oriented to different levels of consumers, and the different professions and businesses individuals choose as occupations. But Routh's sentiment does not take into account that as markets expand, people have greater ranges of goods and services from which to choose, allowing for individuality to be expressed even further. These differences form the basis of economic commerce, both domestically and internationally.

As theoreticians, economists cannot account for the differences in consumers' preferences, but they can account for the impact that aggregate demand and supply have on each other. The differences in demand with respect to the differing products and prices form the basis of economic theory. This holds true for international economics as well as for the domestic economy, and on this basis a theory of international trade will be developed.

Chapter 5

INTERNATIONAL ECONOMICS: CONCEPTS AND TOOLS

Demand and supply curves of exports and imports must not be mixed up with the underlying domestic demand and supply curves for the commodities involved. For example, the import demand curve, even for a consumer good is not a "pure," consumer demand curve, but is the excess of home demand over home supply. It is clear that whenever an imported commodity is also produced at home and an exported commodity also consumed at home, the import demand and import supply will be much more elastic than the home demand and home supply, respectively.

—Gottfried Haberler
"The Market for Foreign Exchange and the Stability
of the Balance of Payments: A Theoretical Analysis"[1]

The basic concept underlying all international transactions is that foreign markets are extensions of domestic markets, in the sense that goods and services produced domestically, and whose quality is reflected in the strengths of the supply and demand curves, can also be sold internationally. This market-extension concept allows for the developing of markets in different countries, regardless of the domestic market conditions. It forms the basis for industries strictly oriented toward export, and also for multinational corporations, a special case of domestic-cum-export-oriented businesses. However, Haberler is correct, that the supply and demand export curves have to be separated from domestic curves for the commodities involved. Foreign markets, as extensions of domestic markets, have their own dynamics, unique to their economies. Therefore, while they are extensions of the domestic markets, they are also as different as the positions on the business cycles, and as the monetary and fiscal policies of the administrations of the countries.

While this holds for countries whose currencies, infrastructures, and government policies differ, it also holds true for those countries whose markets are similar to their trading partners' and which hold to the regulations of a common currency area, such as a well-established customs union. Ours is a world that is both coming together and acting separately. We recognize the need for the general pooling of resources, yet we seek our own economic independence. Customs unions are no different in this respect from nonmember countries, for each country in the union seeks to maintain its own economic identity that it has evolved throughout its existence. Common currency areas thus behave in a manner similar to those countries with their own independent currencies. Any region, any country, within a common currency area, or acting independently of such an area, when faced with a loss of international demand for its products, will be forced to cut its expenditures through a loss of bank reserves and the income derived from trade. The problem is that a country has some control over its domestic supply and demand through monetary and fiscal policies. Can such domestic policies affect the country's position with respect to trade?

The answer to this question depends on the perspective from which it is approached. If considered from the point of view of two separate markets being involved, the domestic and the foreign market, then with respect to the foreign markets, the firms engaged in international trade have to consider the dynamics of their targeted markets. If these markets are in a recessed cyclical phase, then demand for their products will most certainly be affected, regardless of the tendency for inelasticity, should it exist. Demand will decline as foreign liquidity for consumption declines, and the firms engaged in exporting to these markets will have to adjust their planning and production accordingly. As these firms depend on the market conditions of the countries to which they are exporting, the economic conditions of their own economies exert little influence. Their workers will remain employed should their own economies be in a downward cyclical phase, as their sales depend on foreign markets.

On the other hand, the resources they require are mainly from their own economies. Should their foreign markets be strong while their own economies are moving downward on the cycle, their abilities to obtain resources are affected. This is because those firms supplying resources do not engage in business with only those firms that are export-oriented, but also rely on firms that produce for the domestic markets. As these domestic-oriented firms cut back on purchases, the abilities of the export-oriented firms to obtain the necessary materials are affected and production has to be adjusted accordingly. In this sense, the domestic policies affect a country's position with respect to trade.

This ambiguous answer reflects the status of trading businesses, for while they are domestically based, they are subject to the conditions of their domestic economies, and because they are foreign oriented, they are also subjected to the conditions of the countries of their markets. This ambiguity exists because of the inherent instability of domestic markets and is manifested in the instability of world trade patterns. Even countries with common currency areas trading among each other will, at one time or another, be faced with declining demand for their exported products. The extent of this situation depends on the quality of the goods and services being traded, the ability to meet delivery dates, comparative pricing for similar goods and services in other countries, and post-delivery servicing where necessary. These aspects are of extreme importance, for they serve as a basis for foreign trade.

Another basis for foreign trade pertains specifically to our current economic situation. It is the market devaluations, contrasted to government devaluations, that brings about radical shifts in market alignments in the demand for hard currencies. These conditions reflect expectations of the economy's inadequate performances, leading to the withdrawal of investment and foreign currency in that country. For example, the British pound sterling is very strong compared to other currencies, but it was market-devalued in the early 1980s to the extent that it was worthwhile for many Americans to purchase airline tickets and buy goods and services in London, rather than in their own domestic markets.

The U.S. dollar has also been market-devalued because of the continuing expectation of poor balance of trade figures, with expectation worsening these figures even more. It is of little consequence that the United States has become one of the centers of world banking and the largest supplier of goods and services to the most impoverished countries, thereby developing its negative trade balance. The negative trade balance results in the abandonment of the dollar in exchange for other hard currencies.

Market devaluations may be politically useful for governments, to prevent them from taking the political act of devaluation. They may also be politically detrimental as reflecting on the government's inability to maintain a strong currency, especially during election time when a strong currency is a source of national pride, and positive trade figures serve as a reflection of the economy's strength. Market devaluations are, however, beyond the control of governments because they reflect the expectations of people in other countries concerning the values of the currencies in question. There is only a partial justification for market devaluations where the quality of national goods and services is concerned; it does, however, demonstrate the extreme degree to which the deviation from equilibrium—in practice, if not in theory—has affected the worlds' economies. Products are only partially involved, but the countries' currencies, both as commodities in themselves and as reflections of their countries' relative economic strengths through performance, are full participants in the shifts in their values.

As well as market devaluations there are revaluations. These may not be necessarily market-induced, that is based on expectations, but are generally caused by the placing of foreign currencies and investments in those economies that are considered strong or are expected to improve significantly in performance. Even still, the subjective element of expectation, so important in other branches of economics, exerts its influence. While Japan's currency is strong relative to that of the United States because of its trading position, the yen is being threatened by the currencies of South Korea and Taiwan whose markets, looking more promising than before, are expected to make great inroads in those very same markets in which Japan has already distinguished itself. While this expectation has weakened the yen to a certain extent, only in the future will it be known if this weakening process will continue to any great degree.

The question then arises: with advantages held in the fields of agriculture, science and technology, the arts, and those countries with long histories, just how important is foreign trade for an economy? The answer is that it is extremely important for a country's economic survival. A country's currency, for example, is a commodity that is bought and sold, and the demand for the currency depends on a country's economic strength. When either supply or demand pressure is placed on the currency, foreign currencies are needed to offset the deleterious consequences of the pressure; foreign currency can be purchased as well, but if it already exists in sufficient amounts in a country's national financial reserves, there is no need for the purchase. Currencies are so obtained through foreign commerce, and therefore, a country's economic strength is dependent on the extent of its foreign holding reserves. Market devaluations and revaluations inject the element of uncertainty in an economy's performance, and hence result in pressure being placed on its currency, which is why they are so unstabling. While the quality of a country's currency, its value, is determined by industrial output, employment, and the availability of product substitution, the quality of a currency issued is determined by that country's financial leaders. Both supply and demand pressure on a currency reflect the status of that currency's quality and quantity as assessed in the international markets.

Traditionally, the significance for foreign trade is that it provides an outlet for a country's goods and services, so that employment is maintained and profits continue to increase. For this reason, classical and neoclassical economists emphasized the comparative advantage of trade, and the basis for establishing trade among partners whose advantage in production of different goods and services warranted the international exchanges. However, with the production of close substitutes in many competing countries, the comparative advantage concept is no longer valid in contemporary economics. Indeed, because of close substitution production, tariffs are levied to protect domestic industry from foreign competition, while allowing the competing foreign products to enter the domestic markets to insure that domestic products will be exported. This is also why the trade "weapon"—for retaliation against policies that are not acceptable—is effective. Once embargoes are established and then broken—as they inevitably are—it is a great financial cost, usually at the price of foreign currencies, to the embargoed country. Its markets are reduced and its resources restricted in the production of domestic goods and services necessary to maintain a level of economic independence, and for manufacturing those goods and services earmarked for export, usually at profits lower than could be obtained on a more open marketplace. Therefore, foreign trade is a means for achieving prosperity and a weapon against the policies of another country. In the latter case, it must be applied in conjunction with other countries that have extensive foreign trade with the embargoed country; because of the effects it has on the embargoed population and because of possible retaliation in the future, the embargo must be used discriminatively.

THE UTILITY OPTIMUM—1: THE DECLINE OF MARGINALISM

A fundamental concept in neoclassical economics is that of marginalism. Marginalism was important in the neoclassical theory of the firm, when it was necessary to consider the amount of revenue gained from producing an additional product. A cutoff period of production had to be established so that revenues could be calculated and profits realized. Even though domestic and foreign competition is strenuous today and costing has become far more complicated due to the rigors of competition and the diversified production within each domestic and foreign firm competing in the markets, marginalism still has a role to play in economics. For both foreign and domestic commerce this role is limited, however, because the calculations of additional quantities of a product, the revenues received, and the profits realized, are far from certain. We learn from marginalism that the most efficient uses of a firm's resources in production are achieved when the receipts gained from the production of an additional product are equal to the added production costs involved in manufacturing that product, that is, when marginal costs equal marginal revenues. At that point the productive resources engaged in the product's manufacture are used to their maximum efficiency. Should production fall below this point, facilities are still available for increasing production, and should production continue beyond this point, either production will be cut back because of losses sustained as revenues from the increased production are less than production costs, or the product will be phased out due to the firm's limited resources.

Marginal cost can be stated thus: $MD = p - VC$, with p being the price and VC the variable cost of production. VC is the cost of improving the seller's—that is, the firm's—offer sufficiently by raising the sale by one or more production units; VC can also be considered as the savings gained by offering the market less attractive purchase terms, leading to a decline in sales by one or more units. For every sale there is a buyer, so that the elasticity of demand is expressed by $e = p/VC$, which can be written as $e = p \, \Delta \, q/q \, \Delta \, p$, that is, elasticity is equal to the price in relation to the change in quantity, divided by the quantity in relation to the change in price. In the MC equation above, $p \, \Delta$

q equals *p*, *q* Δ *p* equals the variable cost of a single unit with respect to its price. When $e > 1$, the *MC* is rising; when $e = 1$, the *MC* is unchanged; when $e < 1$, the marginal cost is declining.

Another aspect of marginalism that must be considered is marginal outlay, which is the buyer's cost of persuading the seller to sell one more unit. The marginal outlay includes the buyer's variable cost, which is the price change, increasing or decreasing in response to demand. Marginal outlay can be stated thus: $MO = p - VC$. The buyer's elasticity, like that of the seller's, is also *p/VC*, so at the time of the sales transaction the price paid by the buyer must be agreed upon by the seller, so that $[MC = MO] \equiv$ Marginal Revenue is an identity relationship that must always hold for the marginalist doctrine.

This of course means $(p - VC)_s = (p - VC)_b$, with the subscripts for buyer and seller. Since $e = p/VC$ for both sides of the transaction, the *MC* and *MO* equations can be rewritten: $(p - p/e)_s \equiv (p + p/e)_b$, and from this identity derived from the above equations, some unwanted consequences can be drawn.

One such derivation occurs when setting the elasticities to unity. The identity takes the form $Op_s \equiv 2p_b$, but this clearly not the case, for a price does exist at which the transaction was made, at which the seller's and buyer's prices were equal. If the elasticity on one side is greater or less than the other, adjustments will be made until the transaction is completed or abandoned. Equal elasticities, either greater or less than unity, result in similar difficulties, rendering different sale and purchase prices, when in fact only one price is set at which the transaction occurs.

This difficulty represents a case in which there is a clash between situational logic, in this case the logic of marginalism, and reality. According to marginalist reasoning, the transaction price is set according to the marginal propensities to sell and consume; on this point there is no clash. The difficulty arises when this price setting is derived from marginalism and results in a paradox of no transaction price according to the derivation and a real transaction price at which commerce is undertaken. This paradox is not a result of reality but exists because of marginalist logic.

Another difficulty with marginalism concerns the marginal efficiency of capital, a concept employed by John Maynard Keynes in *The General Theory*.[2] The marginal efficiency of capital (mec) is the relationship between the prospective yield of a capital asset and its supply price. An asset's prospective yield, such as an investment, is a series of annuities $Q_1, Q_2, \ldots, Q_n$ that investor expects to gain from selling the investment after deducting expenses. The asset's supply price is not the market price, but that price at which manufacturers may be induced to produce an additional asset unit; this is sometimes referred to as the replacement cost.

Keynes defined the mec as being equal to the rate of discount that would make the present value of the series of annuities given by the returns expected from the capital asset during its life just equal to the supply price, that is, its replacement cost. Because the mec depends on the rate of return expected on money as if it were a newly produced asset, that is, a measure, the historical result of the asset's yield is neglected on its original cost if looked at after the asset's life has ended.

From this argument a paradox can be constructed. Let M $(\text{mec}X)_{t_a - t_c}$ stand for the market value of an asset expected to have the mec of X over the life span of time a to c. If during this period only a few purchases of an asset are made, the asset's mec from the investor's point of view is affected insignificantly, a fact judged with considerable accuracy, so that the real rate of return on the investment is that which is expected. Here, there is no problem.

If during the period a to c a large investment in the asset is realized, the mec will decline accordingly. Let this be represented by $M(\text{mec} - X)$, where $-X$ is the mec of X lower than the mec for its first investor, with the number of assets purchased being many, and existing in time b. Thus, $M(\text{mec}X)_{t_a - t_c} \neq M(\text{mec}X)_{t_a - t_c}$ because during this time span the expected yield of X was lowered in reality to $-X$, so that the logical construction of the mec over time results in the paradox of not being the mec over the same period of time.

In defense of the mec, it may be argued that the reasoning here is unfair, that what must be considered is the entire investment schedule, which would show the aggregate increase in investment and the appropriate decline in the asset's mec. This is certainly what Keynes meant when he cautioned against the confusion the mec has caused because we fail to understand that it depends on the *prospective* yield and not to its current yield.

This can be best illustrated by pointing out the effect on the marginal efficiency of capital of an expectation of changes in the prospective cost of production, whether these changes are expected to come from changes in labour cost, *i.e.,* in the wage-unit, or from inventions and new technique. . . . In so far as such developments are foreseen as probable, or even as possible, the marginal efficiency of capital produced to-day is appropriately diminished.[3]

In the real world where most things are probable if not possible, it may very well be that an investor does not foresee any changes and that his or her personal expectation of the mec is held constant, while others who have invested in the asset have experienced a decline in the mec. In any case, the investment-demand schedule will be altered in reality, whether such an alteration is expected or not. These paradoxes, and the one to follow, will be resolved in the last section of this chapter.

Consider the application of marginalism for international trade. The relationship between imports and national income can be expressed by the average propensity to import, calculated by a country's currency value for imports as a percentage of that country's national income. Should the national income change, according to marginalist doctrine, the percentage of income used for consumption will also change, and for international trade this refers to the percentage of imports consumed. Hence, the marginal propensity to import is altered according to the change in national income. As the marginal propensity to import refers to a specific aspect of total aggregate consumption—as imports are consumer items—then the marginal propensity to import is directly related to the marginal propensity to consume.

Income is broken down in marginalist terms as consumption and investment (savings), with the marginal propensity to consume = 1/marginal propensity to save. Savings (investment) is the opposite of consumption, and importing is the opposite of exporting. As exports are developed through investments, then the marginal propensity to import = 1/marginal propensity to export. The difficulty here is that imports and exports refer to different markets, the domestic market and those to which the exports are directed. Hence, in this case, the reciprocal relationship need not necessarily hold because exports may be increasing to different countries, while imports are reduced in accordance with a reduction in national income. Should the national income increase, consumer preferences for imports may remain constant and consumption of domestic product increase. Still, consumption may remain at the same level, with savings increased. Should the national income decline slightly, the preference for imports may remain steady while consumption of domestic products declines. Of course, should a major recession set in, consumption for both domestic output and imports declines and this may have a negative effect on exports as countries retaliate for the reduction in their exports by reducing consumption of the domestically exported products.

According to the *mpi* concept, changes in national income result in changes in import consumption, with the amount of change being dependent on the elasticity of demand. For a given time, *t,* income fluctuations are supposed to affect import consumption in the same direction as the fluctuations. Hence, the rate of change of imports, given their average divided by the rate of change of national income, given its average, is equal to the rate of import changes and income changes, given both their averages. Setting I to imports and Y to national income,

$$\left[\frac{dI/I}{dy/Y} \equiv \frac{dI/dY}{I/Y}\right]_t.$$

The difficulty here can be realized that over the time span $t_a - t_c$, there is no strict necessity for this equation to hold. It is static, while consumption is dynamic, as stated above. Changes of income occur over time, and the impact of these changes are never immediate. A period of adjustment occurs which cannot be taken into account by a moment stated elasticity equation based on marginalism. For example, if during t_b there are changes and at t_c the changes are altered to the position of t_a, then over the time span $t_a - t_c$ the elasticity remains the same while in fact it did not. The point is that national income does not provide information on individual income and consumption patterns, so no real way of knowing the effects of national income changes on imports can be determined. While there may be changes in import consumption, no strict hard national income measurement can anticipate nor explain such changes. A different approach is required, one that excludes marginalism, yet sheds light on the situation. Marginalism is appropriate here for each consumer in his or her specific situation, but for a theory of international trade, it is of very limited use. The issues of marginalism will be discussed in the last section of this chapter, with reference to utility and entropy, information concepts that are relevant in decision making.

THE UTILITY OPTIMUM—2: ON UTILITY AND ENTROPY

Foreign markets, being extensions of domestic markets, share with domestic markets the property that they thrive only if their products are consumed. Consumption is an individualistic procedure, while production depends on the individuals in the targeted markets, as well as large-scale output in order to attract sales and provide back-up servicing. The ultimate destination of foreign trade is the individual consumer, and just as today's exported goods and services differ from those of the previous era, the consumer of today differs from the neoclassical "economic man" of the previous era.

According to neoclassical economics, the economic man is an individual who acts in matters of economics in a strictly rational manner. The economic man's judgments are supposed to be clear and he opts for the best among competing alternatives in the decision-making process. He acts according to his best interests, as only he knows what is best for him among the available choices. This notion is supported by the notion of an economy acting in dynamic equilibrium, so that at one time one set of alternatives are attractive as choices, and at another time a different set of choices will be available and also attractive. Eventually, a set of choices resembling the first set will appear the better, while later a set resembling the second set will appear better, and so on in a recurring cyclical pattern. The economic man, according to his current economic situation at any one time, is confronted with these alternative choices and will act according to his best interests at that time, only to be confronted with different choices, the acting on which may negate the earlier decisions.

If the concept of economic man were operative, then each man would act to optimize his position. This would bring the economic sectors into an optimum position, so that unemployment would be marginal, referring to those people who are unable to work. Industry would be at a continuing optimal position, and government intervention in the economy would be minimal, only to maintain this ideal situation should signs of a decline in the optimum be threatening.

Of course, this is not the case. Unemployment results from industrial decline, and even the most liberal of the neoclassical tenets maintains a degree of economic intervention by the government if only to develop infrastructure. Recessions and depressions are part of the neoclassical lexicon, and during the

Great Depression, when the Industrial Revolution came to a close, unemployment was high, industrial output low, and government intervention necessary to maintain the economic and social fabric.

Thus, the neoclassical concept that economic man acting in his own best interests brings about maximum economic efficiency has been brought into question by economic realities. Should such a creature as the "economic man" really exist, his orientation would be different from that imposed on him by neoclassical thinking. Indeed, the very concept of "optimum" must be brought into question and its relevance for economic decision making be explained, because an optimum position for one person may differ from that of another person; nor may such an optimum position be obtainable, given prevailing economic conditions. Should one person obtain an optimum position, it may be at the reduction of another person's position. The point is that the situation must be restated to meet our current economic realities in terms appropriate for our contemporary economies. This pertains to the developing and emerging economies as well, for they are under the influence of the developed economies, and in spite of their differences in infrastructure, output, and political orientation, the aspirations of their peoples are the same economically as those in the developed economies: they want better lives.

Hence, the concept of "economic man" requires a new formulation, one appropriate to contemporary economic reality. This is necessary for two reasons. One reason is that the argument to be presented here, in the esprit of contemporary international economics, will begin with the individual qua individual, and then as a member of a sector or sectors, and how, in both instances, the individual performs in the economy. The second reason is that the individual is the basic "unit," as it were, of economic activity, with the individual acting on what he or she considers best. The individual, as economic decision maker, relates to information systems and his or her position with respect to these systems; on the basis of these relevant systems the individual decides and acts.

In our contemporary era the individual acting in the economic sphere is not the "economic man" in the neoclassical sense, regardless of the stage of development of his or her economy. As a member of contemporary society, his or her economic decision making must necessarily be influenced by his or her standard of living, family size, occupation, and expectations from the decisions taken. Therefore, instead of using the term "economic man" with its neoclassical connotations, the term "contemporary individual" will be used in this discussion.

As an economic decision maker, the contemporary individual is rational, operating in all economic circumstances, in a manner that, given the unique conditions and information available, seeks optimum utility according to his or her understanding and liquidity positions. The contemporary individual thus deals with information, which may be scanty—in which case the choice may be taken to avoid decisions—or detailed—in which case the choice to relate to

the information or avoid it will be made with a degree of assurance corresponding to the levels and quality of information.

Information comes in three forms. It may be informal and loose, scanty and
far from complete, in which case it will most likely be set aside and avoided
in decision making. Information may be detailed and systematic and therefore
available to the individual as an information system that can be analyzed and
evaluated with respect to alternative systems, and from which conclusions can
be drawn. Or, third, information may be gathered by the contemporary individual from sources which seem unrelated, but that when put together by the
individual for his or her own use and acted upon, form a system that can later
be avoided or accepted within the decision-making process.

Whatever form the information takes, it must relate to the contemporary
individual as decision maker. For this to be the case, two types of information
systems must be considered, these being the closed and the open system. It
must be stated here that a system closed in time t may be open in $t + 1$, but
this is not a reflexive relationship, for an open system will always remain so
until it ceases to function. This is because by its very openness, its information
content is dynamic and altering, according to the changes in the situation to
which it relates.

The economic information available to the contemporary individual, be it an
open, closed, or informal system, depends on the objective conditions of the
economic area to which it is pertinent. The utility of this information, however,
depends on both the quality and content of the information, *and* the individual's
subjective interpretation of this information. The individual's interpretation may
be affected by his or her peers, or by his or her economic aspirations. As the
contemporary individual is the basic economic "unit," because of his or her
decision, taken in summation of the total decisions and their effects on the
domestic economy, policies are made on both sectorial and political levels. The
extent to which these sectors are viable and the political levels receptive determines the extent of receptivity to imports. This does not pertain to exports,
which nevertheless are a function of this receptivity, as retaliation by other
countries in the form of quotas, domestic subsidies, and outright boycotting of
products may result from unacceptable limits on imports. While this information may very well pertain to conditions in the domestic economy, it is public
information, available to all countries engaged in trade; it must thus be treated
as such, by the sectorials and responsible politicians.

Because information's utility depends on both the objective information and
the subjective interpretation, information—even in the most rigidly closed systems—has different utility schedules for $n > 1$ persons. This, of course, results
in the ordering of utility schedules for the individuals involved with the information. These schedules are expressions of preferences for the various information systems and indicate their utilities and entropies respectively. However,
just as information is both objective and subjective in interpretation, so then
are utility and entropy to be considered.

A closed information system is one that is bounded by a time signature and is isolated from the influence of data that could otherwise alter its contents. Any further data added to the closed information system are therefore redundant and unnecessary, as the system is thus consistent and without ambiguities. For example, on a certain day a transaction occurs in which a specific sum of money for a specific quantity of exports is exchanged between two identified individuals each representing a firm, one for exporting and one for importing. The money exchanged for the exported goods concludes the agreement. Investors who have access to the products shipped and the arrangements for import distribution can determine their utilities of investing in either or both of the firms involved. This information is closed in the sense that the transaction is completed with the strategies of the bargaining process having been formulated and agreed upon before the transaction was made. This information is closed in the sense that the transaction is completed with the bargaining strategies involved having been expired. At the time of closure any further data is redundant and of no value in the decision-making processes for investors.

With the closed information system being time-signature bound and isolated from data that could otherwise alter its contents, the system's utility, nevertheless, varies from one contemporary individual to another. The utility of a system depends on the system's objective probability and the individual's subjective probability. For the information system $S_t = [s_1, s_2, \ldots, s_n]$, where S is the system in toto in time t, and $s_1, s_2, \ldots, s_n$ are the individual statements composing the system. The system's objective utility is assessed by setting each of its statements in turn with the maximum and minimum boundaries of utility and entropy respectively so that the statement s_1, $0 < s_1 < 1$, meaning that the information statement in question lies between the utility and entropy limits and its position with respect to these limits determines its viability within the system in general. Thus, for the system, $0 < S_t < 1$ is valid for all closed information systems for the duration of the time-signature stated.

As well as the probabilistic assessment, for the contemporary individual the system must also relate to his or her preferences. In the example above, for instance, the decision-making individual must be acquainted with the relevant people and procedures involved in the transaction, and the type of product and the markets targeted by both exporters and importers. While the individual may not doubt the information system's content, he or she may be skeptical concerning the actual viability of the product on the market. This skepticism may be due to the individual's consideration of a short time lag before competing products enter the market, thereby reducing profits, or because of his or her understanding of an economic situation that might lead to recession, thereby reducing the sales forecast by the agreement. This individual may therefore assign a low subjective probability rating to the information statements, indicating that in his or her opinion the transaction will not be profitable. Another person may have a different opinion, while possessing the same background information about the market, the state of the economy, and the time-lag potential for close competitors to enter the market. This person may assign a high subjective probability rating in toto to the information system and place his or her liquidity at the disposal of one or both firms engaged in the transaction.

An incomplete system, that is, an open system, is one in which one or both types of conditions occur. Either the system has been "infiltrated" by information elements of other systems, or there is lack of sufficient data within the system to either reduce or eliminate the uncertainty concerning the system's validity and utility, thereby limiting the ability to make specific decisions. Since the system is open, it is by definition a system that is incomplete and thus not subject to a bounding time-signature. Should a time-signature be placed on an open system, it is merely for clarification of the specific time under consideration.

For example, consider the system A in which are incorporated the elements $a_1, a_2, \ldots, a_n \ldots, b_1, b_2, c_3, c_4$ of information systems B and C (it makes no difference if B and C are closed or open). Such a system exists for firms considering engaging in foreign commerce prior to one or both countries' finance ministers announcement of the proposed annual budget, when the investor's decision to place his or her money at one or both firm's disposal must take into account not only the firms' present financial condition, but also the possible effects the announcement and the budgets may have after their enactment. This information contains the firms' positions, information from other systems such as the possible economic forecasts and their impacts on trade, and the political systems involved; because the information system is open and the time is prior to one or both budgets being announced, also included are projections into the future based on expected budgetary considerations. An open information system is subject to conflicting information statements and therefore to contradictions; as both the firms' managers and investors work with the same open-ended information system, they must assess the subjective and objective probabilities with respect to the uncertainty determined by the utilities of the known information statements as they are evaluated, and by the uncertainty of those statements that will enter the system at a future date.

For a closed system, the contemporary individual relates to this system with respect to the system's probability in toto. This is because while each of the system's statements is unique in its expression of a specific point, and as there are no inconsistencies nor contradictions within the system, each statement depends on the others for meaning. The system's probability depends on the probability of each of its statements (that is, elements), and as there are both the objective and subjective probabilities, the objective probability refers to facts, the information as presented and is available to those to whom it is directed. Significant for interpreting and understanding these facts is the subjective probability, as this pertains to the individual's specific requirements for the duration of the information's pertinence. Thus, a closed system may be of utility for some people and be of little or no utility for others, in the same sector or peer group to which the information is directed. Hence, for some, the information may be of utility; for others, it may be entropic, even though its objective probability approaches maximum utility. It is on the basis of subjective probability that contemporary individuals order their utilities.

For the open-ended information system, the individual's situation is more complicated. Not all information is available, and its openness prevents it from being accumulated sufficiently. Moreover, the amount of information possessed by one person may not be the same as that understood by another. Contradictions cannot be ruled out, so that information that may be considered subjectively relevant may be objectively entropic. This difficulty is compounded by the situation in which information available to some people may be lacking to others, so that different objective interpretations and subjective utilities result.

Hence, the difficulty arises when the statements an individual does possess stand in contradiction with those that he or she has sanctioned within the system. Another individual possessing the same statements may also be in possession of additional statements which allow the discarding of the first set of statements as being untenable; yet these are the very statements the first person accepted as viable and of utility. Also, probabilities are often assigned to combinations of statements, as they provide fuller expression of expectations. Taken in combination, these statements may be accepted by some while rejected by others because their recombinations with still different statements provide contradictions.

Nevertheless, on the basis of available information, the contemporary individual must make choices and assign utility schedules. This is to relate the information presented to the reality of the situation as it is understood, thereby bringing the subjective interpretation as close as possible to the objective probability so that sound judgment based on the information is made.

The difficulties of subjective assessment can be minimized by assigning boundaries of verisimilitude according to expectations and allowing these boundaries to represent the utilities and entropies on which choices are made. With the upper boundary designated by 1 and the lower boundary by 0, these limits can never be reached, but can be approached. In the extreme, the upper boundary signifies the complete verisimilitude between the information system as understood and available—that is, either closed and complete or open and incomplete—as a linguistic or symbolic structure describing the situation, with the language corresponding as best as possible to reality. The lower boundary signifies the total absence of a relationship between the information system's language and the reality it purports to describe. For each decision maker, each information system lies between these limits and may be either stationary or fluctuating; the system's position within these boundaries determines its state of utility or entropy. By analyzing the system within these limits, the decision maker combines the highly subjective interpretation and its strong influence on personal expectations, with the objective analysis of reality and the system's language.

For the closed system, the determination of an information system's utility or entropy is a fairly uncomplicated process. Because of the system's closure, the individual confronts an either-or situation, in which the information system describes its domain accurately, or fails to do so. As the system's time-signature states the duration of the system's presumed validity, this can be assessed with respect to the domain of reality to which the system relates. Based on this, each of the system's statements can be broken down into its components that can then be matched with the specific aspect of reality to which it relates, subjecting each statement to utility and entropy measurements, thereby determining the statement's relation to reality. As there are no ambiguities or contradictions in the closed system, the system can be taken in toto and placed between the limits of 0 and 1. While this rating determines its objective status, the contemporary individual has to assess his or her utility rating with respect to this objective rating. His or her expectations may have presented attitudes not allowed for by the information system, but the system's status may allow for revised attitudes. Alternatively, expectations may have been reenforced by the system's status and placed on ground firmer than before. In any case, once the information system's position has been established with respect to utility and entropy, the individual must then act on the basis of this knowledge.

The open-ended information system has a degree of complication lacking in the closed system because of the possibility of contradictory information statements and because information from other systems, not necessarily relevant, may intrude. The time-signature placed on this system takes on added significance because its imposition isolates a system that is dynamic, thereby allowing some control over it. The system S in time t may or may not be equal in the quantity or quality of statements and the import of their content to S_{t2}; this can be determined only by analysis, given the system's dynamic nature. This situation is complicated further, because a statement existing in both t_1 and t_2 may have its nuances altered. Because of the influence of new statements, those in the original S_{t1} may be found to be contradictory in S_{t2}. These conditions require that the system be broken down and analyzed to determine which statements are necessary for the system and which are superfluous and can therefore be eliminated without affecting the system's objective utility—a process that may entail breaking down specific statements and reformulating them so that the troublesome parts are removed.

For both the closed and open systems, objective utility determines the extent to which a system provides an accurate description of its reality; this requires assessing the system's probability. Probability depends on the system's information content and is represented by the letter I, with the expression I/S_t representing the probability rating of S at the stated time t. I/S_t is the general expression of the probability of $SI_s = P(S_t)$, where the left-hand side of the equation means the probability of S, and the right-hand side represents the probabilities $s_1, s_2, \ldots, s_n$ statements of the system. S_t's utility is thus assessed by focusing on each statement and determining its relationship to the reality for which it was formulated. As the probability of an open-ended system tends to vary over time, with S_t being equal or not equal to S_{t_2} in both information content and objective utility, S's utility must be revalued when acting on its information content at different times. Moreover, because of the tendency for this system to vary over time, there is a chance that decisions taken on the basis of this information at one time will yield consequences not considered at that time.

Such is a situation when an individual invests in a firm that presents itself as a dynamic organization exporting diversified products into foreign markets, adjusting the quantity of exports according to its markets' abilities needs and using its excess capital for retooling and engaging in innovative and imitative projects for further exports.[4] When becoming acquainted with the firm's internal situation and markets, as stated in its prospectus, this, together with the firm's performance on the stock exchange, enables the individual to decide if investing in the firm is a sound choice. However, as the firm presents open-ended information bound by a time-signature set down in the prospectus, its future performance on international markets and on the stock exchange cannot be determined as they are excluded from the prospectus. While projections may be offered, there is no guarantee that they will be in fact achieved. This is further complicated by the possibility of new government policies in the domestic economy, in the firm's importing countries, or both, that will bear on the firm's activities and hence on its share price. Or, internal difficulties may arise that have a direct bearing on the status of its shares and performance internationally. The bound information is complete at the time it is presented, but as the firm is dynamic, its total picture is incomplete, and is the system on which the contemporary individual acts. As the information system changes, the individual's calculations must be revised, with each calculation taken as if the system is time-bound, even though its contents fluctuate. The time-signature is placed by the individual on the basis of the information content at his or her disposal, while the reality is in fluctuation.

Two individuals working with a closed information system may choose to act on the system, thereby contributing to the dynamics that the system generates. This system may also be rejected by one or both people as decisions in favor of another system or systems are made. The degree of objective uncertainty is greater in the open system than with the closed system, because the closed system is static while the open system is dynamic and fluid. However, the individual treats both systems as closed in order to study their probabilities and assess their objective utilities. Both systems have time-signatures when the decision is taken, so that when assessing their probabilities, each individual takes into his or her subjective utility and makes the choice with regard to the desired consequences.

In the sense that the actual consequences are those that the individual seeks, subjective utility thus reflects the projected results that the individual desires. Basing the consideration against the future projection, the degrees of uncertainty are related directly to the degrees determined by subjective utility. This utility is derived from and determines the individual's ordering preferences, and personal preference ordering is derived from the information system, which is evaluated with respect to alternative systems; the consequences of future uncertainty is certainly important in this evaluation.

The ordering of preferences requires that each alternative system under consideration be ranked, first with regard to its objective utility, and then in terms of personal subjective utility. The significance of this ordering for international economics is that government programs and business operations on the international markets are information systems. The objective utilities of these systems can be determined within the time-signatures prevalent for their durations and with current domestic and international issues considered. The subjective utilities present another set of difficulties because government planners, when considering economic programs, cannot consider the subjective assessments of the individuals involved; there are other ways for determining the influences of these programs, and these will be discussed in the following chapter. It must be noted here, however, that a relationship exists between subjective utility as determined by the individual and objective utility as determined by the assessment of the system's probability. Should the individual act in favor of the system, then for this person the relationship is positive; a rejection of the system means that the individual finds the relationship negative. Economic activity in general, and international commerce in particular, are generated by the quantity of positive relationships among individuals and information systems; for by utilizing these systems, individuals give life to programs, money is invested, and both domestic and international purchases are made. Those information systems that are inactive soon succumb to entropy.

Whether these relationships are positive or negative depends on individuals' objectives and the systems' contents. Should a person have an established goal and the information system in question fails to provide sufficient inducement toward the realization of this goal, then the person will avoid that system. It is most likely, however, that the person will have established modified goals—a "second best" situation—in case the best goal proves unrealistic with regard to the available alternative information systems. Again, this requires an ordering of preferences on the basis of utility, with the person acting on that system that provides the best future situation as determined by goal modification, with the revised goal becoming the best case.

Schematically, the objective-subjective relationship can be stated thus: $EuS_t = F(P,S)$, that is, the expected or subjective utility of information system S_t is a function of S with regard to its objective probability. With S_t's objective utility approaching the maximum limit of 1, there is no necessary bearing of EuS_t on the expected utility of S, because expectation is strictly subjective and the objective S_t may yield consequences irrelevant or unwanted by the contemporary individual. Hence, for one individual considering the specific information system, $EuS_t = [F(P,S)_{t+1}] \rightarrow 1$, while for another person concerned with the same system, $EuS_t = [F(P,S)_{t+1}] \rightarrow 0$, with the subscript $t+1$ referring to the next time period that would occur when the system is acted upon. Nor are these subjective assessments permanent over time, as they are often altered over time because of the acquisition of greater comprehension and/or due to shifts in subjective preferences. Hence, while S_t may have been rejected in $t + 1$ because of low subjective utility, in a different time period, t_n ($n > 2$), the subjective reordering and possible shifts in S_t's information content with S being open-ended may result in the system's receiving a very high subjective ordering position.

With regard to the decisions based on objective-subjective utility, the sum total of these decisions at any one time period can be considered the sum total of domestic and foreign economic activity for that time. Moreover, because of the difficulties of the open-ended systems, their utilities are reduced over time due to the impacts made on them by decisions taken by those individuals concerned with them. Acting on the open-ended system brings about changes in its information content, as, for example, investing in foreign enterprises brings about a reduction on the rate of return on investment as the demand for investment declines. This reduction of utility is entropy.

In its objective sense, information entropy is the measurement of disinformation in an information system. It illustrates the extent to which the system's elements, its statements, fail to relate to their objective realities, thereby providing a basis for subjective discrimination in the consideration of alternate systems. Symbolized by the letter H, the entropy of a system S_t indicates the extent to which some or all of S's statements no longer correspond to the realities for which they were designed and intended. Just as utility is measured between the upper and lower boundaries, so is entropy, thus making it the negation of utility because where $S_t \rightarrow 1$, then S_t's utility tends to 0, and vice versa.

As the closed system designates a reality relevant only for the period stated by its time-signature, the only way it can be threatened with entropy is if reality is altered and it is revised. For example, the system containing facts 1, 2, . . . , n is bound by a specific future date. If one or more of its statements (elements) has to be altered to correspond to changes in the terms due on that date, the system can become entropic; however, this can be rectified by a reformulation of the statement in light of the changed reality. This is a technical adjustment, restoring the system to utility in light of the change.

It could be possible, however, that such a shift in reality could be so extreme that the information system per se would no longer have utility and would have to be abandoned completely. In the investment in a firm engaging in foreign enterprise, should one of the firm's directors suddenly pass away, bringing instability to the firm and uncertainty in its foreign markets, the transactions would most likely be placed on hold and may even be terminated if it is not too late, until the board of directors can replace the director and redraft the transactions to the foreign partners' satisfaction. There is no time-signature attached here, and objective entropy has replaced utility, thereby breaking down the information system entirely.

For the open information system, objective analysis must be based on S_t's utility being dependent on the probability of all its statements relating to reality as they are supposed to, so that information I of S_t equals the probability of S_t being relevant, that is, $I/S_t = P/S_{t_1}$, with S at t_1 containing a set number of statements indicated by the time-signature. If the probability assessment shows that there is absolutely no relationship between the set of statements and their realities, then $I = H$ and the entire system is devoid of utility. Should the probabilities of the system's elements correspond totally to their realities during the time period, then $I = -H$ and the system enjoys full objective utility.

The either-or situation in which either utility or entropy exists, is the best of all possible worlds, and for utility it is difficult to achieve for more than a brief period of time. As open information systems are formulated to correspond to their realities, it is unlikely that they will be totally irrelevant or absolutely perfect, especially after a reasonable period of time and usage. More than likely, some degree of entropy will set into the system because of slight shifts in reality.

For the bound, that is, closed, information system, absolute utility is far easier to achieve, because of the chances for changes in the realities of the statements being very small. Absolute entropy during the time limit is also difficult to achieve, because radical shifts in the realities are unlikely to occur. It is only when the time-signature has expired, or in case of a crisis or totally unexpected situation, when the realities are altered, that the bound system becomes entropic (to be abandoned) and an alternative system (or systems) should be sought.

Objective determination of an open system's level of entropy is achieved by assessing the probabilities of a system's statements with respect to the realities for which they were formulated. For example, when stated, $S_{t_1} \rightarrow 1$—were this not the case, the system would not have been formulated as is—and over time periods 1 and 2, changes occur in either the reality or in S's content, or perhaps in both. Because the assessment of utility or entropy requires the evaluation of S's statements, it may be found that some of these statements contain glaring inadequacies that can be corrected within the system, or if this is unfeasible, cast out forthright. It is likely that these inadequacies are due to the incorporation of additional statements over $t_1 - t_2$ that have a better definitive relationship to their realities; these provide little difficulty and once removed or corrected, S's utility will be strengthened.

Difficulties arise with those statements whose subtle discrepancies seriously affect S_t's utility and are not subject to alteration because alterations would result in the system being drastically changed, perhaps to the extent of bringing the system into a condition of serious entropy, with the possibility of dissolution. This is due to the culminating influence of shifting statements and/or realities, rendering S_t as such of little utility. For example, a firm may set out to undertake an exporting project and has thus established its information system to attract investors and establish foreign markets. There may be discrepancies between the exporting plans and the exporting process because of changes in either domestic or foreign policies, or both. The consequence is that exporting plans are not quite fulfilled, and the information system moves into an entropic condition with utility declining. If compensated for in time, the movement toward entropy will not be serious and S_t can be revised to cope with the differing conditions prevailing in the domestic and targeted foreign markets. The information system can be reestablished with the entropy temporarily removed, so that $S_{t_1} \neq S_{t_2}$, with $S_{t_1} \to 1$.

The dynamics of international trade are such, however, that new discrepancies will arise that are not accounted for by S_{t_2}, so that over time, this system will also become entropic. The reconstruction process continues until a situation is reached that the entropic conditions that finally evolve will render the entire system not worth the effort or economy to reconstruct it still further. For example, increasing competition for the same markets for similar products may lower the exporting firm's profit-cost ratio to the extent that any "new" changes in the exported products' marketing, or performance, or composition, would not offset the production costs involved in making these changes due to declining sales. The exported market may be so saturated that the product line can be maintained only at break-even costs and profits, or at worst case, at a loss, no matter the changes undertaken to make it more attractive. The decision must be made then whether to maintain exporting the product at its current profit-cost ratio, maintain marketing incentives and advertising at a level sufficient to hold current sales in light of the strenuous competition, or to phase out the export line and allocate the resources otherwise. Should the choice be to maintain the product, then S_t is acted upon to remain viable within its utility boundaries at worse case, and to move to maximum utility at best case. Should the product be abandoned, then entropy is immediately introduced with the system intentionally rendered beyond reconstruction. The latter decision is final, bringing the system into complete entropy, while the former decision still preserves the product's dynamic which will remain active in the market until either a decision is taken to phase it out, or until international consumer demand and the economies' general dynamics no longer provide support for the product but encourage the allocation of resources to other projects.

Discrepancies exist also as a direct result of the information system. For example, revised plans for the product to make it more competitive internationally, no matter how slight the revision, result in difficulties not included previously in the system. Different production and/or distribution techniques, instituted to gain economics of cost, will incur such difficulties as bottlenecks in moving the product in its directed markets. This is due to the conflict between the original plan incorporated in the information system and the revised version which takes time to work out. Another difficulty is reallocating the resources required by the revised system, together with their redistribution, in terms of their previous and future priorities. A further difficulty, especially in highly competitive markets but also in existing new markets, is that when revision results in cost reductions which are passed on to the consumer, it may very well be the case that these reductions are not of sufficient incentive for consumers because of their prior commitments of their liquidities according to their utility ordering preferences. Further, as prices are reduced to move stock, aggregate demand may be so scheduled that profits are reduced more than planned (entropy) so that the project's viability becomes questionable. While lower production and/or distribution costs may result in lower prices in the export markets, in light of this aggregate demand must warrant a sufficient profit; otherwise, the project will be abandoned. In this case, the advantages proposed by cost reductions must be projected onto the export markets and assessed for their utility. If projections indicate that the reductions will yield sufficient profits, then the export lines will be maintained; if not, then they will be either maintained as a loss leader incentive to continue in the markets with other products being introduced, or will be abandoned—the decision on which will be based on projected utilities and entropies. Should the changes be introduced and the difficulties overcome, this would generate similar changes in close competitors' thinking; the initial changes will introduce entropy into their information system and they must calculate their positions accordingly.

Even though open-ended information systems are bound by their time-signatures, they may be subject to various levels and intensities at all times during their durations. This is because the realities of their situations with respect to their changing de facto probability measurements or to the systems' statements and the areas to which they relate during alterations. While the time-signatures indicate the system's durations, as well as indicating their positions with respect to utility and entropy, as time changes, so do these positions. Only through analysis can the extent of these changes be understood, and the reasons for them be comprehended. Measurements of the systems' positions are taken periodically, especially when there is reason to suspect that disinformation has entered the system. Nevertheless, changes are taking place because of alterations occurring in their defined areas, alterations detectable only by proper assessment.

Unlike objective entropy, subjective entropy is not necessarily reflexive, that is, not in response to real changes in the realm of internal structuring. For example, an information system may be approaching maximum objective utility, yet may be considered entropic by an individual with a different ordering for the area that the system defines. The individual will choose to work with an alternative system—one with a lower objective utility and therefore a higher risk—rather than a system with a higher objective but lower personal subjective utility, providing, of course, that the chosen system is not in danger. As the contemporary individual is considered rationally economic in his or her preference ordering, and as his or her reasons for choosing the alternative system may not be understood or agreed to by others for this ordering, this subjective entropy will most likely pose no threat to the other system. There are cases where, subjectively, the person prefers not to act at all but to wait and see what happens over a self-set time span, in which case this behavior is as if all the competing systems are subjectively entropic, regardless of their objective status. This decision is both personal and rational and depends on the individual's liquidity position and the understanding of the possibilities in the time considered significant for waiting before acting.

Subjective entropy is therefore due to personal assessment and depends on the ordering of preferences with respect to the psychological aspect of expectation. Expectation is related to reality by the understanding of current events and how these events may influence the future, so that preferring to work with an information system or opting not to are based on the individual's best understanding of the reality. Hence, there is no contradiction in the situation where $S_{o_t} \to 1$ and $S_{s_t} \to 1$ (the subscripts o and s meaning objective and subjective). Furthermore, S_{t_n} may have a very high utility rating, with t_n being a time in the assigned future, beyond the length indicated by the time-signature.

Unlike their objective counterparts, subjective utility and entropy cannot be analyzed with respect to the probabilities of the systems' information statements in relation to their respective areas. Subjective entropy may be due to personal whims, values, or tastes, or improper or incomplete understanding of the information, or due to an assigned period of waiting for alternative systems that are expected to be of greater utility, but may not materialize when the future is finally reached. As there is no real accounting for personal tastes objectively, preferences for information systems provide expression for these idiosyncrasies that economic activity seeks to control and channel, by focusing on consumer products, investment opportunities, production processes, and foreign markets.

Subjective entropy, nevertheless, also has an impact on the direction economic activity takes. Since the decision to operate within one information system is taken at the expense of using alternative competing systems—the decision limited, in part, by personal and/or corporate liquidity—the impact made by working with a system influences the system's statements, altering their relationships to the area's realities. Rejecting a system because of subjective entropy will affect the system objectively. For the closed system, this rejection inhibits the realization of the system's dynamics, which would certainly be more active by the influences of the individual's participation. As the closed system defines a specific set of circumstances that are valid for the period indicated by the time-signature, the system will undergo a decline in objective utility if not used because of the subjective entropy of the populace to whom it is directed. This situation is usually extreme, but the extent of objective entropy as far as the system's relevance is concerned with respect to its populace, will be determined by the extent of the response of that part of the populace willing to opt for the system. A system without sufficient takers, no matter how efficient it is internally, will collapse.

The open information system is in a different situation because it is formulated to relate to an area uncloseable by the system's statements for more than an undetermined and specific period of time. Dynamics within the delineated area require the system's statements to be revised or discarded as the case may be, and also require that the system take on new statements to relate to area changes if the existing statements are inadequate. In this sense, the system depends on the populace that works with it. For example, consider the extreme case of an open-ended system without anyone working with it; the system will soon collapse because of the objective entropy generated by the changing area for which it was formulated. Subjective entropy, based on the preference ordering that allows the populace to avoid the system, will therefore bring about objective entropy and the system's rapid dissolution. The extreme case is unlikely, however, because managers and business directors are realistic in their judgments and are not likely to formulate systems they think will not attract. Nevertheless, what has been shown is the extent that objective entropy is dependent—this to a large degree—in subjective entropy and the system's use.

There is a qualification that has to be made, this being that subjective entropy in its (near) extreme intensity is not the only way that a system is brought down, in the sense that it is used in the example above. The system, for example, does not have to be avoided entirely, but can be utilized by a very small minority of the populace which, because of its size, is either too defensive and resistant to changes in the area, or too overcompensating in light of the need for changes; in either case, they are likely to act in manners that will bring about objective entropy into the system, this because of their subjective evaluations based on their numbers and need to maintain the system. Still, subjective entropy can act on objective entropy, bringing the system down before its time-signature expires. For example, a closed system that states that on a specific date, conditions x, y, and z will occur; a disagreement ensues over the system's terminology and statements after its formulation, with one individual acting to render the system entropic before the others involved realize this action. The dissenting person acts to prevent one of the system's conditions—say z—from being fulfilled. Since the closed system is so constructed that all its statements have to hold together and relate to their realities exactly as expressed in the system, altering the z statement will bring down the entire system. Subjective entropy can thus bring about actions that generate objective entropy, resulting in the program's collapse, the cancellation of the foreign deal, or whatever the situation may be.

For the open system, the situation is no different. Assuming that the open system is at maximum utility, so that as it is free from destructive entropy, an individual may reject the specific relationship between a statement and its reality, resulting in this person's changing the statement without sufficient consideration for the new statement's probability relationship. This will bring the statement further away from the previously existing probability rating. Over time, enough dynamics will be generated to require alterations in the statements; this is a process that will continue and will eventually bring the system into extreme entropy and its natural decline. But tampering with a statement in a system of high utility, to suit the individual's personal preferences, brings the system into decline faster by generating entropy prematurely.

It is assumed that the contemporary individuals participating in economic activity, whether as producers or importers, exporters or consumers, act rationally according to their preference ordering. These people have their preferences, their subjective utilities and entropies, influencing and in turn influenced by their understanding of their information systems and their realities as they are defined. The economist must deal with decision making, be it based on objective, subjective, or most likely on combined considerations. However, just as people's personal realities change, so are their perceptions of their information systems altered; systems change due to realistic considerations and to personal considerations, but nevertheless, on the basis of these systems, choices are ordered and decisions are made.

THE UTILITY OPTIMUM—3: THE DYNAMICS OF THE INFORMATION SYSTEM

It is necessary to consider further the closed and open information systems because of the impact of entropy. It is impossible to discuss the utility option without taking into account entropy as the dissolution of utility and without examining the methods of repair to the information systems. These methods serve to maintain the systems' integrities until they are beyond repair and abandoned or until they are replaced by systems lacking in entropy and capable of performing as stated.

In both the closed and open systems, the elements define and delineate the realities to which they refer; their elements are therefore information statements about the realities for which they are constructed, and, because of the definition and delineation, they also tell what these realities do not contain. These information statements or elements are isomorphic, with each element referring to only that aspect of the area pertaining to its reality, the scope of which is contained only within the element. This relationship is reflexive, in the sense that each element relates to only its specific aspect of reality, with this aspect relating only to its unique element. When these systems are first established, they lack the difficulties of ambiguity and of metalanguages and metainformation that usually develop through use.

In general, system S_t contains the elements of information and reality, to which the information elements relate. Thus, S_t if and only if R, with R being the defined reality, so that $S_{t_o} = [S, R]_{t_o}$, with the subscript t_o being the time of origin during which the elements in S correspond isomorphically and reflexively with the particles in R. There is no entropy at this time of origin and the system has yet to be worked upon.

In the closed information system, entropy sets in only when the reality is altered and the elements no longer retain their isomorphism. This may be due to a de facto shift in the reality, or because of subjective entropy on the part of an individual changing the reality. As an example of a shift in the reality, consider a project for exporting a type of machinery to an emerging country. The amount of equipment has been agreed to, the delivery time established, the terms and amount of payment set. These conditions are finalized in a contract which serves as the basis for attracting potential investors. With the capital raised, the project begins operations, but there is an unsuspected coup in the emerging country, rendering the contract invalid and the deal cancelled. The shift in reality due to the coup brings down the entire information system into unsalvageable entropy. The system's elements no longer relate to the area particles, and no reconstruction can redeem the system. When order is reestablished, whichever government is then formed may be interested in importing this machinery, but it will be with a different contract and perhaps a different exporting company.

As for subjective entropy, a person involved in formulating a closed information system, such as formulating a prospectus for exporting, may seek to improve his or her personal position by rewriting the prospectus to provide a different slant, or by renegotiating the contract before it is acted upon. If this person's position is important, then the contract may be rewritten, thereby negating the previous contract and the prospectus that followed. Subjective entropy may be due to altruistic considerations, such as realizing that a better contract can be obtained without personal gain, so that terms in the reality to which the contract is directed are altered, rendering it invalid. The point is that the reality is altered so that the system no longer refers in toto to the reality, rendering its information entropic.

It is relevant to note how the change is made. Stating R' as the new reality, the system S must also be altered thereby allowing for a new system to be formed. Consider the relationship $s_d r$, that is, the information element s defines and delineates the reality particle r. When r is altered to become r', its defining element must also be altered to become s', as the shift from r to r' renders s entropic, thereby rendering the entire relationship entropic. Entropy can be reversed by combining s with relevant information and by casting out that part of s no longer adequate without destroying its general defining import. Hence, with s altered to s' and with its general import still intact, r' is covered with the relationship still retaining its viability.

What has been considered here is a slight shift in R with only a single r particle affected. Should there be a radical shift in the closed system's reality, affecting the majority of relationships, either S will be abandoned due to the extent of the entropy, or a new relationship between S and R will be constructed with parts of the previous system not affected incorporated into the new system. However, should such a reconstruction be considered not worthwhile because of uncertainty concerning the new reality, then further research and planning will be abandoned and no attempt at reconstruction will be undertaken.

While for the closed system only the reality is subject to alteration, for the open system both the defining elements and their realities can alter. Because of the system's openness, the likelihood for entropy at any given moment is greater than in the closed system. When entropy does enter the open system, however, it usually is not as devastating as it is with the closed system, because its openness provides it with the ability to expand and thus be salvaged.

Three reasons for entropy entering a system must be considered. First, a change may occur in the reality of the area defined by the system's r-particles. As S contains the elements of S and R's particles, $R_t = [S/S_dR]_i$; as both S and R are open-ended, the definitive relationship holds only for the period bound by the time-signature. At time t_o, n relationships exist, and at time t_1, the c-th particle in n is altered due to the reality shift of this particle, altering c but not to the extent that its identity is totally destroyed. Because of this alteration, the defining element must also be altered, but with the open-ended system, care must be taken not to interfere with the other relationships. This situation is similar to, but not identical with the changes that occur in the closed system; the difference is one of nuances but it is significant because changes in the reality of the particle in question can be brought about by changes in other relationships within the system. This change may be due to improved information in the reality that may threaten the entire relationship. It may be due to a deterioration of the reality particle's significance, which requires a different defining element. It may also be due to a merger of two or more reality particles because of information eliminating the differences responsible for the separating the particles for definition and delineation. The specific instances of changes must be met with the appropriate alterations in the defining elements and their corresponding reality particles if the invading entropy is to be eliminated and the system's viability maintained.

An example of this is a developing country with scarce natural resources, but a highly developed agricultural base—a country that requires intensive importing and exporting activity for its economic survival. The government of this country seeks ways to maintain development while issuing decrees and policies in light of the inherent economic instability. A firm engaged in importing and exporting in this situation has to maintain its information system open-ended for its investors, foreign suppliers, and to those in foreign countries to whom the firm ships finished products of the country's industry and agriculture. Both the domestic and importing-exporting economies are subject to change, rendering parts of the firm's information system entropic. Changes have to be introduced in the firm's information system to account for the shifting realities. Should these changes become too great, the information system loses its identity and becomes intensively entropic. The firm then may formulate another system, or if its dependence on the previous system was too strong, the consequence of the entropic system may be the firm's closing, because of its inability to cope with the changing realities.

The second reason for entropy in the open information system is the improved quality of the defining elements and the manner in which this improvement brings about a break in the isomorphic and reflexive relationships with the corresponding area particles. The consequence is that a statement s_dr, that is, s defines and delineates r if and only if r is so related to s, results in changes in the defining and delineating element, no matter how small, must be met by the area reality particle if the isomorphic and reflexive relationships are to be maintained. s may change due to a greater understanding over the time period, while the reality particle remains stable. The s language, being sharpened, opens new vistas for dealing with its reality. When the considerations for entering into foreign markets are undertaken, the system's defining and delineating elements are sharpened with the accumulation of greater understanding and experience, even though its reality remains stable. For as the dynamics of the system are worked out through its usage, further understanding of the situation requires some redefinition of the problem; differences in the nuances of the system's operations, such as the market responses to the exported products, have to be revised, while the basic reality for which the system was constructed remains unchanged.

The third reason for entropy in the open information system is that alterations occur in the s elements due to a refinement of information *and* in the realities, independent of, and not corresponding to, changes in the s elements. For this condition, appropriate adjustments have to be made on both sides of the definition if the relationships affected by these alterations, and ultimately the system itself, is to be maintained. An innovative product is exported to a country of similar economic infrastructure and output; the product is successful and shifts in consumer liquidity in the targeted country result in greater purchases of the product than expected. The reality has been altered by the product's success and further output is required to meet the foreign demand. The system is revised to take these dynamics into consideration, but also to allow for the further consequences in the targeted economy, considering tariffs, the country's business cycle, and the exporter's ability to meet the new demand. As such changes are not radical—with increased production for the product and increased exporting stimulating marginal consumption in the overall macroeconomic picture—the system's financing has to be restructured to correspond to this new reality. This too has to be included in the changes of its information, resulting in the alteration of the relevant s and r sides. The system is preserved and the reality changed, with entropy on both sides of the definition removed.

In both the closed and open information systems, entropy is at its most destructive form when these systems are unable to handle changes in their respective realities through the reconstruction of their elements and particles. In the long run, the consequences of entropy are either constant reconstruction until the system loses its original purpose and intention, or the system will be retained, no matter how extensive the modifications, until a better system, one clean of entropy and of greater utility, can be constructed. Information systems concerning foreign transactions have to be reconstructed when the economic conditions of the exporting, importing, and/or both types of countries are altered. Should the systems no longer have relevance, they will be abandoned and better systems constructed.

The point is that for every information system S_t, given a change in either s or r—and in the case of the open system only, in both—the system's viability is maintained as a total information system. Should these alterations be neglected, entropy sets in at an increasing rate, bringing about the system's decline. Economic activity requires that the necessary alterations be made when entropy is noticed. This is most important when foreign markets are involved, because of the lack of control an economy has over another. Information systems pertaining to international trade are the most likely to become entropic because of the differences in the domestic dynamics such as the positions on the business cycle, the fluctuations in the currency values, and the potential effects of internal political situations. These factors have to be included in the systems, either as statements or as parameters, to be reckoned with if and when they become sufficiently influential.

THE UTILITY OPTIMUM—4: MAXIMIZING AND SATISFICING

The basic tenet of neoclassical reasoning incorporated into the concept of economic man, that the person knows his best interests, holds for this discussion, in the context of the contemporary individual. The psychology of personal interests is important in economics only when this is given expression with respect to making purchases and to the interests of commercial and/or private advertising, such as peer group recommendations for consumption, and the influences of vested interests on individual economic activity. This basic tenet becomes significant, therefore, when the expression of personal interests is given economic meaning by people distributing their liquidity among the competing economic ends. The utility optimum is the manifestation of this activity as people seek to gain the most from their purchases and economic endeavors, even when close substitutes have to be made due to the reduced liquidity resulting from wage increases lagging behind price increases.

The utility optimum is thus important in decision making, for it is on the basis of the utility optimum that preferences are ordered and decisions taken on the schedule of this ordering. According to neoclassical economic reasoning, maximizing, whether it be for profit or for consumer satisfaction, is the main objective in economic activity. Given individual liquidity with respect to the money supply and the available options, choices have to be made for the distribution of personal income among competing ends, one of these ends being saving. Since the post-Depression economics of large-scale capitalism, some economists claim that the optimum, together with the time-revered concept of the profit motive, cannot be attained. The complexities of contemporary domestic and international markets, coupled with intense competition and the existence of so many close substitutes that the concept of *optimum* is without significance, has eliminated the optimum concept, replacing it with *satisficing*. For example, according to Robin Marris, *satisficing* is the behavior

in which the subject, faced with a difficult problem to solve, prefers to sacrifice some of the rewards of the optimum solution in order to reduce the pains incurred in searching for it. Rather than maximize, he chooses to "satisfice," i.e., to accept some solution which is "good enough" in relation to various criteria such as survival, aspiration, or avoidance of shame.[5]

He further states that the significance of this approach lies in the possibility that satisfactory (satisficing) levels of reward have no particular relation to the optimum solution but are due to various adjustment reactions which are due to stable equilibrium conditions from which there is no reason to depart, and which relate to the optimum solution only coincidentally.

These stable equilibrium conditions offer psychological security as a trade-off against the optimum. Discussing psychological considerations, H. A. Simon, one of the pioneers in satisficing economics, argued that models of satisficing behavior are richer than maximizing behavior models, because they deal not only with equilibrium, but also with methods for achieving equilibrium. In the satisficing models, the individual's aspiration level defines a natural zero-point on his or her utility scale, compared to the maximizing models for profit and utility in which, according to Simon, the aspiration level is arbitrary. The individual as decision maker, whether as consumer or entrepreneur of a business, limits his or her goals by seeking the maximum utility from the decisions. Opting for satisficing allows the person to develop consumption or entrepreneurial strategies that allow for optimum positions instead of seeking only the maximum attainable. Neoclassical economic reasoning stresses only consumer and profit maximization, while proponents of the post-Keynesian managerial school reason that because equilibrium is the goal, maximization can never be reached, and must be replaced by optimal conditions. According to Simon,

When the firm has alternatives open to it that are at or above its aspiration level, the theory predicts that it will choose the best of those known to be available. When none of the available alternatives satisfies current aspirations, the theory predicts qualitatively different behavior; in the short run, search behavior and the revision of targets; in the longer run, what we have called above emotional behavior and what the psychologist would be inclined to call neurosis.[6]

Needless to say that firms are composed of individuals whose aspirations are for profits and who order their utilities according to these aspirations. But psychoses and neuroses aside, Marris describes one way in which a firm satisfices: this is when a firm maintains a substantial put nonoptimal growth rate by deliberately setting an above-optimum retention ratio—which is the ratio between retained earnings and gross earnings—thereby providing its maximum sustainable growth rate at its satisficing level, that is, by setting the growth rate at a level lower than that which can be achieved and thus increasing the ratio of the firm's market value to the net assets operating within this constrained value. For the firm, this value can be pressed on further in the form of higher prices demanded for the shares issued, allowing for increases in the ratio of liabilities to assets and the gearing ratio, which is the ratio between the money borrowed and money reinvested in capital structure, according to the market demand for the firm's shares.

For the individual, however, this translates to setting goals higher than can be initially afforded, and investing whatever liquidity is available after consumption in shares and funds that yield an extremely high interest rate and dividend to offset this reduced liquidity that could be used for consumption. This also translates for those who are self-employed to having the accountant find the most possible loopholes in the tax scheme and to use these to the advantage of reducing taxes while increasing personal wealth. For those employed, it translates into finding a financial consultant who can best advise on the uses of liquidity, thereby increasing personal wealth without damaging one's consumption level.

For the contemporary firm, whether dealing domestically or for exports, Simon argued that satisficing models are the only valid models for describing the contemporary firm's operations. Such practices as those Marris mentioned are indeed valid and legitimate in the operations of corporate decision making. Moreover, the theory of the managerial firm is important in international economics to determine under what domestic and international policies the firm's behavior will be influenced to reallocate resources. Simon thus commented that

the satisficing model vitiates all the conclusions about resource allocation and are derivable from the maximizing model when perfect competition is assumed. Similarly, a dynamic theory of firm sizes, . . . has quite different implications for public policies dealing with concentration than a theory that assumes firms to be in static equilibrium.[7]

In this comment Simon identified the problem of satisficing—it is effective only when dynamic equilibrium prevails; for in such a setting firms of different sizes compete and equilibrium is maintained in spite of each firm's ability to control its resource allocation and resource potential with respect to its share of the domestic and/or international market. According to the framework of dynamic equilibrium, the necessity for resource allocation exists and is controlled by the dynamics necessary for maintaining growth and stability and is underwritten by countries' governments by their monetary and fiscal policies.

As for the individual, replace firm sizes with levels of income, and the firm with the individual. Simon's argument is thus translatable from the firm to the individual. The individual, according to Simon's argument, operates in an environment of dynamic equilibrium in which maximizing is unrealistic; it cannot be achieved because close substitutes do not allow for maximizing. With the wide variety of choices for each product available, maximizing is not possible, unless the individual's demand for a specific product is inelastic. Even this is usually short run, because the close substitutes and the uniqueness of each substitute brings about experimentation, thereby weakening consumer loyalty. With the economy in dynamic equilibrium, for Simon maximizing is replaced by satisficing, so that the consumer seeks to satisfice his or her tastes through the specific consumption at any one time, based on liquidity.

Yet the question here is not one of dynamics or statics for those firms and individuals whose policies and consumer preferences have direct impact on economic welfare, for the accumulation of aggregate national wealth, and the influence on monetary and fiscal policies. The post–World War II use of statics has only been for the monetary analysis of programs and policies, affixing on them a single time-signature; statics have not been used in the formulation of policies, programs, or individual preference ordering for consumption. Moreover, the use of dynamic equilibrium theory has been for the construction of economic models to demonstrate how the economy could operate in the ideal world where an economy produces the same goods and services and requires the same resources in permanently fixed ratios of allocation. The de facto dynamics, those operating in the economy and considered by business people in the big firms and to some extent the managers in the auxiliary businesses, are the dynamics of disequilibrium. The difficulty with the satisficing approach in contemporary decision making is accepting that since the advent of post-Keynesian managerial economics the areas of concern for managers are the generation of market dynamics for new products, domestic or imported, the maintaining of those products that retain an acceptable profit-cost ratio, and the phasing out of those products whose profit-cost ratios are not acceptable. Therefore, the derivation of satisficing conditions from maximizing models where perfect competition is assumed is, again, an important analytical technique for the formation of policy alternatives, but no more than that. Releasing the perfect-competition restraint brings the model that much closer to reality, even though the control on the model is reduced; in this way, greater flexibility is provided between maximizing and satisficing. The point is, however, the closer the model approaches the real situation of the economy, the closer maximizing and satisficing become.

In other words, when plans are drawn up with a realistic appraisal of the domestic and targeted foreign economies in the restricted domains for which the plans are formulated, maximizing and satisficing become unity and at that point the utility optimum is reached. This does not, of course, mean that there are no best-case and worse-case scenarios, strategies planned for taking advantage of the most profitable situations and possible difficulties. The problem with these strategies, however, is that they are formulated before the program is acted upon, while best- and worse-case situations develop while the program is in force. Strategies are not, however, goals but means to achieving them, and the goals to be achieved are the optimum results and benefits accorded by the reality of the situation as understood by the planners and decision makers. This optimum is determined by the program's utility with respect to how well the program relates to the reality which it defines and delineates. While the program is still "on paper," proposed as a project and even accepted and acted upon by the firm, it can still be faulted for inconsistency and irrelevance with respect to its reality. At this stage the probability criteria are established and the relationship between probability and the program's information stated. The time-signature is then placed so that for the closed information system, its validity is stated for its assigned duration and for the open system, its validity is stated with respect to the changing time periods indicated by the signature.

If, at this stage, no inconsistencies or other difficulties are exposed, then the program is set into motion and relates to its assigned reality. While the closed system is terminated when its time-signature expires, the open system continues and is revised according to the extent of entropy that has invaded the system. For the closed system, the utility optimum is stated and is either achieved or not over the period allotted by the time-signature. For the open system, the utility optimum is maintained only by making the alterations necessary to insure the system's continued viability, without the system's original identity and purpose being destroyed as a result of the changes undertaken. As long as the system's utility is maintained and entropy held in check, it is at its maximum, and maximizing and satisficing are equal and identical with utility. Should entropy become too pervasive so that the system can no longer be corrected without the system's identity being destroyed, maximizing and satisficing are irrelevant for the system no longer exists. This eventually confronts all open information systems, and results in programs that were once useful being phased out and other programs formulated to take their places, only to run their courses and meet the same fate.

This is why new lines of foreign commerce are developed while lines whose profitability has declined are phased out. Profitability in foreign trade is not merely a function of consumption as it is in domestic business. Both domestic macro policies and those policies of the importing countries have to be considered. Changes in foreign governments or established governments' economic policies bear influence on consumer liquidity in those countries, sometimes directly. Devaluations or revaluations, the reporting of the quarterly balance of trade and foreign reserve holdings, the leveling of value added taxes and increasing income taxes all influence how consumers allocate their liquidity. These are aspects of trading that the exporting countries cannot foretell, never mind the monetary policies of their own governments. This is why programs are being formulated increasingly by the big corporations that can diversify their production and, if considered profitable, establish branches in foreign countries where a better knowledge of the labor force and government political decision makers is available. This tendency is increasing as a result of the collapse of the Bretton Woods agreement in 1973, when the OPEC countries disrupted whatever economic stability existed among the world's countries by raising the price of petroleum at drastic rates. While stability has been achieved to a large extent since 1980, the development of multinational corporations and the big corporation impact in international economics has been shown to be profitable and hence directing resources into its expansion. This is even more so with the European economic union being formed in 1992, and with the current dissolution of the Eastern Communist bloc.

However, with the prevailing stability there is also uncertainty. The European Economic Community will be a formidable competitor for the United States, and its impact on the East European countries has yet to be assessed properly, mainly because of the lack of information on how events will continue to develop there. The big corporations and their multinational branches have the resources to develop along with these conditions and change their programs accordingly. The contemporary trade situation is that in one sense, markets are opening up, responding to products not available, such as in Eastern Europe and the important markets of China; on the other hand, they are closing in on themselves, such as with the European Economic Community, making the challenges of continuing trade that much more important and perhaps difficult.

Trade is an economic activity that has tremendous influence on the world's economies. It allows for greater sales for an economy's products, it provides foreign currency necessary for dealing with other countries, and it allows for the downswing of the business cycle to be softened in its severity by maintaining foreign markets when domestic demand declines. One of the consequences of the Great Depression was a decline in world trade because of beggar-thy-neighbor policies, taken to protect the domestic economies. This in fact contributed to the decline in domestic economic activity and prolonged the duration of the Depression. For these reasons, the Bretton Woods Conference was held; its policies stimulated trade and was very effective in achieving increased commerce.

With the OPEC price increases and the noncyclical recession they generated, the beggar-thy-neighbor policies of the previous era were not undertaken. Instead, three consequences of the oil price rises occurred. There was a search for alternative supply sources for petroleum and the bringing on-line those sources that were hitherto uncommercial. There was also the development of nonpetroleum energy sources, such as solar and to a lesser extent wind energy. Moreover, greater efficiency was introduced into machinery requiring oil and its by-products, thereby reducing the quantity of oil demanded.

The second consequence was a looking inward of the economies, to see how the recession could be cushioned. The neglected field of economics, that of welfare economics, took on a new interest, only to find its contributors confronted with an overlapping and greatly inefficient system, one unable to cope with the serious unemployment resulting from the recession. Incentives were provided to industries by local, state, and federal government agencies to increase production and employment, but many of these incentives proved to be noneconomic because of the lack of sufficient demand, and were abandoned by those businesses whose losses exceeded the value of the incentives.

The search for alternative energy sources and the applications of those that demonstrated efficiency, together with the overhauling of the welfare system—with still many inefficiencies existing[8]—would have been impetus enough to move the economies out of the doldrums and back into production and near full employment. But there was the third consequence that also proved important, this being the looking outward into the arena of foreign commerce. Many multinationals were established, tariffs lowered, and one important consequence, that of the economic union of Europe being considered in earnest, were the outcome of the economic recession of the period. International competition sharpened with new products entering the markets and with close domestic substitutes being developed and exported as well. New programs are being formulated while other are entropic and abandoned, and trade, as a result of rejecting the response of the Great Depression, is flourishing.

The situation is far from being stable, however, with the uncertainty of the European Economic Union being somewhat of an unknown factor, in spite of the strength of its member economies. Also, with the changes being undertaken in Eastern Europe and the Soviet Union, uncertainty exists with respect to the roles these countries will take in the trading situation. With the Cold War's thaw, however, the Eastern bloc economies are seeking to enter the world's markets as genuine competitors. This is a slow process because of the necessary economic reorientation, but it is made even slower because of the political uncertainty in these countries. Their viability as participants in international trade depends, as with the developed trading countries, on their ability to produce quality products. This depends on their labor force, industrial development, and on the acumen of their governments to establish sound monetary and fiscal policies. These points will be discussed in the next chapter.

THE PARADOXES OF MARGINALISM RECONSIDERED

Marginalism has been an important concept in the development of economic thought, especially since Karl Marx's *Capital,* when, during the height of the Industrial Revolution the focus was on the firm and its ability to reap profits. But even during this period when marginalism began to develop as an economic tool it was not without its difficulties. For example, we learn in the economic textbooks that a firm is at its maximum production level when marginal revenue equals marginal output. Any furthur output would result in lower profits and output at a lesser amount means that increased output can be achieved for increased profits.

The difficulty with this specific marginal concept is that it directs attention to the firm's internal economies with respect to output, but avoids the firm's major concern of generating markets. If, for example, greater demand can be exploited by production increases over those necessary to meet current demand, then while marginal revenue equals marginal output, this is no real statement of the firm's revenue—and hence profit—generating position. Also, while for current demand this equality holds, it says very little about the firm's real productive capacity, even in the very short run when no changes in the firm's productive capacity are made. The firm's productive capacity may be far more extensive than its marginal output indicates, and if this is so, it is up to the firm's managers to expand production to capacity, by either continuing along the same lines and seeking through advertising to generate more demand, or through product diversification. These alternatives do not depend on marginalism, however, but on the utility optimum. The utility of these alternatives has to be taken into account with respect to the third alternative of continuing as is. Market conditions, the extent of close competitors, the cyclical phase of the economy, the availability of new resources for alternative or increased production, and the ability to obtain funding if necessary are all considerations that have to be analyzed with respect to their utilities.

Even the strict neoclassical sense of maximization being reached when marginal revenue equals marginal output is in question with respect to the utility optimum. In the very short run, if unused productive capacity exists, yet marginal revenue equals marginal output, then both revenue and output can be increased through promotional advertising, providing that market saturation for the product does not exist. If production is running at full capacity, then market diversification through different products can be undertaken, perhaps at the cost of reducing output for the product and rechanneling the resources into other production lines. This can be undertaken without altering plant capacity, but by rescheduling production programs. These considerations, however, depend on their utilities as determined within their respective information systems.

With respect to the paradox of the buyer and seller stated in the section "The Utility Optimum—1" in this chapter, setting the elasticities for the buyer and seller to unity, $Op_s \equiv 2p_b$; but as was stated, this cannot be the case for a price exists for which the transaction was made. This difficulty can be resolved if another approach is taken, in which the utilities of the buyer and seller are expressed by the agreed upon price. If the price is x, then the negative sign for the seller is replaced by a positive sign, as this is the utility the seller establishes for the product. The seller trades off the product for x which provides the product's utility exchange rate. The buyer purchases the product x as this is the amount considered of utility for the exchange. Hence, the formula transforms to utility outlay equals price minus alternative costs of selling for the seller, and equals price minus alternative uses for liquidity for the buyer. Multiplying both sides by -1 eliminates the negative sign so that the seller's price equals the buyer's utility consideration for the product with respect to alternatives when the purchase is made. Marginalism has no role here as it is replaced by the utility outlay, that is, the utility consideration involved in both making the sale and the purchase when the transaction is undertaken.

Consider the paradox of the marginal efficiency of capital derived from Keynes's *General Theory*. As was stated earlier in this chapter, the mec of an expected yield of asset over the time periods a to c is lower than real yield over this time, as the expected yield X was lowered to $-X$ so that the logical construction of the mec leads to a paradox, that of not being the same mec over the same period of time.

This paradox can be resolved with the application of utility. The construction of the mec over time is not the mec over time because expectation was not realized can be approached from the utility position. When the mec is replaced by utility, the role of expectation remains strictly personal and psychological and is not included in the asset's actual utility. Granted that the total of expectation is the basis on which the investment is made for the projected yield over time, but nevertheless this expectation may or may not correspond to the asset's actual utility. There is, therefore, no paradox, because expected and actual utilities must be kept separate. Thus,

$$[M(u^X{}_{t_a - t_c}) \equiv M(u^X{}_{t_a - t_c})] \text{ if and only if } [u_{t_a - t_c} \equiv u_{t_a - t_c}].$$

Where $EuX = uX$, that is, where the expected utility is equal to the actual utility, the expectation is confirmed in reality; when $EuX \equiv uX$ over the time period, say in time b, then the expectation is not realized and only the actual utility should be considered. Keeping expectations separate from utility eliminates this difficulty, and while expectations are important in ordering subjective utility preferences, reality which is the deciding factor and expressed in objective utility is certainly more important. Considering both aspects of utility eliminates this paradox of the mec.

With respect to the marginal propensity to import, this indeed is a function of aggregate liquidity. It is an error, however, to maintain that changes in national income result in changes in import consumption. Developing countries, whose industrial bases are being formed, rely heavily on imports and this regardless of the national income levels. It is correct to state that changes in national income result in changes in import consumption only if such changes in income affect aggregate liquidity and the utility of importing. For this reason no matter what changes have occurred in importing with respect to national income in the interim period t_b, should the ratio of importations remain with respect to changes in national income over $t_a - t_c$, then the mpi is inaccurate. Of course, the aggregate liquidity may have altered with respect to national income changes. If so, then this would bear directly on the utility of importing with respect to domestic consumption. But this is not the entire picture, for as was mentioned, developing economies and certainly those economies that are emerging lack the sufficient industrial base to supply the needs of their citizens. Changes in national income in these countries may bear on the importing patterns, in which some products are no longer purchased while others even more so. But it is unlikely that substantial shifts in the total importing package will occur.

Moreover, the concept of national income has to be sharpened. The value of a country's income depends on the utility of its currency, and this, on the strength of the country's industry to produce and on its government to regulate the economy and maintain growth. Changes in national income, that is, changes in the amount of currency in circulation, tell nothing of the economy's viability. What is important is the currency's utility with respect to purchasing and saving. Domestically, this depends on the welfare utility function relating industry, government, and labor into a general economic dynamic, with each of the components interrelated. This concept also will be developed into an international utility function in the following chapters relating the domestic economy to trade.

The trouble with marginalism is that it seeks to objectify the subjective aspect of expectation. This was shown in the first argument given, where the differing elasticities of buyer and seller were attributed to the subjective perspectives of the parties to the bargaining process. The second argument illustrates this by showing that the decline in the mec is due to the subjective expectation and the objective reality in which the asset is regarded. In the third argument, this is shown by the expected changes in importation brought about by changes in national income, while importation may in reality remain the same in monetary value while perhaps there may be changes in the imported product list. As utility is both objective and subjective it combines expectation as subjective preference ordering with reality as objective reality. Both aspects of utility influence each other in the decision-making processes, but expectation and reality are kept separate because of the different requirements of each.

Chapter 6

THE WELFARE UTILITY FUNCTION

To determine if the natural equilibrium of the economy is optimal or suboptimal we must introduce additional empirical material, painting a picture of the dominant forces in the real economy detailed enough for us to derive at least a coarse idea of its motion. Unfortunately, to do so we will have to step onto considerably thinner ice than that which has borne us till now, since the economy is an enormously varied and complex thing, valid generalizations concerning which are hard to come by.

—Jacob T. Schwartz,
"Mathematics as a Tool for Economic Reasoning"[1]

DYNAMIC EQUILIBRIUM AND TRADE

Granted that the economy is a complex thing, and that an economy's international commerce most certainly adds to this complexity, valid generalizations about an economy, no matter how difficult to come by, form the basis of economic theory. An economic theory is indeed a set of generalizations, set in a working order, from which conclusions can be derived and tested against economic realities supported by empirical data. In this sense, economic theory is just like theories of the natural and physical sciences.

The theoretical concept of equilibrium, whether optimal or suboptimal, is certainly one that has been around for a very long time, and one whose validity must be examined. This must be done not only with respect to the economy in general, as is the focus of Schwartz's comment, but also with respect to international trade as an extension of domestic economic output and market orientation.

According to the economic concept of equilibrium, macro equilibrium is in its optimal position when aggregate supply and aggregate demand are interrelated to the extent that increased supply will not find buyers and increased demand will not find the goods and services to be purchased. Hence, supply and demand in the aggregate are equal. Suboptimal equilibrium exists when, even though the tendency is toward aggregate supply and demand equilibrium, various important markets have not yet obtained this position, but are dynamic by their being suboptimal. They are shifting with the currents of supply and demand for closely competing products; as these remaining markets settle down with the reaching of stability among the competitors, they too will fall into the equilibrium pattern and the removal of suboptimal equilibrium will bring the macro economy into its natural equilibrium position.

According to this approach, trade will also be stabilized with the amount of goods and services being produced for export being sold and the amount targeted for import being consumed by the specific populations for which they are directed.

Employment will be full, with frictional employment due to the relocation of labor and seasonal variations being very marginal and thus having no significant bearing on the natural equilibrium position. Industry will be operating at the point where marginal output equals marginal revenue but as consumption is stable there will be no need for increased production, so revenues will remain stable.

This is an interesting model of the macro economy, and as foreign trade is stable, its equilibrium position means that the world's economies are also stable. As a model, it offers the investigation of economic stability and the dynamics that can bring such equilibrium into fruition. Political stability, for example, has to be achieved, competition among businesses has to have ceased, with each business being content with its share of its respective markets, and for international trade to be stabilized, political stability throughout the world has to be accomplished and levels of economic sophistication reached among the world's economies for exported and imported goods and services to be absorbed at the rates they are produced and delivered to the targeted groups.

This also means that innovation, the introduction of new products into markets, would have ceased, for as soon as the innovation process begins, the natural equilibrium is disturbed and competition flourishes once again.[2]

The theoretical concept of natural equilibrium, for all its interest and knowledge that can be gained in the construction of its domestic and global models, is certainly unrealistic. The profit motive, one of the main reasons for generating economic activity, will not allow equilibrium to remain for long in its natural state as defined here. Business people will seek greater profits and these cannot be obtained in the static natural equilibrium situation. Innovations will be encouraged in both the domestic and international markets, in order to draw demand from close competitors so that profits can be increased. With innovation, spurred on by the profit motive, should this natural economic equilibrium ever exist, it will have a short life span.

With respect to equilibrium, a more accurate model is that of the suboptimal dynamic equilibrium, generated by innovation and subsequent imitation. According to this concept, the dynamics of equilibrium are maintained by innovation and imitation as new markets are developed and if demonstrated successful by the amount of sales and consumer interest, imitators bringing into the market close substitutes reduce the original profit levels of the innovating firms.[3] Consumers are drawn to the competing products, either because of price, or subjective preference, reducing the original profit level of the innovating firm and bringing the market into saturation in which no economic viability exists for another close competitor to enter the market, as consumers will not respond to the competitor's product with sufficient consumption to make the venture profitable.

Market saturation is another approach to equilibrium. The market has stabilized, demand and supply are fairly constant, with shifts only among competing firms as product loyalty diminishes with consumers substituting products because of price, shifts in the nuances of individual tastes, and because of what Robin Marris terms "sheeplike behavior," that is following the purchasing patterns of peer groups.[4] The market is in its natural equilibrium position with supply equaling demand in the aggregate, and will remain so until a firm seeks to increase its profits and initiate the innovative process with another product that, if commercially successful, will generate further imitation and bring the entire dynamic process into operation again.

As well as being a dynamic process with respect to market development, innovation is an internal dynamic process with respect to the firm as it requires the internal reallocation of resources for the production of new product lines. This requires the phasing out of product lines that are considered by the firm's directorate to be of low profitability due to their production costs and market prices. However, this phasing-out process enables the firm's competitors to obtain greater market shares of the product. As this is a dynamic process, moreover, these competing firms will also evaluate their product lines to see which of their products can be phased out, with the released internal resources to be used with greater utility.

New products are brought into the markets as a result of innovation; their commercial progress determines whether close competitors will enter the market, or whether they will direct their resources elsewhere. For some firms, maintaining products with low profitability may be to their advantage, because sales are usually always guaranteed. Hence, stimulated by the profit motive, innovation and imitation are recurring situations in an economy, bringing to the markets dynamics, but also tending toward equilibrium when market saturation is reached. This suboptimal equilibrium is the economic rule, as even within the framework of dynamic equilibrium, growth is generated, resources reallocated, and new products are made available to the consumer.

With respect to trade, dynamic equilibrium operates along similar lines, as
innovation generates new products that can be commercial internationally. There
are, however, several factors that have to be considered before a firm, even in
this artificial situation of dynamic equilibrium, can engage in trade.

One important factor is the ability to market the product.This depends on the
level of economic growth in the targeted countries and the ability of the targeted countries to respond with imitative products, or whether such products
already exist and the exported product is to be another competitor with a "foreign flare." If the product is strictly innovative, understanding the targeted
countries' abilities to respond with competing products must also be part of the
calculation, to determine the long-range commitment which is usually necessary for beginning relations with distributing and marketing firms in these countries. With respect to innovation, the product has to be marketed to relate to
national tastes and moods for trying something foreign and new. This is more
than advertising, for there has to be an attraction to the product on which the
public relations firms can relate and promote. Innovations that do well domestically have to be researched internationally before they can be exported, unless
the firm's directorate is willing to rely on its initial judgment and engage in
international commerce without such research, given the certainty of its product. Here, the information system is open and its utility will be tested in the
real markets.

In order to explore the dynamic equilibrium models of trade further, additional comments are necessary to clarify the concept of dynamic equilibrium.
It is an extension and variation of the general equilibrium concept, in which,
to quote Emmanuel Farjoun and Moshe Machover, "all its internal forces neutralize each other, so that if left to its own devices the system will continue in
the same state, and will be perturbed away from it only under the influence of
external forces."[5] The equilibrium state, in its natural condition, is stable, so
that all perturbations by external forces are those generated by innovation and
the subsequent imitation that follows the commercially successful innovation.
Resources are reallocated, existing products either reduced in their production
levels or phased out entirely according to profit calculations, and different markets are exploited according to the product's ability to generate back-up products to accompany it. Once market saturation is reached, however, the forces
of innovation having ceased leave only marginal and insignificant imitation
remaining. Equilibrium is restored and the natural equilibrium is reached when
all market activity retains its stability.

This condition describes the domestic economy, and the exception to this
condition lies in international trade. Market saturation and hence stability may
be achieved in the domestic economy, but for those products exported, the
dynamics are somewhat more complicated. Firms dealing in trade have to ac

count for their own domiciled economies and those of their targeted countries as well. The domiciled economy is important because it provides the labor force for manufacturing the product, the banking system for providing the instruments for the transferring of funds and for credit when necessary. The monetary and fiscal policies have to be considered by the exporting firm's directorate when planning to open new markets and when maintaining those already established. Given foreign commitments, a recession in the domiciled country results in the reduced labor force. While the exporting firm's labor force may not be so affected, the ability to acquire product parts, the basic materials for manufacturing, the necessity for shipping within the economy as part of the allocation of resources, and the ability to maintain financial liquidity necessary for maintaining trade are necessary operations of the firm.

The targeted economies have to be considered for the very reason that they contain the markets to which the firm is exporting. The conditions in these economies may differ significantly with respect to culture, general tastes, and domestic production. These are important factors, for they serve as a basis for establishing markets by providing products that do not already exist, or providing competitive products in a market that is still open, or perhaps by providing products whose attraction is the "foreign flair" effect.

These factors are also important for the marketing of the products for the respective countries in that they are inputs in the information systems as they relate to both the internal processes of production and the external processes of generating market interest in the foreign countries. This is important internally, for a common basis for the product has to be established that will allow for its appeal in countries with diverse consuming patterns and tastes. As the product is usually one manufactured for the domestic market as well, its appeal has to be universal in the sense that its purpose is specific and its appeal strong for those in the exported markets for which it is targeted. In the rarer situations, where the product is strictly for export, the appeal has to be universal in order to cover the diversified tastes among the targeted economies. This is established in the product's manufacture in any case; it is part of the internal information system pertaining to the product's development, manufacturing, and the advertising strategies.

The actual marketing of the products depends on the type of advertising already established, and the abilities of the advertising firms—be they incorporated in the exporting firm's business, or local firms employed by the exporters—to stimulate interest among the targeted groups. If the product is innovative in these economies, advertising has to indicate the product's advantages and it must do this by adapting the concepts and styles of the targeted economies as well as those from which the product is imported; its benefits have to be emphasized and its drawbacks, should they exist, minimized by way of guarantees and/or financial remuneration in case of complaints that cannot be handled by domestic businesses that the exporters may employ. If the product is imitative, the "foreign flair" effect has to be exploited, so that the product's advantages over its domestic (and perhaps other foreign) competitors can be enhanced and brought to the targeted consumer groups.

This approach of dynamic equilibrium is thus manifested in both domestic and foreign innovation and imitation, with the markets reaching saturation, that is, equilibrium stability, and with natural equilibrium eventually setting in. This natural equilibrium state will be temporary as further innovations break into the domestic and foreign markets, either by firms domiciled in the domestic economies or by those exporting to targeted economies. Consumers will alternate their spending among the various innovative and imitative products bringing about the condition of dynamic equilibrium again; but this will eventually settle into general equilibrium, with aggregate market stability prevailing once more.

According to the natural equilibrium approach, the economy will always enter into the natural equilibrium position; the dynamics of the markets are temporary and will result in the stability of equilibrium when markets are saturated. While this is an interesting model for representing economic movement, it is certainly unrealistic, as the Great Depression so vividly and painfully demonstrated. Markets are not established because innovation pierces the saturated state of previous markets, neither for domestic nor foreign economies. The natural equilibrium position is that of neoclassical post-Marx's *Capital* economic theory and is based on Adam Smith's "invisible hand" concept and the later refinement of this concept in Say's Law of Markets. It found its most eloquent expression in Pigou's *Economics of Welfare,* and was respectfully subjected to critique in Keynes's *General Theory.*[6] The difficulty, as Keynes stated, was the assumption of full employment, allowing for consumers to shift loyalties from one product to another. The Schumpeterian position that after a period of gestation markets will be revived as inventories are restocked, is also a manifestation of the neoclassical theory.[7] Full employment, as a concept of economics, was cast aside when confronted with the realities of the Great Depression; it should never have been adapted into working economic models for it never was actual in the best of economic conditions. Schumpeter's business cycle theory never held because of the unemployment situation which prevented existing stocks from being moved sufficiently for new inventories to be purchased and sold. With unemployment, money is scarce, consumption minimal, and there is insufficient incentive for innovations and imitations to be undertaken.

Foreign commerce is also affected during periods of unemployment for the same reasons of insufficient consumer liquidity, insufficient incentives for undertaking innovation and imitation, and the lack of movement of existing inventories necessary for aggregate restocking that could bring about a revival of employment and the markets. The only advantage for international trade in this equilibrium model is the lack of synchronization of market dynamics among the trading economies, so that depression in one economy can be relieved somewhat by importing to an economy in a state of recovery or prosperity.

The final movement toward natural equilibrium is one in which the inventories of shops are full as the markets are nearing saturation. Consumption cannot keep up with the levels of inventories and as they are not moved fast enough salaries cannot be paid to the workers in the shops and in industries that manufacture them. Inventories remain high and unemployment increases so that consumption decreases as consumer liquidity is reduced because of unemployment. Profits are reduced as sales try to induce increased consumption; this may be a successful policy at the margin, but its impact on the economy in general is insignificant.

Natural equilibrium exists when the final dynamics cease and markets are saturated and demand has declined. This will pressure those businesses that cannot sustain the decline to go out of business, thereby increasing further the ranks of the unemployed in those businesses and the industries that supplied them. Those businesses that can sustain the decline will cater to the demands of the consumers. As the consumer aggregate liquidity is reduced, the stocks held by those existing businesses will be the very goods and services the consumers can afford and need. Here we have a Say-like situation in which existing supplies in stock equal the aggregate demand, and the economy is in its natural state of equilibrium, with its dynamics having ceased.

Trade may still continue as international contracts are fulfilled. For these contracts the necessary labor force is maintained, but resources become increasingly scarce as they are derived from other aspects of the economy that are also dependent on the domestic markets. While trade will be maintained—even at declined profits or perhaps at losses—no new trade will be initiated due to the lack of labor and resources already unemployed and removed from market considerations. When the existing contracts expire and natural equilibrium still prevails, depending on the firm's ability to muster resources and employment necessary for contract renewal, international commerce may be halted or slowed down according to the terms of the renewed contract. The consequence is that the firm's profit declines, its influence in foreign markets declines leaving the way for firms in other countries in various phases of dynamic equilibrium to enter as close competitors take over the market, and unemployment will be increased according to the decline in demand for resources to maintain trade.

In pre-Newtonian physics, it was considered that the natural condition of motion is rest, with motion itself being a special case of rest. Newton changed this approach by arguing that motion is continuous and rest relative to motion. This was a great revolution in the thinking of physicists.[8] Economics has also undergone a revolution in which equilibrium has been rejected as the natural state, to be replaced by dynamic disequilibrium, with economic activity constantly in motion. Our contemporary era is one in which government participation—due to the lessons learned from the Great Depression—is necessary for keeping the economy in motion; this is its natural state, because the idea of mass and long-enduring unemployment of the labor force and resources is unacceptable. Intervention is necessary for maintaining consumer liquidity sufficient to enable the real spark of economic growth, innovation with its subsequent imitation, to take place at levels of intensity that will maintain economic motion. As natural equilibrium is severe recession or depression, and as dynamic equilibrium leads to natural equilibrium, this concept does not provide the means for maintaining economic growth in light of the business cycles that are inherent in the economy. The natural condition of economic activity is one of motion, of dynamic disequilibrium. When the extremes of the cycle begin to prevail, responsible government activates policies that eliminate the uncertainty and provide enough confidence for the innovative and imitative process to continue. The conditions of another severe depression are most certainly unacceptable for both domestic and international economies; a state of equilibrium in which no significant activity occurs is completely unnatural.

THE WELFARE UTILITY FUNCTION: DYNAMIC DISEQUILIBRIUM AND TRADE

The Industrial Revolution was an era in which the new science of Newton and those who followed were merged with the processes of production in order to manufacture with greater efficiency and hence at lower costs and consumer prices. This required the training of a work force to make it competent to handle the new machinery that resulted from this merger. This resulted in the situation in which great cities were formed around industrial plants, bringing into their confines great populations who took advantage of industrialization and the cultural and social amenities that developed.

Another aspect of the Industrial Revolution were the business cycles that resulted from the disequilibrium between production and consumption, and from the fluctuations in the value of currencies in their purchasing power as a result of these fluctuations. The wealthy easily fell to levels of poverty as the cycle moved downward, while those in poverty, albeit with greater difficulty, could amass great wealth through initiative and daring. The cycles were destructive in their downward motions, but as industrialization was developing and gaining in momentum, new geographical areas were opening for those whose opportunities were limited in the established cities due to the downward swing of the cycle. Science and production had sealed a bond that was never to be broken. The benefits of this bond—technology—certainly brought about better living conditions. It led to the restructuring of employment, moving rural workers who had become redundant due to the new machinery into the cities where their work contributed to their betterment and to society's in general.

It also contributed to the development of economic theory, beginning with Adam Smith's division of labor in the production process, to the advanced theories of Alfred Marshall in his discussion of the relationships between production, revenues, prices, and profits.[9] There was another consequence of technology and industrialization that had relevance for both economic theory and the practical world. This was the formation of three factors that had to work with each other: government, industry, and labor. The relationship between industry and labor was fairly clear as industrialization developed. This was the symbiotic relationship in which industry needed labor to produce and labor required industry for its livelihood. The third factor, that of government, was somewhat uncertain because of the liberal tendencies in those countries undergoing industrialization. In Great Britain, for example, the leading economists were liberal and in the country that claimed to be the "mother of parliaments," the upper class hold on society was weakening as workers earned in industry and bettered their economic positions. In France, with its antimonarchial sentiments, liberty held sway and the government treaded very lightly where civil rights were concerned. In Germany, with its history of militarism, its efficiency was exploited by industry and its citizens were engaged in a social struggle between its militaristic past and the liberal influences of other industrializing countries. The U.S. government was formed by its founding fathers who had the awareness of the new country established free from the tyranny of government. Its liberalism is written into its Constitution and the struggle of its citizens has been to safeguard this liberalism throughout the years, with the changes in the social dynamics of industrialization and postindustrialization.[10]

The new liberalism unleashed by the merger of science with the means of production and the jobs and opportunities industrialization brought, was tempered by the concept that the best government is that which governs according to the conditions at the time. The government was the custodian of the nation's land and other natural resources; moreover, it was the custodian of the nation's currency and provided legislation for dealing with its uses. Still, the role of government was less certain than those of industry and labor; the reluctance to suppress the liberalism that was developing along with industry made the governments during periods of economic recession and depression reluctant to act, for this would be interfering into areas that are in the private sectors of society. This reluctance to participate actively in the economy became part of the liberal creed, and the concept that the government governs best according to the conditions of the time still prevailed in its liberal sense of noninterference in the economy. Recessions and depressions were certainly painful, but the economy seemed resilient enough to come back even stronger. Hence, when the Great Depression hit, the policy was still of noninterference, nonintervention, based on past experiences of recessions, depressions, and economic recovery.

The Great Depression was different from all previous depressions because of its impact and the loss of confidence that resulted. Many great fortunes made on the stock and commodities exchanges were wiped out almost instantly. There were runs on banks as people tried to salvage whatever savings they had in order to survive the crisis. Moreover, governments took the first approach that they should refrain from intervention in the industrial and labor sectors in order to prevent the establishment of dictators. Theirs was the classical and neoclassical position that this crisis too would be resolved as soon as markets were cleared of their inventories and the pressures of demand were exerted for restocking. This would result in reemployment as business once again resumed. The difficulty was that the full-employment assumption of the neoclassical economists was invalid, and that therefore there was no pressure by aggregate demand for moving out inventories and their restocking. With high unemployment demand declines accordingly and whatever consumption there is, is channeled toward the basic necessities; consumption of these necessities was insufficient for economic revival on the scale that had previously existed, and the crisis worsened.

In Germany, the old militarism asserted itself once again, and the democracy of the Industrial Revolution was replaced by one of the world's worst dictatorships. Unemployment was eased with the rechanneling of the unemployed into the arms industries. But in Great Britain, France, and the United States, governments became active in the economies in other ways. Instead of preparing for war, they sought to salvage the dynamics of the Industrial Revolution, and with the concept that the best government is that which governs according to the conditions of the time, competed in a sense with industry by hiring the unemployed. This hiring was not for commercial profit but in order to provide the unemployed with income by moving workers from the bread lines and soup kitchens to productive labor in the nonindustrial social sector. Hence, reforestation, building noncommercial structures, and for those who were scholars, working on government research projects, eased the situation considerably, but still, this was no substitute for industrial employment and the economic growth derived from it. The Great Depression was ended as abruptly as it had begun, but this time by World War II.

During the Great Depression the Industrial Revolution had come to an end. The depression itself was a result of the conflicts on industrialization and the business cycles that had developed because of it. The neoclassical assumption of full employment had given way to the realistic concept that employment is a function of growth and is related to industrial output and government activity. The governments could no longer remain passive in economic affairs in light of the history of that depression, and formed an alliance with labor and industry to insure that cyclical downswings are not so destructive as in the past, and that policies will be enacted to genuinely underwrite economic activity.

The period also had great moments for trade. The beggar-thy-neighbor policies proved counterproductive for easing the Depression, and trade was reduced significantly. Tariffs, devaluations, and in some cases the ceasing of commercial ties altogether, were activities of governments in a period of great uncertainty and groping for policies that would improve their situations. In the postwar period, the Bretton Woods agreement, the IMF and GATT, provided a basis for reestablishing trade on terms that would not be counterproductive. However, both the new trade conditions and the government approaches to economic activity were tested again in 1973 with the oil crisis that followed the Yom Kippur war. This led to strengthening of the relationship between government and industry, and government and labor, which was the process that had begun since the Great Depression.[11]

There is still another factor to consider in this relationship with respect to government reluctance to become too active in these sectors, maintaining its liberal outlook, even though the merger among the three economic sectors has been stronger than ever. This reluctance is due to the conditions that existed after World War II and that have developed since the oil crisis of 1973. This factor is the new historical era that had emerged as a result of the last world war, an era that had come to rely on knowledge systems to an extent greater than at any other time. This new era resulted from the development of the computer—a concept that had its foundations in the work of the British mathematician, Alan Turing, prior to the last world war.[12] It also resulted from the realization of a concept that had its origins in the writings of the ancient Greek philosophers, that of smashing the atom;[13] finally, it resulted from the realization that the Cold War was not to be waged only on simulated battlefields, or with hostile Allied and Communist bloc forces confronting each other across agreed boundaries, but also in the academic institutions, when the Soviet Sputnik was placed successfully into outer space.

Our contemporary era of knowledge began after the war with the shifting of industry from war-time to peace-time production. This required the retraining of a labor force, the majority of whom had been mobilized into military service, instructing them in the new methods of production that had been developed for wartime output. Moreover, with the lesson of unemployment learned from the aftermath of World War I, when demobilized servicemen were left to their own initiative to find employment, the government became active with various programs to provide education and technical training for those who sought this assistance. Knowledge was also required in the organization and reconstruction of the war-torn countries in Europe and Asia, but knowledge in the more sophisticated forms of computer applications and the restructuring of the education systems to enable these countries to compete economically in world commerce and trade.

In the aftermath of the dictatorships that had ruled in Europe and Japan, the knowledge of harnessing atomic energy was withheld from the conquered countries; their education systems, and especially their universities, were brought up to standards that would offer competition to Great Britain and the United States. Moreover, with the new concepts enabling the easing of trade, the extra incentive to reconstruction was reentering the world of commerce through economic growth and trading quality goods and services for goods and services in kind or for hard foreign currencies. The production of prewar type goods continued, so that automobiles, refrigerators, and the like were still manufactured, but also being produced were televisions, jet-propelled aircraft, sophisticated computers, and new medicines for fighting diseases that were nonresponsive to previous methods of treatment. The role of government had been to underwrite these economies, to insure that growth was unhindered by the recurring cyclical movements in business, and that society benefited in general as a result of the renewed economic activity. These were the conditions of the times and the government that performed best was that which functioned in response to these conditions.

These conditions altered, however, when the world was thrown into turmoil because of the sudden rise in the price of oil, a previously inexpensive form of energy. The world's economies ran on this cheap energy and when the prices were raised dramatically, the world's economies, especially those already industrialized and those undergoing the processes of industrialization, were thrown into a deep recession. Production prices had to increase to compensate for the radical increase in energy costs, and these were passed on to the consumers; consumption was decreased accordingly, and this led to a decline in employment. As prices increased, brought about by increasing oil prices, unemployment deepened, bringing the economy into a recession.

This economic decline was not cyclical, not brought about by the natural dynamics of disequilibrium economics. It was artificial in the sense that it was caused by noneconomic influences of rising energy costs, with oil used as a political weapon to exert influence on the industrial and the industrializing countries. In politics, such an action is legitimate, especially if the desired results are achieved. In economics, after a period of adjustment, such politics are self-defeating. Alternative oil and coal sources were brought on-line, nuclear energy was advanced in its conception and also brought on-line in power stations, and the revenues obtained by this policy were recycled mainly into the developed countries in order to gain interest and to multiply through investments. Money was, of course, brought into the economies of the oil producing countries in the attempt to raise the living standards and bring these countries in line with the industrialized economies. The consequence has been a serious conflict between those sectors which seek modernization and change, with those of religious orders seeking to remain true to their beliefs in spite of the availability of new modes of living—the fall of the Shah of Iran is one example of this conflict.

As well as seeking alternative energy sources to maintain the economies, two important consequences resulted from the energy crisis. First, with respect to international trade, the Bretton Woods agreement, which had established fixed but adjustable exchange rates, had collapsed, with countries moving into floating exchange rates. This was due to the fixed but adjustable exchange rate system to confront the imbalances that had resulted from the additional costs of importing oil, and the insecurity of dealing with the trading partners that ensued, reminiscent of the trading situation of the Great Depression. Trade had become destabilized, as previously cheap oil had become expensive and agreements had to be rephrased in order to cope with potential losses.

While the industrialized countries felt the impact of the oil crisis, their economies were sufficiently resilient to come back, after a period of recession and of placing alternative energy sources on-line. Their currencies remained viable with respect to one another and they still remained the coinage of trade.

The emerging, developing, and newly industrializing countries, however, felt the impact that much harder. Their currencies were not wanted in the international arena, and only hard currencies served as the basis of trade. As a result of the recession in the industrialized countries, hard currencies were that much more difficult to come by. In a sense, the flexible exchange system that resulted was beneficial, as it reflected the demand for a country's products and thus led to a liberalization of trade. In another sense, however, it was most certainly detrimental to the economic welfare of the nonindustrialized countries. As their currencies were unwanted and as they could not readily obtain hard currencies because of their limited products in a highly competitive and at that time uncertain situation, they suffered by paying extremely high prices for energy, draining the foreign reserves of these countries. Moreover, as the revenues from oil were recycled into the industrialized economies, their currencies were that much more valuable to the nonindustrialized countries, and hence that much more difficult to obtain. The flexible exchange system was certainly a liberalization of trade, making economies more efficient; for those economies in which the concept of contemporary economic efficiency did not yet exist because their stages of development had not reached competitive industrialization, this was a major setback to their progress in achieving growth.

The second important consequence was that it resulted in a more workable relationship among the components of economic activity. Governments confronting the recession did so with the memory of the Great Depression revived because of the suddenness and severity of the recession, even though it was not cyclically initiated. Labor had to retrench, especially because of the heavy losses in employment. Industry had to restructure to remain viable as it waited for alternative energy sources to be profitable and provide price competition with the previously cheap source of oil.

In light of the historical development of these three economic sectors, the merger was made only because of the circumstances. Government, in the liberal tradition of the Industrial Revolution, sought to maintain a distance from industry and labor, becoming involved only when necessary to maintain their viabilities in times of crisis. Labor, as a natural antagonist to industry, sought to exploit the best conditions for its members in all situations. Industry, antagonistic to labor, sought to reduce labor costs and pass on the savings to consumers in order to survive competition.

During the Great Depression, after much animosity, these sectors cooperated somewhat to overcome the economic crisis. After World War II, this cooperation remained, but loosely, with the natural antagonism existing between labor and industry, and with government remaining somewhat aloof, operating in neo-Keynesian frames of reference to counteract the extremes in business cycles. Because of the sudden severity of the recession brought about by the oil crisis, this cooperation was strengthened, resulting in the welfare utility function.

The historical traditions of these sectors have not been abandoned. Governments, in the liberal tradition of the Industrial Revolution, still seek to govern according to the conditions of the times, as perceived by the responsible officials. Industry still seeks to achieve the greatest output for the lowest production costs, and this includes labor's wages. Labor still seeks to obtain the highest possible wages for its work, but at times is willing to trade off wage increases for retraining employment.

It must be understood that while the recession brought about by the energy crisis was not cyclical, it was a severe recession nevertheless, with all the complications this entails. Trade was reduced, and for the United States and other advanced countries, international assistance was granted to those countries which were struggling with the high costs of oil to maintain their output to some extent so that their countries would not claim international bankruptcy.

To cope with the high levels of unemployment and the consequences of reduced industrial output for agriculture and for social development, the concerns of welfare economics were raised. Various governmental agencies, at the central, state, and local levels, attempted to alleviate the unemployment situation and to revive industry. However, while this crisis had all the appearances of a major recession, it was nevertheless brought about by the noncyclical cause of the oil price rises. Only when alternative energy sources came on-line was the crisis eased and economic growth and trade revived, but with flexible exchange rates.

The welfare utility function has become an operable concept for dealing with the business cycle and has its extensions into international commerce in the form of the international utility function. In order to understand its ramifications for trade, the utility function has first to be described for the domestic economy.

Considering the function first in a stationary setting without dynamics, and letting W stand for the welfare utility function, $W_t = U(I, G, L)_t$, with the enclosed letters standing for industry, government, and labor, respectively, for time t. As these are generalized terms, they can be broken down into their components. Industry, for example, contains the subsets of all industrial firms, secondary businesses, and their auxiliaries. Government contains the subset of all government activity bearing on the economy, such as defense, taxation, and welfare payments of all kinds.[14] Labor is organized labor in all branches of industry and government, viewed in terms of wage bargaining and strike action as they affect the economy.

The utility of W is determined by the same manner as the information system S_t, with the utility of W at any time t being $0 < W < 1$. As for components, there are subsets; the I component of industry including business is composed of subsets for the various industries such as steel, the automotive industry, electronics, and so on. For each of these subsets there are further subsets, such as the various automotive companies, the several steel and electronics companies, etc. The utility positions of the individual firms within each of these subsets shows the firm's ability to compete within its specific market. This depends on the firm's information system and the responses from investors and consumers that this system evokes. Moreover, while one firm may not be able to compete effectively, other firms competing in the same market may be doing very well and thus show a rise in profits. The total of these firms at time t gives their respective utility positions, so that if some of these firms' utilities are low while the majority are high, then for these firms, say from F_1 in the complex for firms with high utility, tends to 1, while those with low utility tend to 0.

The low utility rates for those several firms may be due to several reasons. There may, for example, be reduced efforts to market the competing product, as their managers seek to rechannel their resources into developing other products, either innovative or imitative, for other markets. Or, there may be conflict within the firm at the decision-making level and managers seek to liquidate their own positions and seek employment elsewhere. Still, another reason may be the opting for liquidity instead of maintaining production for achieving strong positions to fend off corporate raiders. Should the utility rates of all or the majority of firms be low, while those of the few be high, this is an indication that the market itself is changing, in the sense that the cycle is beginning to act with greater restraint in purchasing. This pertains to foreign as well as domestic goods and services, because as the cycle moves downward consumer liquidity is diminished in the aggregate due to increased unemployment. Hence, for all firms and businesses symbolized by the letter I for industry, and at time t, $0<I<1$.

The situation is similar for the government, G. There is a difficulty, however, because while the domain of business activity is clearly demarcated in economic activity, as businesses act within their respective markets, the impact of government economic activity is not so well delineated. Government can order from business products that may or may not be necessary for the smooth functioning of government activity—a condition of all bureaucratic entities—and while business may profit from this order, it may be wasteful on government's part. A big spending objective is defense. This spending, while motivated in the best interests of the citizenry, may not be in the best economic interest. Wasteful defense projects, for example, may seem impressive, but they may have very low military utilities, making these projects extremely wasteful, while the firms contributing to these projects achieve high profits. Still another big spending objective is foreign aid. This comes in the form of direct assistance to developing and emerging countries, as well as purchasing their goods and services, resulting in competition with the domestic markets. Agricultural produce is an example, with sugar, tomatoes, and other homegrown crops competing with foreign produce, as a means of helping these economies. The utility of this type of aid is determined by the purchases of the foreign produce with respect to purchases for the domestic produce.

The area of governmental economic activity where there is not this difficulty is in the building of infrastructure to provide for long-run economic activity. Such projects as constructing dams and building roadways and investing in regional (state) and local education are examples of this activity. Although these projects rely on the contracting of businesses for their construction and realization, their utilities can be determined with respect to the growth they provide to the economy—even though this may be over the long run. Measuring G within the W_t equation is thus somewhat problematic, but as the government exerts a powerful economic influence, its position with respect to utility must be considered. As the government's various economic functions are subsets of its overall economic activity, assessing the utility of each of its economic functions within the upper and lower utility boundaries at time t provides the overall utility of G. Hence, $0 < G < 1$, for time t provides the general utility of the government's economic policies—including health, welfare, and foreign economic assistance—for that time.

Labor's situation is not ambiguous, but very clear-cut. For labor, no distinction exists between the government and industry as employers; they are both employers and labor has to reckon with them, as well having to reckon with labor. This distinction holds for those governmental jobs—and in this sense, regional and local governments as subsets of the national government are also considered—whose employees are prohibited by law from taking work action against the governing bodies, such as the police and fire departments as well as the armed forces. As these are workers with well-defined jobs, because they are in public service they are represented by organizations that enter into collective bargaining on their behalf. For these employees, it is understood, as part of their contract, that strike action is deprived them; in collective bargaining, therefore, they must have good contracts that prevent discrimination and provide incentives that will continue to make their jobs attractive and motivate others to join them.

But with organized labor in a variable market system with mobility, it is clear that the labor-industry dichotomy still exists. The variable market system is one in which business cycles regulate the supply and demand for labor, thus imposing on labor mobility, so that it can move into areas or regions in which demand is high, from areas or regions affected by declines in the demand for labor. As governments operate in the same principle as industry with respect to labor, then the dichotomy is broadened into employee-employer relations. Workers want high pay for their efforts and employers want workers to work long hours for low pay, and the utility of labor must be viewed in light of this dichotomy. For international commerce, bargaining for higher wages in an industry engaged in international competition depends on the industry's position with respect to this competition. If the industry is weakened, then the likelihood of labor's bargaining representatives achieving a higher wage is low, and hence labor's position tends to entropy. Similarly, if the industry successfully competes internationally, then labor's utility is high and its bargaining position tends to 1, so that most, if not all, of its requests are met. For the domestic market, should there be a recession, bargaining for higher wages is of little utility, but for those workers engaged in successful international commerce, regardless of the recession, their bargaining position is stable or perhaps even strong with respect to their industry.

In general, the welfare utility function's three economic forces have utility ratings with respect to the cyclic position, but for international trade, industry, government, and labor, are dependent on the domestic as well as the foreign cycles of their trading countries. This provides the basis for the international utility function.

The interactions among the industrial, governmental, and labor sectors of the economy determine the general economic situation. As the individual in the economy belongs to one of these sectors or is directly affected by their policies, the individual's welfare is derived from the economic conditions of these sectors and the manner in which they interact with one another. Thus, as the individual is a member of society, and as these sectors are the society's economic forces from which goods and services are produced, from which the socioeconomic infrastructure is derived and generated, and from which employment is sought and maintained as best as possible, the interactions among these sectors, and the utilities of their programs and the interactions that may result, determine the economy's domestic strength. To the extent that foreign trade is dependent on the domestic economy in supplying the raw materials for production and the labor force for executing production programs, this is a subsector of industry. It is, however, also dependent on the utility functions of the trading partners, and this is a component of the international utility function.

In general, the individual can compute his or her utility functions with respect to income earned, the goods and services available for consumption, the possibilities for employment in domestic and foreign-oriented businesses. Ultimately, in the industrial sector, the contemporary individual's utility function with respect to domestic and foreign goods and services available, determines, when taken on aggregate, which domestic—and to some extent foreign—firms will survive and which will not, which firms will continue their production lines and which will alter them, which firms will maintain their labor compositions and which will either hire more workers or lay off those already employed.

While excluding consumer influence as a sector does not mean that consumers as a force have been neglected. Indeed, the consumer is the ultimate beneficiary and the subject of all economic activity. By so being, the consumer is intrinsically involved in the economy, either in industry, the government, or the labor movement. The welfare utility function reflects the consumer's position with respect to the economy as it relates to the dynamics of innovation and imitation in toto.[15]

The dynamics of the welfare utility function must now be discussed in order to make the transfer to the international utility function. For a utility function to be viable it must be dynamic, moving with the changes in the economy and providing the opportunities for evaluating these changes with respect to utility and entropy. An automobile company, for example, may embark on a new image for a car and seek to use this car to capture the markets of its competing domestic and foreign firms. In the static situation, this may seem to be good marketing for an innovative product; over time, however, this project may be a drain on resources for the domestic market, while being successful in the foreign markets. Only dynamic analysis with respect to the firm's position (and the firm is a subset of the industry, which is, in turn, a subset of the classification Industry in the welfare utility function) can the state of the firm's viability with respect to single projects or to its total production lines be understood. The static position signatured by t indicates a moment in time; dynamics provide a clear understanding of the situation.

As the welfare utility function is a measuring function of the utilities of the industrial, governmental, and labor sectors over time, it also takes into account that the economy is an entity in which these sectors are intricately related in the dynamics of economic development and expansion. The function does, however, measure the utilities of each of these sectors as they operate, with the inclusion of the other sectors in them. The purpose is not to isolate these sectors, but to assess their utilities in their dynamic settings over time, and through the international utility function, to analyze their dynamics with respect to foreign trade.

The notion "over time" refers to the time period of cyclical fluctuation, for their utilities depend on the cycle's position. For example, during prosperity (just as the cycle's upward motion is increasing at a decreasing rate),[16] innovation may not yield expected profits for a firm. Saturation is setting in, and in spite of the prevailing optimism, profits in the industry to which the firm belongs are declining, albeit slowly. Innovation in a similar market will then yield declining profits, in spite of the expectation of higher profits, and the firm's utility thus declines with respect to these innovative projects. This is measured by the firm's utility position and then the particular industry's utility position, the status of which may have direct bearing on the I sector, depending on the weight that the industry has.

Government projects during the cyclical downswing, for example, tend to alleviate difficult economic conditions, because—in Keynesian terms—the increased money as wages and investment stimulate demand, and this regenerates restocking of inventories, bringing about further employment. It also stimulates innovation as the risk element is reduced because of the increased aggregate utility. These projects, over the recession phase of the cycle, have high utility, and their influences on industry and labor are both noticeable and positive for economic growth.

With respect to foreign competition, during the recession phase there is no serious competition for both industry and labor, because of the diminished aggregate consumption. Even during the early period of recovery, when labor regains its strength in its relations with industry, labor unrest is of very low utility, because as aggregate utility increases, so does aggregate consumption, with foreign goods and services again becoming competitive. The electronics industry, for example, may be experiencing renewed demand because of the increased aggregate liquidity; this influences innovations and imitations within the industry because of the increasing consumption, serving as an incentive to introduce new products. As innovation generates imitation, and as there is an international imitation effect in which foreign companies seek out the newest domestic products and attempt to manufacture competitive imitative substitutes at lower prices even when tariffs are considered, labor unrest will not benefit that part of organized labor engaged in sanctions or strike action.

As $W_{t+n} = U(I, G, L)_{t+n}$, and as the utilities of these sectors depend to a large extent on the cycle's position at the time of measurement, then the welfare utility function is, to the same extent, dependent on the cycle's position. This dependence is as weak or strong as that of its components during the measuring period and indicates the components' utilities as a result of this dependence. As the measurements rely on the time factor, circumstances considered relevant during one part of that time may not be so significant during another part. Hence, the utility measurement does not account for the events that had occurred during that time, but merely assesses the utilities of the sectors over that time range.

In general, then, the welfare utility function $W \approx 1/C_p$, where C_p is the cycle at its phase during the measurement, and the approximation sign indicates that a strict equation does not exist because of the variations in the subsectors due to responses that are not general, but specific. For example, a single firm during recession may generate demand because it has undertaken innovation, thereby bringing imitation into the dynamics. For the industry in general in which this firm is included, however, the utility rating may be very low due to the recession. Thus, as $W_{t+n} = U(I, G, L)_{t+n}$, then $U(I, G, L) \approx 1/C_p$. Joining the cycle's phase p with $t+n$ allows for the time element as well as the cycle's phase to be considered and measured accordingly. Should the time element for a given imitation be one year, and during that very time the cycle has moved from, say, recovery to prosperity, then as $p = t + n$, the time period can be substituted by recovery.

Substituting the cycle's phase for the time period allows for the isolation of each sector for observation, and the components of each sector for further scrutiny, evaluating their performances for both their general compositions and their specific utilities. For example, consider the I sector during recovery. Partial derivation allows for I's isolation from the other components, and the corresponding partial derivative of $C_{recovery}$ allows for I's position in the cycle during recovery to be evaluated. Hence, $0<\partial I<1/\partial C_{rec}$. Moreover, this allows for examining a specific industry to evaluate its position, so that for I, $i \in I$ can be substituted. This also provides for the evaluation of a single firm within an industry, so that $(F \in i) \in I$ can be considered with respect to utility and entropy. This holds for those industries engaged in domestic and foreign commerce as well, but for the utility measurements of those involved with foreign markets, the international utility function has to be considered as well. This will be discussed further in the next chapter.

Another advantage of this approach is that the cycle's phase, say recovery, can be further broken down. Recovery, for example, may be a very long-term process. But with I being considered for only the first two months (or for whatever period is considered necessary for evaluation), the approximation welfare utility function takes the form $W_I \approx 1/I_{C_{t(2\ months)}}$ from which the utility position for I can be derived: $0<\partial I<1_{t(2\ months)}$.

Moreover, this equation can take into account two of the three sectors, so that, from time a to c, for, say, industry and labor, the situation takes the form:

$$W(I,L) \approx 1/C_{I,L_{t_{(a-c)}}},$$

so that $0<(\partial I\partial L)<1$ can be evaluated. Another advantage of this utility function is that it provides for the breaking down of each of these sectors into their components and subcomponents for still further evaluation. As $\Sigma(F\epsilon i)\epsilon I$, and as $\Sigma(gp\epsilon g)\epsilon G$, with gp being a specific government policy, and as $\Sigma(lp\epsilon 1)\epsilon L$, with lp being a specific labor policy—with the sigma being a summation of these policies and the "ϵ" being the inclusion sign, then such a breaking down is readily accessible.

For example, consider a specific firm in an industry, for which its utility is sought over the past three months. The firm in question, F_j, can be placed in this equation in the following manner: as $W_I = 1/C$, and $\Sigma(F\epsilon i)\epsilon I$, then this summation can be substituted for I in the approximation equation. As F_j is one of the subcomponents for I, then the equation can be written $W_{F_j} \approx 1/C_{(3\ months)}$, for which the derivative is stated $0<[(F_j\epsilon i)\epsilon I]<1$, and as F_j is a component of the summation, then it can also be placed within the utility evaluation separate from the other firms and industries. This holds for those firms engaged in either strictly foreign commerce, or in both foreign and domestic commerce. It applies to those firms engaged in only foreign commerce, because of their base of operations and their final center of decision making and financial operations. For multinational firms, this provides a difficulty of definition as to center of operations, but this must wait until Part III. The isolation of any sector or sectors provides no difficulty, on the condition that at the most only two sectors are involved; otherwise there is the general utility position of the economy in its current phase that is being assessed. By analyzing two sectors, the influences of the policies of one sector on the other can be determined in the way that the information of one sector relates to that of another sector in open-ended analytic fashion as discussed in chapter 5.

It must be understood that so far the discussion has pertained to the utility measurements over time *past* up to a point in time, from the stipulated past to the present. This itself involves a dynamism because the measurement—in the example above of three months—takes into account the changes over the assigned time, and also because the point in the present is somewhat difficult to capture, without the dynamics surrounding it. If the present were to include today and the next five days, this is a very small time, but it is far from static. Other firms, other government policies, and other labor issues are likely to come up and be acted upon during this period, but the greatest dynamic lies, again, with the "engine" of domestic and foreign economic activity, the single firm in the industry, where programs of innovation and imitation are devised, planned for, and acted upon.

The present, in this sense, is a sufficiently small amount of time not to allow for cyclical considerations in *most* cases, but economic crises never announce themselves in advance, as the October 1987 market crash testifies. While this was not cyclical in its nature, it was financial, and hence an extremely disturbing event. Economic events such as that crash, unpredictable and unexpected, cannot be ruled out and their effects will certainly be made known in the very short time of even a few days allowed by the concept of the "present" in the welfare utility approximation. In general, then, using the past with respect to the present, or whatever the cutoff point is for analyzing the utility situation, refers to a time period in which, while there have been changes in the domestic and foreign economies in which trade is in progress, there have been no radical deviations in the path that the domestic economy has been running, while such deviations in the emerging countries, such as revolutions, or famine, cannot be ruled out. A strong domestic economic base will enable firms engaged in trading with these types of economy to cut their losses by focusing on either domestic commerce and/or direct their trade to other and perhaps better established economies. However, this also includes such less extreme events as a president's or prime minister's speech reporting on the conditions of the economy and perhaps proposing a tax reform or replacement of finance ministers or secretaries of the treasury due to previously known clashes of opinions or because of indicated plans for retirement.

Nevertheless, the question remains: if the past and the present as defined above can be treated in this manner, what about the future? Cannot the future utility of a program be estimated? When firms, governmental agencies, and labor organizations undertake projects, cannot the consequences of these programs be predicted? This brings up the issue of expectation discussed in Chapter 5. While a project can be assessed for internal utility, so that there are no contradictions in its formulation and the necessary resources and technologies exist for its execution according to its planning, its overt utility can be assessed

only with respect to its performance. Hence, if the accepted response is within
the range according to the program, then the utility approaches 1; if the response deviates from the allowed boundaries, then the project becomes entropic
and should be treated in the appropriate manner, of either altering it or rejecting
it, should the direct and alternative costs be too high, with resources involved
being considered better used elsewhere.

However, while the welfare utility equation describes utility and entropy with
respect to the analysis of information systems and the applications of expectation of these systems, what can be said with respect to the approximation equation? Stated another way, while the future is unknowable, is there something
of the future about which we can know and to which we can apply our technologies and exert some control over our activity as a result? The answer to
this is affirmative. Economic activity deals with the problems of everyday commerce, with the tasks of developing projects and making them viable for domestic and foreign markets, and bargaining for higher wages and offering better
work techniques as a result; and doing more than trying to determine what the
government's next fiscal and monetary steps will be, and how to find protection
if they are detrimental, and how to exploit this to the best advantage, if positive. Economic activity occurs within the phase of the trade cycle, and this can
be understood and addressed.

Chapter 7

THE INTERNATIONAL UTILITY
FUNCTION

What a pity Lycurgus did not think of paper-credit, when he wanted to banish gold and silver from Sparta. It would have served his purpose better than the lumps of iron he made use of as money; and would also have prevented more effectually all commerce with strangers, as being of so much less real and intrinsic value.

—David Hume,
"Of the Balance of Trade"[1]

Banishing gold and silver from Sparta, and replacing them with metals with imputed monetary value, certainly affected commerce with strangers. For while Lycurgus and the people of Sparta recognized lumps of iron as currency, strangers certainly found this difficult to accept. Gold and silver are certainly more appealing to the eye and more difficult to obtain than iron, and these traits, as well as their durability, made them acceptable as measures of wealth and currencies for commerce.

There is a lesson to be learned from Lycurgus's action, however. Had the Spartan economy been sufficiently strong and productive, then those lumps of iron with the Spartan seal would have become on par with gold and silver in commerce. The value of a country's currency is determined by that country's economic strength—actual and potential. This economic strength depends on the politicians' acumen in running the fiscal and monetary affairs of their country, and on the abilities of people in business to conduct their financial affairs in accordance with the government's policies, while at the same time earning profits, investing, and engaging in successful innovative and imitative projects.

Paper currencies and credits were certainly unheard of during Sparta's era; nor are they very "Spartan," appealing to the warlike mentality of the people. Iron, the symbol of strength at that time, was more appropriate to those who wielded weapons of iron. Iron is tangible, capable of being molded into construction and weaponry. Paper currency is far more abstract, easily destroyed, highly symbolic. Stamped with the seal of Sparta, iron as a currency took on the added dimension of representing the strength of Sparta, its armies, and its capacity to conquer. The symbolism was not abstract but direct, for iron was the means of power.

But as a currency, it certainly restricted foreign commerce. Gold and silver were certainly preferable, as their imputed values were much higher than the coarse iron. Iron was the symbol of strength, gold and silver, the symbols of accepted wealth. But these too have the difficulty of portability in commerce, and their melting down, or counterfeiting, was common practice. Neither with iron, nor with gold and silver as the currencies, could economies develop and expand; their bulk made transactions awkward, and the tampering with these metals made their values questionable. Paper money became the standard of nations, each currency representing the nation's wealth and capacity. This provided for banks to ease commercial transactions, both domestic and foreign, enabling commerce to expand. As economies became more complex due to increasing transactions and foreign commerce, currencies were sought after more than the precious metals, with these metals relied upon in times of economic crises in case the national currencies were no longer acceptable.

During the Industrial Revolution, there were economic crises, and both governments and private citizens relied on gold and silver to protect their interests. These precious metals, after all, have a longer history of representing value than do the paper currencies, and were therefore accepted as means of exchange. As the economies became more sophisticated because of industrialization, governments acquired the positions of monetizing these precious metals, making sufficient amounts available to jewelers, dentists, and others whose work required them.

With the end of the Industrial Revolution, manifested in the Great Depression, the realization was finally accepted that neither the precious metals as means of exchange nor their storage in government institutions, but the productive capacity and potential economic activity are the measures of a nation's wealth, and its currency is a symbolic expression of this wealth.

Nevertheless, in order to maintain the people's confidence during this troubled period, removal from the metal standard was not undertaken. Silver replaced gold, however, for backing currencies, while gold was held as the ultimate symbol of economic strength. In the post-Depression period, in our contemporary era, the metal aspect of wealth has certainly been diminished, replaced by the productive aspect of economic activity. Hence, the pegging of currencies to fixed exchange rates after World War II to maintain stability as the world recovered from that war served the purpose of allowing economic growth and foreign exchange without relying on the amount of gold and silver mined and stored. With the collapse of stable exchange rates due to the oil crisis, gold and silver remained demonitized although still held by governments for psychological reassurance. With the bringing on-line of alternative energy sources economic stability was again established, but the focus turned again to the business cycle, as the crisis brought about by the OPEC energy policies was not cyclical, but nevertheless resulted in a severe recession.

FURTHER COMMENTS ON
THE WELFARE UTILITY FUNCTION

During the Industrial Revolution the three sectors responsible for economic growth and development had established patterns that were to forge into working systems, each dependent on the other. The situation during the process of industrialization was, however, that of liberalism, of each sector caring for itself, and acting with the other sectors only when conditions deemed it necessary. Government, for example, seeking not to interfere directly in the business of industry and labor, provided infrastructure and territory when necessary. Railroads are an example of this, for as custodians of the nation's land, government had to approve the building of rail lines across countries. Moreover, they allowed for monopolies for public utilities, such as electricity and communications services, but with control over their operations, so that fair services at fair prices could be obtained. This enabled industrial expansion as transportation and communications services were necessary for the ordering of resources, of placing orders for goods and services, and for moving productive equipment as well as finished goods and services throughout the country.

Of course, industry provided the means of employment and of taxes. Labor, working in industry, acquired the skills that enabled them to become a political force. Granted that workers needed employment in order to provide for their families, but industry needed workers in order to manufacture and expand. Once sufficient skills were developed, workers formed into unions and demanded higher wages and better working conditions. Because they were essential for industry, they achieved their goals and established themselves as a political force. This was accomplished with a great deal of difficulty. Ideology, union busting, and terror methods used by some industries set back the unionizing process, but could not prevent it because of labor's necessary position in the production and distribution processes of economic activity. Taxes were used to regulate the money supply, thus exerting some pressure on inflation and deflation. Moreover, local, county, state, or parish, as the case may be, used taxes to finance projects and maintain their localities in operation. Without industrial activity providing employment and goods and services for sale, these taxes would not have been available.

Labor's position, even before unionization, was one of being the ultimate objective of industrial activity, for people employed had money to purchase, and through purchases, profits for both middlemen and industrialists are earned. Through the strengthening of labor's position because of unionism, those products so affected rose in price, but the workers could afford them due to their increased salaries. Moreover, interindustrial competition maintained prices at reasonable levels, so more could be purchased at affordable prices.

Nevertheless, in spite of these working relationships, the ideology of the Industrial Revolution continued to prevail and distrust among these sectors was maintained. Hostility of industrialists to unions and unions to industry continued, and both unions and industry distrusted government, as organized labor considered government in debt to industry for financing campaigns, and industry distrusted government for trying to curtail its development through legislation and for providing the legal justification for the existence of unions.

Nevertheless, these three sectors became dependent on each other. This was certainly made clear when the Industrial Revolution came to an end with the Great Depression, and the three sectors had to cooperate to move the economy out of the crisis. In the aftermath of World War II, however, the relationship was somewhat uncertain. Countries had to rebuild their industries, to convert them from war-time to peace-time production, and demobilized service personnel had to be retrained for the new economic situation that was opening up to the world.

Prior to the 1973 energy crisis, there were of course cyclical fluctuations. These were built into the economic system that arose and developed during the Industrial Revolution, and the most severe was the Great Depression. In the aftermath of World War II, cycles still persisted, as they had become inherent in the dynamics of economics. The lessons of that depression were learned, however, and the three sectors merged into a working relationship, in spite of their evolved mistrust and different objectives.

It was the energy crisis, however, that placed a different emphasis on this relationship, for the cycle that was initiated then was not caused by the course of economic events, but because of the sudden increase in energy prices that resulted in drastic price rises and the diminution of aggregate demand sufficient to bring industry into a severe recession. Moreover, as the sudden rise in energy prices was unexpected, the welfare institutions formed to cope with unemployment and retraining were caught completely off guard, unprepared to handle the problem of recession-level unemployment.[2] The relationship that was formed among the sectors was strengthened to cope with this situation, to which the welfare utility function gives expression.

Of the three sectors of the economy, industry is the most volatile as it generates growth, and growth is subject to consumer purchases of industrial output, both domestic and foreign. In this sense, labor serves industry and government regulates the growth process in light of the cycle's phases. However, both government and labor have their constituents—these as with industry being the consumers, the contemporary individuals to whom industry, government, and the labor movement are ultimately answerable and accountable.

Individual tastes and opinions vary among people, and within the individual over time; tastes are therefore not fixed, and this is exploited by industry through innovation and imitation. Opinions are also flexible, and this is utilized by governments in formulating economic policies. Moreover, workers' opinions are expressed in labor meetings, and these are taken into consideration by labor management and manifested in the formulations of different and newer policies.

There is, therefore, a relationship between individual utility functions based on information systems and the aggregate welfare utility function based on the business cycle's fluctuations. Individual utility functions are formulated on the basis of rigorously stated information placed in an operational-area language isomorphism; this strict relationship exists because of the expectations to be derived in the reality of the situation. These utility functions are attempts to impose order on a seemingly chaotic reality, an order based on individual wants, desires, and tastes. With respect to firms, government agencies responsible for economic policies, and labor organizations responsible for their workers, this poses little or no difficulty. The leaders in each of these sectors and sectorials— including the micro level of the firm, the specific government agency, and the specific labor branch or union local—are managers, and their decisions are made with respect to their organizational positions and their personal conceptions, tempered by the opinions of those with whom they work.

These information systems often clash and are thus subject to entropy, the extent of which depends on their performances in conflict with systems. Firm's managers often have to consider their workers' responses when new projects are placed into operation. Workers have to consider their strategies with respect to management's predicament in the firm's competitive position. Both business and labor managers have to consider the effects of government policies on their operations, these considerations influencing their relationships with one another as well as with the government.

When deemed important, this information is included in the system. The system is open-ended if having a time-signature longer than the immediate very short-term period, and this open-endedness allows for both alterations and responses to alterations generated within the system by the influences of the markets. Firms engaging in foreign trade have to be responsive to domestic as well as the conditions in those countries with which they have commercial relationships, making their positions more susceptive to changes and their information systems more flexible and responsive to alterations. Changes are made within the system whether by management's intentional alterations based on new products and/or methods of production, thereby altering the operational and/or area languages, or because of the reality's imposing changes within the system for which alterations have to be made in one or both languages. This is a dynamic process, continuing until the alterations outweigh the original system and entropy is too intense, or until the system is abandoned for other projects. This process holds for the information systems of domestic and foreign-oriented firms, for governmental agencies, and labor management; the systems of each of these must take into account not only their competitors in their respective areas and markets, but also the information systems of the others as they affect the individual firm, governmental agency, and labor organization.

The decisions of business managers, governmental managers, and labor organization managers are thus based on their information systems; these systems, in turn, depend on the business cycle. For example, innovation and imitation will be greatly reduced and in most cases will refrain from being undertaken when the cycle approaches the peak of prosperity. Government economic decisions tend to be counter cyclical, in order to eliminate as much as possible the difficulties of unemployment and the problems of people being on welfare when the cycle declines, and to prevent too much liquidity, hence inflation brought about by increasing aggregate demand because of excess consumer liquidity when the cycle rises. During the peak of prosperity and the following movement toward recession as well as the obvious situation of recession itself, organized labor realizes that it has to refrain as much as possible from taking sanctions and strike action, and that the best time for these policies is when the cycle has moved well into recovery.

How, then, does the individual consumer relate to the welfare utility function? The contemporary individual as consumer, outside the framework of employment and managerial level decision making, does not have information systems formulated rigorously, as do business managers, directors of government agencies and of labor unions. Consider, for example, the contemporary individual as a manager of a large firm. This individual constructs the information system using operational and area language to attempt to define the problem situation and form a working relationship that will provide the conditions for using the system effectively, one that allows for expansion and alteration as the circumstances prescribe.

Consider this same individual as consumer. This person has tastes, preferences, income limitations in his or her allocation for consumption, and is open to new products in spite of these tastes and preferences—the last condition being necessary in an economic situation of expanding markets, domestic and foreign. In one very important sense, this individual shares with the general economy the property that his or her consumption is influenced to a great extent by the cycle's phase. When the cycle is in the depths of recession, goods and services, limited in quantity because of declining output, are sold at relatively high prices, so that there is both inflation and stagnation, "stagflation," as this situation has been named. Business managers then share with government managers and those of labor the same situation as that of the employee of the firm, the government, and the rank and file union member—this being that consumption is restricted to the relatively small amount of goods and services available at prices that are fairly high. The consumer, no matter what his or her job may be, is thus restricted by this condition. The restriction is one of degree that requires that each consumer budget his or her purchasing according to the liquidity possessed with respect to alternative purchases.

With the rise in the business cycle, the opportunities for consumption increase, with competition forcing prices down. This process continues throughout the various stages of recovery[3] and into the prosperity phase until innovation ceases and imitation follows suit shortly after, plunging the cycle into recession once again, only with a broader based socioeconomic infrastructure, so that the next movement to recovery will bring a greater variety of goods and services due to innovation and imitation. The completion of each cycle enriches the economy that much more.

From this, it can be stated that consumers' utilities are cyclically oriented, so that setting UC for consumers' utilities, $UC_p \approx 1/C_p$, where the subscript p stands for the period in the cycle's phase. We could also substitute p with t for time, but it is important to note the cycle's period in its phase when discussing consumers' utilities, for this indicates the general pattern of purchasing of goods and services with respect to income.[4]

From $UC_p \approx 1/C_p$, the individual consumer's utility function can be explained. As $UC \equiv \Sigma UC_1$, then $uc_i \equiv UC$, and therefore $uc_{i_p} \approx 1/C_p$, i being the individual consumer, uc being i's utility function. This can be analyzed still further: $uc = m(y_c + y_d)$, that is, individual consumer utility is a money function of income for consumption and income for saving and investing. The main component of this function is y_t for from this, most, if not all, consumption is made,[5] used for the purchases of individual goods and services having the set-elements $<1, 2, . . . , n>$ at time t, and these may include imports, depending on individual preferences and alternative prices. At $t+1$, there is no necessity that these elements will be identical to those at time t, but as people tend to be creatures of habit, the deviations will most likely not be too profound. This depends, of course, on the impacts of innovation, imitation, and the quality of imports. While innovation may stimulate different purchasing patterns, imitation depends on the competitive variation of the type of product, perhaps due to price, better packaging, effective advertising, or a better product of the same type as with different automobiles, one offering more options than the other and having a longer warranty.

The assumption that each contemporary individual as consumer knows what is best for him or her is upheld in this argument. For this reason consumer tastes differ as much as the consumers themselves and renders attempts to quantify over the individual consumer within the consuming public impossible. Tastes are as fickle as the weather, so that while general patterns of consumption can be established, individual details cannot. On the basis of generalization, innovation and imitation are undertaken to influence the consumer to change direction—in the case of imitation, perhaps slightly—of purchases.

Hence, general statements can be made about consumption that are valid for the entire consuming populace. For example, consumer purchasing patterns are influenced directly by the cycle's period and phase. On the basis of this, substitution of purchasing takes effect when, for example, inflation is high due to the peak of prosperity, or in the beginning of recession, when the consumer will seek competitive lower priced goods. Substitution is not limited to inflation, for it forms the basis of imitation, as firms, both domestic and foreign, compete for consumer liquidity. This, as a variation of substitution, is another generality.

Another generalization is that as the cycle moves up in recovery, less of the consumers' income will be directed toward consumption, because prices decline through competition, with increasing competition being undertaken at fixed rates of income allotted for consumption, thereby releasing a greater part of disposable income for investments. This does not necessarily have to occur throughout the cycle's upward movement, but the tendency is for more of income to be saved during this phase and movement. For this reason, fixed rates of return are popular savings incentives, as they allow for hedges against uncertainty, even though the rates of return are far lower than the risk-investment rates.

There is still another generalization that can be made about the consumer as a member of consuming groups. The term *group* is used loosely here in the sense that it refers not to organizations or organized behavior in consumption set by others to follow. It does mean that certain living standards, specific appliances, and modes of consumption expected by these living standards provide the basis on which commercials are directed, packaging oriented, and innovation and imitation vie for the consumers' aggregate liquidity, broken down into income classes as manifested in the differing living standards.

Nor are these groups rigid, for while they may be targets for production and advertising, they may prefer to venture into the purchasing patterns of other groups, providing that their income allocated for consumption allows it. Thus, while expensive wines can be enjoyed by those who have the money, they can also be enjoyed by those who decide to "splurge" and cut back on consumption later. This mobility does not have to be always upward, as is the case with wealthy people eating at a fastfood restaurant.

What determines these consuming groups, and how does a consumer decide to which group he or she belongs? These groups are socially oriented to the status of salary and position within the economy. A doctor has a higher status than a street cleaner and the doctor's consumption patterns based on medical skills, demand for the doctor's services, and tax loopholes to which the doctor takes advantage, determines the group to which he or she belongs. While aspirations are important here as professional people move from one occupation to another—in the doctor's case, specialization is a form of occupational mobility, while the street cleaner will most likely remain so employed. It must be noted, however, that while salary as a social determinant is socially oriented and quantifiable, personal feelings, either held within or expressed openly through aspirations, are strictly individual and hence unquantifiable.

What is quantifiable, moreover, is the contemporary individual's total consumption, and this is expressed by the *uc* function over the time period considered. As consumption varies with the business cycle's period and phase, for each consumer, $uc = m = (y_c + y_d)_t = m < 1, 2, \ldots, n >_t \approx 1/C_{p_t}$. The consumer's utility function is identical to the welfare utility function, which approximates the economy's position with respect to the cycle's period and phase. This is so, intuitively, for during recession and unemployment, the consumer cuts back on consumption, and during recovery when the economy is active with innovation and imitation, the consumer expands consumption according to his or her income. That this is so, logically, has been derived from the argument.

With both the contemporary individual's utility function and the general welfare utility function being approximations of the business cycle's period and phase, the economy's welfare, output, and wealth, as well as its position with respect to its trading partners, requires both the individual as consumer and organizations—be they business, government, or labor—in which they work. Their work generates income, part of which is allocated as salaries which generate liquidity for consumption of the products of innovation and imitation, part of which is allocated for savings and investments for personal security and for industrial restocking and production. But while this is so, business, government, and labor have specific roles in maintaining the economy, and its competitive position with respect to international trade.

This is especially important in light of the changing world economy, in which dictatorships, considered so firmly established, have yielded to the realities of the present and are preparing for the near future. Recent changes in the world's balance of military and economic power have required different analytic approaches to the markets. Planned economies, for all their ideological humanism, have been shown to be greatly inefficient, with the citizens of these economies suffering as a consequence. The world's markets are thus becoming freer in the sense that neo-Keynesian economics is replacing the worn ideologies; this, to the extent that in Eastern Europe and to some extent in China, Adam Smith's theories are being discussed among economists, where previously his name was considered taboo. The difficulty with neo-Keynesian theory is that it too has become worn, subject to the paradox of Say's Law, and therefore must yield to a theory appropriate in its terms and analytic power for our contemporary era.[6]

In light of this approach, it has already been stated that business is the generator of economic activity for both the domestic and foreign markets, for the firm initiates programs of innovation and imitation, producing for domestic and foreign consumption. Moreover, through the aggregate activities of the business sector the cycle is generated, with the firm responding to the cycle's dynamics through innovation and imitation, when cyclical conditions allow.

While the firms generate cyclical dynamics, the government's role, through policies of investing in infrastructure and in specific projects, is to counter the cycle in its extremes and hold it steady when moving from recovery to prosperity. The government has to prevent the cycle from moving too fast during the recovery phase, enabling firms to withstand the pressures of production to the extent that inflation rises with increased demand generated by increased aggregate liquidity as a result of rising employment. For example, should the psychological atmosphere of the recession be one of caution even though recovery is progressing, then the firms' liquidity options will be stronger than otherwise. While profits are gained through successful innovation and imitation, the liquidity option acts as a form of security, but this is somewhat unrealistic because fixed costs are reducing unproductive liquidity. Other firms act on production, and as demand increases, supply does not follow the pace. The result is inflation and the government has to enact policies under these conditions to reduce inflation.

Taxation is an easy policy to enact because it is historically acceptable and a method that requires no new thinking. But it is economically questionable as a policy because it restricts spending only marginally but mostly affects the rates of personal income allocated for saving, and this is money necessary to maintain the liquidity flow of businesses. Consumption levels are largely maintained, applying pressure on limited supplies manufactured, and hence increasing inflation still that much more. As the problem is psychological, so is the solution. The government should invest in social infrastructure and maintain the current tax levels, thereby providing a more positive economic picture that will encourage businesses to drop the option of maintaining liquidity and direct liquidity into production so that supply can be increased and the full dynamics of disequilibrium, through the changing production patterns of innovation and imitation, be realized. Moreover, this will reduce production costs for exporting businesses as competition will reduce the costs of materials necessary for the manufacturing for these markets.[7]

Labor's policies are perhaps the most important for our contemporary era. The traditional labor policies of strikes and sanctions to gain worker's rights and win government legislation are fair play, when labor's policies are in agreement with the requirements of this legislation. However, another aspect of labor must be considered, and this involves labor's approaches to changing industrial production procedures, and to new and upcoming industries. There are the traditional industries that evolved as a result of the Industrial Revolution, such as the steel, automotive, and aviation industries—although the latter developed greatly after World War II, when the advantages of air travel were increased through jet propulsion. However, in our contemporary era of economics, industries have developed that do not require "blue collars" and "hard hats," but require skills of very high levels of technical proficiency. These are the computer industries and those industries necessary for their development and maintenance, as well as their manufacture. These industries are domestic and foreign in orientation and because they have become essential in running economies and for personal recreation, both domestic and foreign competition are extremely rigorous.

Because of their hard fought struggles and the concessions that were won from business, labor has tended to become conservative, requiring stringent procedures, such as long periods of apprenticeship and long waiting time before such apprenticeships can be obtained, together with the restricted mobility of workers within plants, in order to maintain labor's own position of authority and bargaining power with respect to the firms.

This conservatism is understandable historically, but has little bearing on our contemporary economic situation. Contrary to popular opinion, technology does not have to be specialized in orientation; with its advancement and increasing sophistication, technology requires conceptualizations of mathematics and physics, among other disciplines. But the image of the blue-collar worker, hard-hatted and assembly line–oriented, is being replaced by the workers who are acquiring higher degrees and greater sophistication in their work. The necessities of innovation and imitation impose on labor to maintain its competitive work edge, both domestically and internationally, in order to remain employed. Labor cannot, therefore, rest on its traditions of the struggles of earlier decades but must make efforts to insure that its members are kept abreast with the latest in technological advancements and developments, and how they can be applied in industry.

Labor is thus in a period of transition, with the unique opportunity of bettering its position without the wasteful sanctions and strikes, yet without relinquishing these tactics and applying them when absolutely necessary. The strike funds can be rechanneled into courses for workers involved in the technologies of industrialization. As the cycle turns downward, funds previously allocated for buffers while strikes are being undertaken or while sanctions are being applied with employers holding back wages, could be invested during profitable times and applied to reeducation during periods of unemployment. Moreover, this should not be considered a policy of discrimination against technologically unskilled workers, for apart from marginal businesses, in our modern economy technology is demanded from workers. During the cycle's recession phase workers receive unemployment compensation and in conditions in which unemployment is prolonged, welfare payments are made. These types of funding, together with retraining and updating of work in specific fields, will allow workers to maintain a level of self-esteem, instead of being idle as in the past, preparing them for the next upturn of the cycle.[8]

The cycle of one country affects its commerce with others. Since the Bretton Woods agreement and the establishment of parity for currencies, the world has come together economically. Trading stability brought stability through the world, with countries trading according to their output and specific cyclical positions. This stability has not deteriorated since exchange rates have been floating, but has certainly made countries much more sensitive to the policies of others. The United States Federal Reserve Bank raises or lowers interest rates and the economies of the rest of the world are affected by the influences exerted on consumer liquidity and purchases. The dynamics of change in Eastern Europe affects the exchange rates of other countries as the new liberalization in the Eastern bloc is resulting in citizens holding hard currencies. Thus, the exchange rates are floating not only according to the relative strengths of trading economies, but also because of the supply and demand of hard currencies. The dollar and the mark are replacing gold as symbols of financial security.

There is an international utility function and an international disequilibrium effect associated with these policies and with successful private business ventures. As countries become even more active in trade, their domestic economic policies will influence the foreign trade positions of their trading partners, to the extent that disequilibrium and the international utility function become representative of these economies' domestic positions.

Such expression has already been given expression in Leontief's Paradox, with the calculation that an average basket of United States exports employed substantially less capital per worker than a basket of comparable U.S. import substitutes. This is the $2 \times 2 \times 2$ problem mentioned earlier in this work. In fact, this is not really a paradox if considered from a point of view other than its original expression. For the United States, being a capital-intensive economy, should employ *more* capital in the exporting of the average basket compared with other countries. In order to resolve this paradox, it must be considered that a capital-intensive economy does not necessarily require the over-abundant supply of capital equipment in production; within the limits of utility and entropy, such productive capital is employed, and in light of domestic and foreign competition, greater efficiency is sought in order to manufacture quantities according to projected market demand, at costs low enough to gain the competitive edge and lower sales prices. This drive for manufacturing efficiency tends to reduce both the costs of production and the quantity of capital equipment involved in the production of each unit. Hence, this paradox can be resolved by considering that a highly competitive economy such as the United States has lower capital per worker than other industrialized countries that lack the quantity and quality of domestic competition found in the United States. While according to this paradox, import substitutes are of greater capital intensity, this does not necessarily have to be the case, so long as competition is flourishing in both the domestic and foreign markets. This will motivate production at lower costs to insure greater profits, thereby utilizing capital that much more efficiently, reducing the capital/worker ration in production. Hence, by increasing worker utility with respect to the production program, the capital/worker ratio is reduced, insuring a greater competitive position with respect to domestic and foreign markets. The paradox is thus removed.

THE INTERNATIONAL UTILITY FUNCTION

The Great Depression demonstrated the intricacies of foreign trade, as expressed by the interrelatedness of the world's markets. Both as suppliers of resources and of finished products, and as the importers of these commodities, the crash that began with the decline of Wall Street spread throughout the world. Demand declined and with unemployment supply was lacking. Within the old conceptual framework countries took measures of devaluation and increasing tariffs in order to protect their industries, but as other countries retaliated in kind, the amount of trade decreased considerably and unemployment was the "commodity" that was both exported and imported.

As well as portraying the interrelatedness among the world's markets, the Great Depression also showed how prolonged economic depression could result in world instability. With all the positive intentions of the world's leaders to revive their economies, the easiest policy to follow was that of assuming a dictatorship and taking control of the means of production. Of course, dictatorships rely on the wisdom of the dictators, and this wisdom has yet to be demonstrated to be superior to the market forces regulating the economies. While in Italy the trains ran on time, industry remained in the doldrums, and while in Germany, the traditional efficiency was again amassed, it was applied not to genuine economic revival, but to placing the unemployed into the armaments industries and other such services of the state.

The democracies whose people refused the dictatorial path provided relief for the unemployed in such government programs as works projects and national insurance (social security) payments. Scholars were employed in research projects, while laborers were employed in construction and reforestation and other such projects. The armaments industries were only marginal and became centers of focus only when the instability of the European countries and the strength of Japanese militarism became threatening. Even then, however, appeasement as an alternative to another global war was sought. The instability and militarism had gained in their own momentum and the conclusion was World War II.

The Great Depression also demonstrated that the economic system of the Industrial Revolution had come to an end. Depressions were not uncommon during the Industrial Revolution; nor were business cycles and economic growth unique to this historical era. But prior to the Industrial Revolution, cycles were long run and determined the economic fates of countries, while during the period of industrialization cycles were production-oriented and depressions lasted as long as it took for retooling and new economic production to make their impacts in the markets.[9]

There was always revival, no matter how painful the depressions were. The duration and extent of the crisis brought about by the stock market crash of 1929, however, attested that this was a situation unique to the Industrial Revolution and signified the decline of resiliency that had existed during previous depressions. Active government participation in the world's economies had to be undertaken in order to achieve economic revival, but policies such as tariffs, devaluations, and taking control of the means of production only exacerbated the situation.

Stable exchange rates, fixed after World War II, served the purpose of

achieving a degree of world economic growth; moreover, they were very effective during the reconstruction of those countries damaged by the war. These
rates were periodically altered as economies sought to deal with their situations,
and when devaluations were undertaken they were not met with retaliatory actions by other countries. With the dissolution of exchange-rate stability due to
the pressures of the energy crisis, another consideration came into economic
reality, that being the de facto economic strengths of the world's economies.
This was manifested by the abilities of industry, government, and labor to
perform within the welfare utility function, maintaining employment and growth
in light of cyclical fluctuations.

These three sectors in the post-war economies of Western Europe and Asia
had formed a strong working relationship and had resulted in these reconstructed countries developing strong economies, capable of competing effectively in the world markets. In fact, the stabilized exchange rates that had
served in the reestablishing of their socioeconomic infrastructures were no longer
viable and hence unnecessary. The purpose of trade is to acquire goods and
services of quality at competitive prices, so that if one country can produce
alternative commodities at lower sales prices, they should be purchased. Stable
exchange rates that were necessary for these countries to regain economic strength
had become unnecessary once this strength had been acquired. The OPEC energy crisis only resulted in the inevitable breakdown of the stable exchange rate
system, without the possible trade wars that could have resulted.

Still, the chaotic situation that had existed during the Great Depression years
was not to be allowed to recur. Economies were severely affected by the initial
impact of the energy crisis, and with the breakdown of the fixed exchange rate
parity, a floating exchange rate system was established. This prevented the
free-for-all situation of beggar-thy-neighbor policies that prevailed during the
Depression, but also allowed for countries to adapt a help-thyself attitude in
light of the crisis. Countries' currencies were to be considered with respect to
their economic abilities, and these were evaluated with respect to the abilities
of the three sectors to work together and insure economic growth.

With respect to trade, then, the focus of each country had to be on its welfare
utility function. A country with low industrial output, a labor force with low
utility in output, and a government more concerned with its own affairs than
those of its citizenry has a welfare utility function measuring toward entropy.
While those countries that managed to demonstrate real concern for their citizens, countries in which industry, government, and labor, worked together to
provide for employment and industrial output as well as seeking to maintain
viable welfare systems in light of the crisis brought about by high energy costs,
had welfare utility functions measuring toward utility.

While alternative energy sources brought on-line eased the energy crisis, the
three sectors had merged into an operative force capable of dealing with economic problems. Where this force was effective those countries reestablished
their economies on the basis of new strength as the sectors that were once
antagonistic had managed to overcome this and work together; those countries

that were unable to forge the three sectors into a working relationship eventually entered into periods of revolution, war, or economic decline.

While the domestic economy is evaluated according to its welfare utility function, a country's trading ability—its ability to produce and deliver for foreign markets at prices that are competitive—is determined by its international utility function. When currencies were fixed, prices of imported goods and services were determined by the local market's ability to reap the highest profits in light of competition from domestic alternatives. However, with exchange rates fluctuating, domestic prices for foreign goods and services have to account for the differences, as well as the profit element in the domestic markets in light of domestic competition.

Moreover, a country's exchange rate is determined by its balance of payments situation with respect to other countries. The United States, for example, has a high balance of payments deficit with respect to Germany (a powerful country in the European Community, itself to be united in 1992) and Japan. Its currency is therefore not as strong as it could be, but with a lower relative currency value, this is an incentive for other countries to export from the United States, as the prices of its goods and services tend to be competitive both in price and quality.

A country's trading position is determined with respect to its international utility function, $\bar{I}$, a utility function of a country's currency value and its welfare utility function. Hence, $\bar{I}_t = U(c,W)_t$. The status of a country's currency, c, depends on the supply of that currency in foreign markets, and the demand for that currency as a hedge against other currencies. The situation with currencies is that they are in a somewhat ambiguous position of being the money of countries and hence part of the countries' welfare utility functions, as well as separate commodities, to be traded, bought and sold, somewhat as other commodities on foreign markets.

For example, inflation is the overabundance of a country's currency with respect to the country's domestic and foreign products. It is considered with respect to the purchasing power of the country's currency, where a representative "basket" of goods and services are compared in price over differing time periods. If that basket costs more, then there is inflation, at the percentage in the rise of the basket's price. While this currency is devalued in its domestic purchasing power, foreign demand for that currency may be high, and hence its price higher than other currencies because they may have higher inflation rates, or because of the country's inherent stability making its currency strong on the foreign markets, or because the dynamics of speculation involve the currency, bringing many buyers into the purchase and thus driving its price upward. The ambiguity of c, due to its being a part of the country's economy and a commodity in itself for foreign trade, nevertheless requires that it be treated separately within the $\bar{I}$ equation, for the very reason that its influence is incorporated in the W component for the domestic dynamics and because it is significant as a commodity in international trade.

While the W component of $\bar{I}$ is an approximation and depends on the country's cycle and its position, $\overline{I}$ itself is an equation, holding at time t for all foreign transactions at that time. As contracts are signed for international commercial agreements, unless otherwise stipulated—and thereby allowing for flexibility over time for exchange rates—the transactions are conducted at the exchange-rate ratios of the currencies of the countries involved at the time of signing. A contract of long duration may stipulate that transactions will be paid at the rate of exchange at the time each transaction is undertaken or there may be some leniency on this, depending on the financial situations of the exporter and importer—this, however, depends on the specific situation at its terms of trade.

$\overline{I}_t$, representing a country's situation with respect to trade, must portray two types of conditions. One is the ability of the country to export, and this depends on its W component for any specific time. For example, when a country is in recession, its ability to export is diminished because of reduced employment, hence, comparatively low output. Even in the heavily industrialized countries, with a high capital/labor ratio, recessions reduce demand for industrial output, resulting in unemployment and disused capital equipment. The developed country's currency may be stable in spite of the recession, because other countries may be experiencing recession and their currencies may lack the potential economic backing, thereby placing heavy demand for the industrialized country's currency. As floatings are not wild in this situation because of most countries being in recession, demand for the country's currency will make it stable instead of rising. Moreover, the country's central bank will step in and sell if there are deviations in the stability, making whatever exports profitable as the trading currency will most likely be in the developed country's coin.

During recovery, employment increases and so does demand and output. Foreign markets are sought, but the success in securing them depends on their cyclical phases, indicated by the international utility function. For the prosperity phase, the same condition holds: exporting depends on the targeted markets' ability to absorb the products, and this depends on their phases of the cycle. However, with the country in recovery or prosperity, demand for foreign goods and services increases accordingly, providing incentives for foreign countries to increase output—at least for the domestic market of the importing country. This, then, provides for the country's ability to import. When the recovery and prosperity phases occur, demand increases and for foreign products, the increment may be slight, but as employment increases, so does demand for foreign products. This provides the incentive for importing, resulting in further employment for those businesses engaged in importing, thereby providing further stimulation to the domestic economy and ultimately to the exporting economies.

Hence, in general, trade is both internal and external in orientation. An economy's ability to conduct trade—both as exporter and importer—depends on the status of its international utility function. As $0 < \overline{I}_t < 1$, when $\overline{I}_t \rightarrow 0$, this means that $W \approx 1/C_{\text{recession}}$, and that the economy is sluggish with respect to trade, both importing and exporting. The c component usually reflects this condition, but the currency may be at a high float because of speculation, thereby increasing demand. This may also have an adverse affect on $\bar{I}_t$, because with a high currency and sluggish economy, demand for that economy's exports may be reduced because of the high exchange rate involved in possible transactions. But the tendency is that the currency's value reflects the economy's condition, so when it is in recession, the currency's value is comparatively low.

Moreover, keeping the currency's value relatively low may be intentional as this may stimulate the demand for the country's exports, thereby aiding in the cycle to be shifted upward. The extent of the demand, of course, depends on the potential importing countries' financial ability to pay. The dynamics of innovation and imitation enter here, for through innovation new markets are established, and through imitation competitive alternatives are offered.

While innovation is primarily domestically oriented, it is also directed to foreign markets. The success of both domestic and foreign innovation depend on the firm's open-ended information system, whether it is of utility or entropy as the innovative project becomes marketable. During recession, the opting for production instead of liquidity has the risk of failure, and careful planning and advertising are required. With a stable or low currency exchange rate, competition becomes more profitable in foreign markets, especially where innovation is involved. Again this, however, depends on the cyclical phases of the countries; entering into new markets, however, is never without risks and the firms' information systems must take into account the risks, providing a basis for flexibility in situations where expectations and reality are in conflict.

With respect to differing cyclical phases, there is an international imitation effect, based on the success of a product in its country of origin. Success is determined by two factors. One is, of course, the profits from sales of the product, so that the greater the profits, the greater the product's success in the markets. The word *markets* is intentionally plural, because when a product is planned and its targeted groups projected, only a certain amount of profits can be earned from these consumers. One sign of success is when the product does not remain only for those selected consumers, but is purchased by other groups, perhaps of different social or income classes. Hence, the greater the consumer exposure, the greater the consumption and the higher the profits. The markets have thus expanded, incorporating a greater consumer awareness and willingness to devote the necessary liquidity for consumption.

While this aspect of success raises profits, the other factor tends to reduce them. This is imitation that follows from successful innovation. While substitutes are always close, there are always differences that distinguish them. The innovative product competing successfully in markets it originally initiated thus maintains a respectable profit rate.

The point is that while a product is successful in its domestic markets, these markets tend to become saturated over time with imitators. To protect profits, firms will seek to export the product, so that domestic saturation will not have such an effect on business. Successful communications are necessary in the form of advertising, and this often requires portraying the product in its original domestic setting. There is usually a short time lag after market research and advertising are conducted before the product is introduced in the foreign markets, and if successful according to the criteria of consumer liquidity being allocated for the product, the international imitation effect takes hold with the importing countries entering into imitation.

The international imitation effect also operates when firms in one country, possessing the necessary infrastructure and perhaps the appropriate competitive products, enter the markets of other countries with these products on an imitative footing. In this case, the important point of consideration is not which country innovated the product, but how well the exporting countries can compete through imitation.

The international imitation effect contrasts with the international demonstration effect, the latter being, to quote Charles P. Kindleberger, "under which underdeveloped countries have learned about the existence of goods in developed nations which will lighten their burdens, satisfy their physical appetites, and titillate their innate sense of self-expression or exhibition." [10] There are several reasons for the contrast between these approaches. One reason is that the international imitation effect holds for developed, developing, and underdeveloped countries. Imitative exports, or exports that result in imitation, require sophistication and economic infrastructure in the importing countries. While sophistication from the point of view of consumer orientation may be present, in the emerging countries infrastructure is a serious problem. Exporters are aware of this, and they export to those countries in which their products can be distributed with relative ease to their targeted markets. Whether imitation is originated in the exporting country's domestic markets and then imported by other countries as innovation, to be imitated by the importing countries' industries, or whether the imitative products are imported as such to compete with similar products, has no influence on the dynamics of the markets once the products are absorbed. A product which is imitative but enters into a country as innovative will generate imitation if successful; a product exported to compete with similar products will increase competition within the market through further imitation. In the first instance, the product will generate competition; in the second, it will increase it. In both instances competition is stimulated to the benefit of those consumers directing their liquidity into purchasing the product.

The international demonstration effect refers to underdeveloped and indeed developing economies. As for imports, the demonstration effect is valid, but its validity is limited. It does not explain, for example, how domestic markets develop as a response to imports; nor does it explain how these imports are to be paid. The international imitation effect does explain domestic market development as imitation of successful foreign and domestic products. Payments for imports are therefore supplied by money earned through imitation within the economies and from innovations that they also export. The demonstration effect prevails in those countries whose economies are hindered from growth because of natural restraints such as drought and insufficient techniques for soil treatment and agriculture, and man-made restrictions, such as politics and war. In countries with relative political stability and the willingness to acquire and apply knowledge for development, these restrictions are nonexistent, and while the imports from the developed countries generate demand, this demand is soon met by domestic industry producing close substitutes. The demonstration effect is thus a limit case of the imitation effect, especially since multinational enterprises and customs unions are bringing the world's economies closer together, making imitation that much easier and innovation more likely to be exported. [11]

The international imitation effect can be derived from the $\bar{I}$ equation. As the equation representing a country's exporting and importing abilities and capabilities, the $\bar{I}$'s W element describes the economy with respect to its cycle. With recovery, employment is increased, increasing general aggregate liquidity. Industry increases production and exports are planned. Moreover, imports are increased due to increasing consumer demand. This sets off the imitation effect when exports are successful and firms seek to reduce their liquidity option for production. Those firms not engaged in innovation will be active in imitation, part of imitative production being in competition with foreign products that have demonstrated their success. Therefore, the imitation effect is included in the category of imitation within the economy and provides a source for market dynamics, in the same way that these dynamics are provided for by domestic imitation.

With respect to the international utility function, the concept of comparative advantage has to be reconsidered. Comparative advantage is a classical-cum-neoclassical concept in international economics, and as such was an answer to the mercantilist and physiocratic concepts of favorable balance of trade and of land as the sole sources of wealth. The mercantilist concept of exporting more than importing and having the difference made up with hard currency, had no place in the new economics formulated by Adam Smith and his followers. Neither did physiocracy, which maintained that all wealth comes from the land, as the land provides the necessities of life: agriculture for food, cloth for clothing, and the building materials for construction. Therefore, according to the physiocratic doctrine, those who owned land owned real wealth, especially since the products of the land could be exported and hard currency earned.

The new economics brought these two concepts into repute. The mercantilist approach was questioned because possessing another country's currency did not prevent this currency from fluctuating in value, according to the demand for that country's products and the ability to meet the demand. Moreover, with gold underwriting currencies, through mercantilist expansion and the discovery of gold mines, inflation set in as merchants increased their prices to increase their share of the money backed by gold. In this manner, currencies were devalued, making the mercantilist approach doctrinaire and easy prey for the new economics.

The physiocratic approach also suffered because it emphasized land as the source of wealth, and not the production resulting from land. Owning land in itself provided title and prestige, but not wealth. It was brought out by the followers of Smith that the real cause of wealth is how the land is used, and this means how efficiently it is used in production, and in alternative products and methods of production. Land itself as the source of wealth thus became doctrinaire, and like its mercantilist counterpart, became rigid and invalid in light of the new economics.

Adam Smith and his followers maintained that production is the source of wealth, with wealth increasing as productive efficiency increases. Of course, there are market considerations, but the successful entrepreneur will be flexible and deviate production according to market fluctuations.

According to the classical economists, a country will produce those products that can be manufactured at costs less than would be paid if they are imported. For example, if countries A and B both produce textiles and steel, but country A has better pasturing lands and therefore better wool from its sheep, and country B has higher grade iron ore in its mountains, A will reduce its iron output and import it from B either as ore or as finished steel, while B will reduce its textile production and import from A. This relationship has been expressed in the Hecksher-Ohlin model of trade, an important assumption of which is that the two products differ in their capital input and labor costs. Should a multitude of products be considered for trade between A and B, the political factor also enters in, as producers lobby for tariffs and governments impose taxation on imported goods to raise revenues or reduce spending, as the case may be.[12]

In a free trade situation, the exploitation of nations' comparative advantages results in economic efficiency and low consumer prices for all trading countries, even when transportation costs are involved. One component of comparative advantage is location, and this is important when trading partners are considered. Two countries with similar factor endowments competing for markets will sell to those countries closest to them. Countries with limited capital and natural resources will exploit whatever they have to obtain trade, such as tourism and historical sites. Even when competition is restricted because of taxes and quotas, tariffs and even embargoes because of international hostilities, the theory of comparative advantage provides efficient trade, given these restrictions, for the economic model of the world.

However, what must be brought into question is the validity of this model, for if this is found to be wanting, then the theory of comparative advantage must be abandoned and replaced by one adequate for our contemporary international economic situation.

Upon analysis it is found that the theory of comparative advantage relates to basically two markets: home and foreign. It discusses within the context of the Hecksher-Ohlin theory factor endowments and their exploitation for trade. The real difficulty with comparative advantage is that it refers to countries, to the home country and its foreign trading partners, but in reality trade is conducted on an entirely different basis.

This basis is that of individual firms as well as governments, and in modern economics, a country deficient in natural factor endowments but efficient in production and marketing will not suffer in trade relations. Firms import raw materials and if necessary, skilled labor, to manufacture its products. Where the materials are lacking, in whatever combination, they are imported, with the finished product consumed domestically and exported. Governments, as consumers of surpluses from domestic markets and as stockpilers of strategic materials from foreign countries for times of crisis—the holding of crude oil is one example, uranium another—can purchase these materials either through barter, through monetary payments, or a combination of both, according to the requirements of its trading partners. These government-held supplies, such as surplus gains, can be shipped to regions that are in need, such as the Sudan in times of famine, with payment being in the currency of good will, or with the Soviet Union, to help defuse the Cold War situation. Governments act on the basis of the utility of their alternatives in the decision-making process; the utility-ordering is political in orientation and not economic as is the case with firms engaging in international trade.

This aspect of the home market, then, contradicts the comparative advantage approach to trade as an economic concept, because it is based on politics and not strict economic considerations. Indeed, in situations of assisting famine areas, the financial costs are calculable, while the political benefits may not be forthcoming.

Apart from government restrictions on trading with specific countries, the political considerations have no bearing at all on the commerce of firms. Here, again, the concept of comparative advantage is inapplicable, for firms trade from the advantage of being innovators and establishing markets in foreign countries, or as imitators, perceived by the managers to be able to make profits in markets at different stages of saturation. With respect to firms, the issue is not the natural resources available in each country, but the abilities to muster resources, either domestically or through importing, and to form them into products that can sell abroad, covering expenses and reaping profits sufficient to make the projects of utility among other competing projects. This, of course, requires planning as well as the assembling of the necessary materials, each of which has its costs.

Comparative advantage has, therefore, to be replaced by a concept relevant to contemporary economics, this being the international utility function. This is expressed by each trading firm with respect to its utility within its specific markets. The utility is determined by the success in terms of profits and other objectives within the firm's information system, such as market expansion, the accumulation of other consuming groups outside those originally targeted, and the market-assessed receptability of other products that the firm may seek to export into those markets. Hence, in general terms, a country's $\bar{I} \rightarrow 1$ if its firms have high utilities in their various foreign markets. If the firms' successes are mixed with respect to their goals stated in their information systems, $0 < \bar{I} < 1$. Logically, if the firms fail to achieve their goals, then $\bar{I} \rightarrow 0$, which is a situation that exists when the country's government is unable to provide the necessary economic stability for internal development, thereby affecting its firms' abilities to export. Countries that are emerging in their political and economic development, subject to power struggles and coups, are in this situation, and it is resolved when political stability allows for the country to establish its business cycle and move into the contemporary economic era.

The two aspects of trade for a country are, therefore, governmental and private; the dynamics of each of these aspects depend on the value of the trading countries' currencies at the time the transactions are agreed upon. For the importing country, a lower currency value for the exporting country means that domestic sales prices can be adjusted to bring about high profits, depending on the percentage of tariffs levied on the products. For the exporting country, lower foreign currency means that, in general, less of the domestic products will be purchased—the exceptions are when demand for the product is held constant or rises because of appeal, or when the products are raw materials and the price is less of a concern than the possession of the material themselves, with high costs passed on to the final consumers. Again, the discussion of trade among countries is in need of clarification. Discussing trade in this manner is helpful in the accounting of the balance of payments with respect to its trading partners, and this includes those countries also trading in currencies to bolster their own in the international markets.

Thus, to consider a country's trade situation, it is necessary to consider it with respect to its firms and its government's international commercial transactions. This requires the analysis of the country's international currency value, as well as its position with respect to the trade cycle, for these two factors present its international utility function and the willingness of other countries to engage in trade.

Given $\bar{I}_t = U(c, W)_t$, c can be removed from this functional equation by partial differentiation. Variable c is the country's money, which domestically is composed of money for consumption and money for savings and investments. The utility of money in the domestic market depends, of course, on the cycle's position, and in the domestic markets money is measured in value with the cycle's movements, as was discussed in the previous chapter.

For international commerce, however, money takes on a different significance. It becomes a relative measure for both the exporting and importing countries' transactions. For example, the U.S. economy may be turning downward according to the projections of the nation's indicators. But trading with another industrialized country having its own economic difficulties may make the dollar a stronger currency in the transaction, in which case fewer purchases will be made from the U.S. firms than would have been previously had the currency values been reversed, subject to the reservations on purchases stated above. Therefore, money has three commercial uses: one is for consumption, which entails the purchases of domestic goods and services and those imported; it is used for savings and investments, the distinction between them being the source in which the money is placed. Savings in a bank differs from investing in a business, although both are done to gain returns on the money placed. Third, money is the measure of foreign transactions, in which their value is determined with respect to the currencies involved. The trading process, in which barter is not in consideration, depends on the goods and services being traded, on the demand that they can generate, and on the value of the partners' currencies with respect to each other and to the other currencies in circulation in foreign trading. A country's currency is in demand, that is, it is hard and highly negotiable, if its utility approaches 1. While this, to some extent, reflects the country's internal economy, this is certainly relative. For example, when the United States approaches recession, with all the internal diseconomies this involves, its currency is still stronger internationally than the currencies of the developing and emerging countries, and in demand more than some of the developed countries' currencies. This is an expression of the relative cyclical positions of the various trading countries, as well as their political stability, and their potential as well as actual abilities to produce and manufacture and market effectively its products in the domestic and foreign markets.

Hence, a country's political leaders can set the exchange rate for their national currency at whatever level they choose, but the actual trading will be conducted within the value of that currency set by international demand, or in a hard currency agreed upon by the partners. In emerging and developing countries where hard currencies are often obtained on the black market with a premium as payment for hedging against the uncertain future, banks try to purchase foreign hard currencies legally and lend them, for a premium, to traders. The extent of the black markets is a reflection of the lack of confidence the people have in their own currency, which in turn reflects their lack of confidence in their finance ministers and perhaps their entire government. This is expressed within the country's cycles and the value of money in purchasing during the cycle's phases. The raising of taxes, the abolishing of subsidies, and the ratio of businesses closing or in financial difficulties to those opening and those solvent, is usually greater than ever, and sometimes very high as a reflection of the lack of confidence in the government as overall financial manager of the economy. As a country's currency is of utility when its political and economic systems are sound and its economic potential is great, opting for hard currencies in an economy is a statement on the part of the citizenry that confidence is seriously lacking in both the political leadership in managing the economy and in the domestic industries' abilities to compete within their own markets and most certainly internationally. Competition, in this sense, refers to

successful innovations and imitations in domestic markets and the marketing of
the products in foreign markets. Countries in situations in which innovations
and imitations are far from frequent and which rely on imports for a large
portion of their supplies, often undergo devaluations to reduce the purchasing
of foreign products and encourage exports of domestic products on the basis of
a better currency ratio for importers. In these situations not only are devaluations often repeated, they are also ineffective for encouraging exports. A country's currency is only one factor in the $\overline{I_t}$ equation, even though it reflects the
currency's value internationally. Without effective management of the W_t factor, devaluations are merely short-run measures without any significance. They
result in inflation at levels higher than the devaluation because of price spiraling
and labor sanctions and strikes to protect their wages. The consequence is that
while prices rise, so do wages, and aggregate consumption remains fairly stable.
Moreover, the increased export currency ratio brought about by devaluation has
no real effect on international trade, because the economy's structural reasons—found in W_t—are not corrected, making W_t more efficient in the dynamics of the economic cycle. A policy for changing W_t, that is, changing industry,
government economic policies, and labor attitudes, requires great acumen and
energy on the part of the country's leaders, but these are too often sapped by
political infighting and the concern for each politician's own personal welfare
that results. Instead of going to the source of the problem, in the W factor,
devaluations are easier to implement, lower the price of a country's currency
and provide political propaganda to show how active the government is in boosting
exports. Without working with the source of the problem, it will not be too
long before devaluation is again undertaken and the same reasons given to a
public that will continuously sell and buy on the black market.

In contrast to devaluations initiated by governments, there are market devaluations, as well as revaluations, depending on the demand for the country's
currency. This also relates to the W_t factor, to the country's industrial output
and potential for innovations and imitations, to its government's ability to act
in response to the cycle, and to labor's interests in maintaining a skilled and
up-to-date work force and responsible behavior during periods of recession and
recovery. Currency fluctuations depend on buying and selling of foreign currencies, to make profits on flexible exchange rates as currencies move in value
between points established by agreement among the trading countries. Should
a hard currency become overvalued, rising in value with respect to other hard
currencies at rates that may possibly hinder foreign trade, central banks inter-
vene and sell off as much of its holdings of that currency as their directorates
consider feasible, using the money from the sales to purchase their own and/or
other hard currencies to raise their values with respect to the overvalued currency. Hence, in this situation, currencies fluctuate in value as do other commodities, because of demand for them; their demand, however, is based on
their economies' abilities to remain dynamic and maintain the innovative and
imitative processes, expanding the domestic economy and its international com-

merce. Indeed, an economy's ability to maintain innovation and imitation and to expand its foreign commerce are the factors of its currency's value, and this ability is what makes its currency in demand, making it hard.

Soft currencies, therefore, reflect economies that are unable to maintain successful innovation and imitation; these economies often rely on those with hard currencies for their products and financial assistance. Their currencies are soft because they are nonconvertible into hard currencies, and they reflect their economies' inability to maintain the dynamic processes of activity so necessary for growth and development. Their foreign transactions are conducted in hard currencies and their imports exceed their exports, with the major part of their cash exports going to countries of similar economic positions, while their imports are mainly from countries with hard currencies.

The point is that while in the $\overline{I}_t$ equation, c and W are separate, as they are intricate factors in an economy, they are indeed related, but as they pertain to different aspects in the economy they are treated separately. The W_t factor is internal, in the sense that it pertains to the economy's ability to develop within its cycle. It relies on the utilities of firms' policies, of government's economic policies, and on labor's activities on behalf of its members. It also relates to the value of money in its purchasing power and the interest on savings and investments that it can obtain during the cycle's phases. Variable c is the factor that relates the economy to others in the international market, and if hard, is also traded internationally, with its value fluctuating with respect to other hard currencies and other alternatives available for foreign consumption.

How does an economy's international utility function therefore relate to international trade? As $\overline{I}_t = U(c,W)_t$, and as W represents the economy's ability to produce, to innovate and imitate, and as its foreign currency's value is assessed with respect to its productive ability, then the economy's ability to export and import depends on its $\overline{I}_t$, that is, its ability to absorb imports and generate exports. This ability is manifested in the two types of markets that make up an economy, those for imported products and those that are generated in foreign countries through export. Hence, as the economy's currency value and its ability to produce determine its international utility function, c and W can also be written as Market$_{domestic}$ and Market$_{foreign}$, so that $\overline{I}_t = U(M_d, M_f)_t$. Factoring out the foreign markets for their consideration weakens $\overline{I}_t$'s relationship to these markets, as they are as dynamic as the economies engaging in international commerce, and because the c's value shifts according to its demand and the demand for alternative purchases. Therefore, while both M_d and M_f provide an equation for $\overline{I}_t$, with only M_f being considered, $\overline{I}_t \approx (\Sigma M_f)_t$, with the sigma sign summing the import and export markets. The approximation sign with respect to the time-signature demonstrates the fluidity of trade. It captures agreements being formulated but not yet finalized, it portrays the currencies' values in fluctuation according to their demand, and as both imports and exports are the result of W_t's ability, it demonstrates the innovations and imitations directed for imports and exports and the possible market dynamics they may generate with respect to the firms' information systems with respect to trade.

The utility of the foreign market summation can be assessed with respect to the upper and lower boundaries. If there is a greater amount of domestic money spent in toto on imported goods and services than the foreign markets spend on that country's exports, then that country is in a general balance of payments deficit, because more income is diverted to imported goods than for those goods exported. This, however, is a very general picture and as such sheds little light on a country's import-export balances. For example, to speak about a country's position, again both the government and the private firms have to be considered. The government's actions are not conducted from commercial considerations alone, because the government is a political organization and not one geared to profit maximization. Government-contracted deficits are therefore not based on the same motivation as those by private firms; there are no innovations nor imitations exported by governments, only surpluses in production purchased from firms for political leverage both domestically and internationally. Again, consider the example of grains. The government purchases surplus grains from private farmers and stores them, to be resold to farmers and processing companies for the commercial markets, thereby preventing the type of gluts that prevailed during the Great Depression, as well as preventing shortages in times of diminished agricultural output. These grains, however, are used as exports to countries in times of famine as is the case with Sudan and Ethiopia, or to supply the grains to countries with low commercial agricultural output, such as the Soviet Union. Payment may be demanded in the form of hard currency or may be expected as international good will, depending on how the government officials consider the significance to the grain shipments. There is also the problem of long-term government loans to the developing and emerging countries, and their need to reschedule payments on these loans also has to be considered for the government's payment balance. In this case, there is more than an accounting problem involved; it is a problem of the receiving countries' utilities in the application of the liquidity. This must be postponed until Part III, but it suffices to state here that this is a manifestation of these economies' relationships to their domestic and international situation, with respect to innovation, imitation, and the dynamics of their cycles.

The utility of government policies in the realm of economics is determined by the achievement of the objectives as stated in the information system of each policy. As the financial profit motive is not necessary, social and/or political objectives are the aims of these policies. Hence, with respect to these policies the balance of payments for goods and services exported is not at issue, as governments rely on private firms engaging in foreign commerce to make up whatever financial losses are so accrued.

Even in socialist state-run economies—slowly becoming relics of a bygone era—those state firms engaging in foreign commerce are expected to compensate for the government's balance of payments deficit by exporting more than importing. This expectation is often not achieved because of the absence of sufficient economies within the state-run firm to allow for effective competition with those firms privately owned. But, as the influence of democratic ideas are penetrating these countries and as the inefficiencies of state-socialism are being revealed, private initiative in business is being encouraged, and the consequences of this initiative on innovation, imitation, and foreign trade should be interesting, but still remain to be seen.

Private firms, by the very nature of their ownership, cannot allow themselves the luxury of trading without making profits, for if they did the business would soon find itself in default of fixed payments and into bankruptcy. Their trade is motivated by profits and the utilities of their business ventures are determined with respect to the expected and actual profits gained from each venture. Hence, engaging in foreign trade requires planning and some degree of comprehension of the markets that are being entered into. This is easier now to obtain than in previous eras, because of the influence of the Western countries throughout the world after World War II, and the dominations of the world's markets by these countries. A degree of ''commonness'' was established, enabling the export of soft drinks, clothing, and eventually products merging on high technology, such as computers and automobiles. Exporters have acquired the acumen of developing markets in which the culture of the exporting countries is preserved, while using this cultural appeal to promote sales of their products. The prestige of British products, the durability and quality of U.S. exports, and the flair of the taste of France, are important selling points for these countries' exports. Moreover, they are exploited by the domestic importers who market and sell these products in their own countries.

Exposure to these cultures because of increased travel and the impact of World War II and the Cold War that followed, helped to promote exports. Additional help in the export markets is gained by the thaw in the Cold War, with the once-closed Eastern bloc countries becoming exposed to the Western-oriented markets, importing and exporting as much as the hard currencies and market absorption will allow.

Market absorption, of course, depends on the cycle's position. In those countries whose markets were dominated by the ruling political parties, there were no business cycles in the sense of the cycle in contemporary economics. There were, however, bottlenecks in planning and production, due to the absence of signals from the markets as to which products need to be increased in quantity, which need to be reduced in output, and which distribution points are in need of increased and reduced supplies. Hence, the long lines of consumers, often finding the shelves empty when their turn has come. With the diminution of state authority in the economic realm and the increasing emphasis on private enterprise and the profit motive, these economies will enter the contemporary dynamics of the business cycle when the profit motive stimulates innovation and imitation.

The effects of imitation are already being felt in these countries due to the easing of import restrictions, making available greater products from the developed economies' industries. Moreover, grants from government to government, and favored country trading concessions, serve to reduce tariffs on their imports to the developed countries, thereby stimulating production for export. Export production cannot have the same market exposure as domestic production, so that these incentives stimulate production increases across the board, but this time motivated by profits and therefore generating economic efficiency in production. Moreover, the products have to be of quality so that they will sell in the imported markets. Efficiency and quality are necessary in competitive production; applying these principles results in innovation as new products are conceived to gain consumer liquidity. As the economic liberalization continues, these countries will enter the business cycle as a result of their production, the consequences of which are: expanding of their industry, increasing their internal and external competition, and bringing their economies more in line with those of the industrialized countries. Their international utility functions will then be considered within the same frame of reference as those of the industrialized nations, with the value of their currencies changing from soft—unwanted in international commerce—to medium, respected in trade according to the relative strengths of their economies.

With respect to a country's trading position, again this depends on the policies of the government and the success of its firms. Although the government operates from other than economic considerations, there is still an economic cost for its actions. Humanitarian shipments of food to disaster areas in the various needy regions of the world requires logistics and payments within the countries receiving the shipments. This has a cost that must be considered when calculating a country's balance of payments position. Extensive aid, financially and materially, has costs. The financial aid could be used internally to reconstruct parts of the domestic economy that are in need; the material aid could be applied, again, to the domestic economy in the form of regulating supplies to stimulate or cool down markets as the case may be. While firms, on the other hand, seek profits in export, they may not always be successful according to the requirements established in their information systems. Indeed, it may even be to their advantage to take losses to reduce their taxes, but this calculation requires the decision of the firms' directorates.

The point is that a country may be in a surplus balance with respect to some countries and at a deficit with others, when aggregate accounting is considered. With respect to trading, countries are in functional relationships with each other. This relationship is manifested in the elements of the country's international utility function. For example, as industry, government, and labor are elements of the welfare utility function, and as W is a factor of the $\overline{I_t}$, then the elements of this function generate economic activity and provide international value to the country's currency. The utility of this function is measured within the upper and lower limits of 0 and 1, which determines whether or not the country is performing well or badly in the aggregate with respect to trade. This measurement includes the government's economic policies, which may be undertaken at a strict accounting loss, but which may pay off in political dividends. But as the $\bar{I}_t$ is strictly an economic concept, financial gains and losses are the only relevant consideration here. Industry may be exporting and importing at gains and losses, but to determine which industries are at surplus and which are at deficits requires the analysis of each industry and its firms. Labor is the contributor to the manufacturing process, carrying out the plans established within the various information systems. Sanctions and strikes hinder firms' abilities to export, to meet existing agreements, and to open new markets. Such policies by labor also have effect on a country's $\bar{I}_t$ position.

Hence, to state that a country's international utility function is between the upper and lower limits is, in itself, insufficient. A country's trade position has significance only with respect to its trading partners, with their $\bar{I}_t$'s being inter-related with that country's. The significance and importance of international trade are such that countries with political hostilities over many centuries are now forming into common markets, customs unions that allow for the free movement of goods and services across national borders without tariffs or other quotas. While most of a country's business is conducted within its borders— the W of $\bar{I}_t$—an important part of commerce is international, prompted in part by the possibility of domestic market situation, and at all times by the profit motive. Even in customs unions, however, each member country has a balance of trade position with the others, and with the world outside the union, based on its share in exporting and importing. While customs unions will be discussed in Part III, it suffices now to state that they behave as single countries with respect to the international utility function generated on aggregate by their economic activity.

World trade is conducted on the basis of countries' international utility positions, and each country has to be considered with respect to its $\bar{I}_t$ when its firms and economic leaders consider trading. The firms' utility positions with respect to trade can be projected within their information systems, and when trading is in process these positions are adjusted according to the situations of the foreign markets and the domestic ability to meet the assigned deadlines for manufacturing and shipping. The government utility position, assessed in terms of accomplishing its goals, is often of longer duration before the information can be received; it is also less controllable, as various political influences tend to enter the situation, affecting the government's information system's expectations.

Hence, there is flexibility in the trading process, depending on the international utility positions of the partners involved. Cyclical fluctuations among industrial countries tend to move in the same patterns because of the interlocking economic and political relationships. This tendency is lacking among countries of different levels of development, so that while an industrialized country trading with a developing country is undergoing recession, the only effect this will have on the developing country's cycle is that the reduction of commerce may exert a downward pull on the cycle. This can be offset by diversifying trade ties whenever possible, and this requires an alert directorate among the trading firms, scouting out new markets for exports and imports while maintaining the levels of commerce acceptable to the information systems of each of the partners.

In general, then, as a country's $\bar{I}_t$ position is measured within the boundaries of utility and entropy, this measurement can be understood only within the relationship to the country's trading partners. Country A, at time t, trades with ten partners, some of these partners will be in debt to country A, while others may break even and others still may be in surplus. The concepts of debt and surplus are both financial, that is, accounting concepts with the country holding more hard currency as a result of the transaction being in surplus over the country with less hard currency.

However, there is more than the accounting of debt and surplus in hard currency involved. A country's economic strength is based on its productive ability, and while greater or less hard currency may be important in the calculations of governments when considering their countries' positions in trading, the very processes of trade stimulate the economy, mobilize resources, invigorate the dynamics of innovation and imitation, and therefore influence the cycle's movement. Hence, the necessity for the time-signature, for as a country may be in debt to its trading partners, this will stimulate its firms and managers to move into innovation and imitation, to build new markets and to reduce and perhaps eliminate the debt position. Moreover, countries in surplus will have greater hard currency at their disposable to make trading that much easier, and their advantage should serve to maintain their position.

A country with a trade debt has acquired greater foreign goods and services than it has exported. There has to be the ability to consume these goods and services, otherwise there has been a misreading of the cycle's position with respect to the exporting firms' calculations and the importing firms' awareness of their country's economic circumstances. In either situation, when the products are consumed, this stimulates the domestic market into imitation to eliminate the foreign influence and to perhaps establish export markets similar to those in the partner countries. The international imitation effect takes hold, with the processes of production becoming integrated into the business cycle.

The point is that countries that are debtors can move into the surplus position by the very dynamics that hold for the domestic markets, by innovation and imitation, innovating products that carry the cultural identities of their countries, and imitating those the domestic economy has successfully manufactured and sold as well as those that have gained profits internationally. The notions of surplus and debt, while reflecting the currency positions of the countries, can nevertheless stimulate greater production, especially for international commerce. The summation of the $\bar{I}_t$'s for the trading countries therefore reflects their internal dynamics with respect to their business cycles and the values of their currencies in the international markets. The importance of world trade was understood sufficiently by the drafters of the International Monetary Fund, the World Bank, and the General Agreement on Tariffs and Trade; given the contemporary economic and political world situation, trade is certainly of the greatest importance now. How countries implement their dynamics to generate trade depends on the acumen of their political and economic leaders, with respect to their business cycles and the values of their currencies, that is, to their international utility functions.

HELP THY NEIGHBOR HELP THYSELF: FURTHER COMMENTS ON THE EXCHANGE RATE

With the developments of our rapidly changing political and economic situation, a flexible exchange-rate system is not conducive to trade in the developing and emerging countries, while it is very suitable for the developed countries. The linkage of soft currencies to hard currencies burdens those countries whose economies cannot afford to obtain hard currencies through regular trade. Hard currencies are obtained either through aid or through special trading terms, each of which relegates them to second place in the world economic order.

The peoples of the emerging and developing countries are industrious, but they seek remuneration for their efforts. Often, they have to cope with political regimes that are often repressive and competent in economic matters. There is a linkage between oppression, incompetence, and the lack of genuine industry that can compete in the world's markets. Both oppression and incompetence stifle individual initiative and encourage economic favoritism, so that some people prosper while others are subjected to government decree and policies to regulate the economy; often the fortunes of those who prosper change with the whims of the ruling classes.

These countries are the recipients of assistance, given with the sole purpose of allowing them to become economically solvent and able to compete internationally. The antidote to oppressive and incompetent governments is a strong domestic economy that can extend itself into foreign markets successfully.

The argument to be presented here is not against the flexible exchange-rate system that has accommodated the developed countries so well. It is, however, for a two-tier exchange system, one flexible and the other fixed to a basket of currencies. The fixed exchange rates can be set on a per country basis, agreed upon by the country and the World Bank, and altered as the country's conditions require it, with the agreement of the World Bank. This will provide a solid basis for trade with the developed countries as with other countries in similar economic situations. With this system there is the stability of the currency with respect to the hard currencies, and the flexibility needed when required. Truly flexible exchange rates are luxuries these countries cannot afford. Rates that are both fixed and flexible according to their needs will encourage trade without the reliance of obtaining hard currencies.

An economy engaged in trade will produce to meet its commitments. This will provide employment, consumer liquidity, and sales within the economy. Competition will stimulate competence in government and will eliminate favoritism as more people become involved in the economic processes. Government will then work with industry and labor in a welfare utility system, and as this economic development continues, the country's currency will become stronger through industrialization. Eventually, the tie to the hard currency basket will be cut by mutual agreement with the World Bank, and the country's international utility function will take it to the levels of development sufficient to be a full competitor in trade.

The single-tier system is inadequate for our complex and changing world; it keeps those developed countries on top and hinders the emerging and developing countries from trading, as they have to rely on other countries' currencies in their transactions. The two-tier system will allow these countries to trade among themselves and with the developed countries on the basis of their own currencies.

These soft currencies can be redeemed by the developed countries from the World Bank at exchange rates that are determined by the currency basket's supply and demand by the developed countries, and/or by the aggregate flexible rates of the currencies other than that of the redeeming country. Through this method, genuine world trade can be stimulated and the need for financial assistance to the developing and emerging countries be reduced significantly, or eliminated altogether.

Part III

THE CHANGING
ECONOMIC WORLD

Chapter 8

INTRODUCTORY REMARKS

Only a few industrial countries are able to repay their external debts in their own currencies. Because of exchange controls, the currencies of the developing countries are not fully convertible and, because of the past record of inflation and depreciation, they are not widely respected.

—Tim Congdon,
The Debt Threat

The world economic stability sought by the founders of the IMF, the World Bank, and GATT has, in our contemporary global political and economic situation, become more elusive than ever before. With the dissolution of the Cold War and the establishment of the European Economic Community, there seems to be a unification of the world's economies; with each country seeking to exploit its own unique resources and cultures in international trade, there seems to be diversification in production and export. One of the objectives of the founders of the IMF, the World Bank, and GATT, is that, through trade each trading country would establish its economy on a solid foundation so as to make their ability to trade operate competitively. This requires a strong internal economy, and such internal strength was a promising objective in the aftermath of World War II.

This was the period of a new optimism for the world, in which the United Nations was established and in which the promising global economic organizations were to prevent the occurrences of economic international behavior that existed during the Great Depression; indeed, these organizations were founded to serve the world's economies and to provide assurances that such trade practices would never occur again.

This new world optimism was short lived, however, as countries that were once allies in war were again adversaries in the developing Cold War. It was more than political ideologies that were the sources of the new global conflict; it was also the competition between the systems of capitalism and communism, both in the domestic economic development and growth among the Cold War countries, and in their competition for economic development of the newly emerging and developing countries.

At first, the Cold War persisted along the lines of the big power blocs, with the United States and the Soviet Union as the main adversaries. But as Communist China achieved power through the control of the many groups that had previously splintered that country, unifying them into a central government and supported by the armed forces, the Soviet hegemony was confronted by a Marxist-Leninist competitor, one that sought dominance over Southeast Asia, and at times over India. The United States, while leader of the Western Alliance, did not prevent France and Great Britain from acting independently, to the extent that France resigned from NATO and established its own foreign policy.

During this time, money that could have been used for economic development was in fact used in the development and expansion of the arms industries and the defense establishments. The Cold War could not have ended by decree, and this increased international suspicions and hence the need for arms of increasing sophistication. Moreover, the arms industries provided employment and the development of technologies. While armaments were necessary because of the Cold War, their increasing quantities and sophistication only led to the deepening of suspicions and the furthering of animosities. The consequences of this were the Korean War, the continuing conflicts in Indochina leading to the U.S. involvement in Vietnam after France's withdrawal, to the India-China conflicts, and to the Soviet intervention into Afghanistan. Moreover, the Israel-Arab wars were allowed to continue due to the arms supplied by their U.S. and Soviet sponsors, respectively.

In the arena of international economics, arms trading became increasingly important, to the point that not only was this trading conducted among governments, but also private arms contractors entered the markets and sold to governments as well as to private armies. While this type of trade was legitimate in the sense that it provided the demand for arms with the supply and led to the development of alternative sources of arms suppliers, it was certainly illegitimate with respect to the dynamics of the very economics necessary for establishing imitative markets internationally. This resulted in the sharpening of the distinction between economics and finance, with finance being conducted with the exchange of hard currencies for arms purchases, and with no economic benefit because the arms industries do not enter into the dynamics of economic growth and the business cycles.

This was further compounded by the fact that the countries importing most of the arms were those whose economies could least afford such luxuries. They were the developing and emerging economies, those with insufficient industrial infrastructure to produce their own weapons systems.[1] This of course was justified by the foundation of new countries having to defend themselves against their neighbors, some of which were also newly formed and some of which had already been established and were wary of the new countries that had within them the seeds of internal revolution and external expansion. Moreover, there were the revolutionary groups based on ideologies alien to the countries in which they resided that were in need of weapons. There was no discrimination here, as established countries and newly formed countries alike were fair prey to these groups, and they needed arms to carry out their revolutionary programs. And there was no discrimination among the arms dealers: those who had the money, regardless of their ideological proclamations, were able to purchase weapons. The arms industry was certainly good business, but also certainly bad economics.

Together with heavy investment in the noneconomic arms industry, there has been, in the latter half of the twentieth century, the expansion of the public sector throughout the industrialized and developing economies.[2] This was due to the extensive role in the economies that the governments had to undertake during the Great Depression, and on the continual reliance on the government as the main generator of economic activity in the aftermath of World War II. There was the demobilization that had to be undertaken with respect to the fear that unemployment, which followed the demobilization of World War I, would not occur again. Moreover, the extensive welfare services that had evolved since World War II in light of the Great Depression had to be strengthened because of the severe recession following the rapid increase in energy prices as a result of the OPEC cartel's increase in oil prices and across the board price rises that resulted in all sectors of industry and labor being severely affected.

In light of this noncyclical recession, governments began to realize that both economic growth and successful trading depend solely on the domestic economy's ability to manufacture and sell. As inflation was increasing and interest rates on loans also rising, liquidity was scarce compared to the previous period. Sales were down, unemployment high, and trade seriously affected. The relative tranquility that had persisted until then in the international markets was also shattered as fixed exchange rates were abandoned and floating exchange rates accepted instead. Moreover, the role of gold was altered. This precious metal that had provided the basis for international trade—this prime symbol of wealth—was demonitized, and the countries' currencies were to stand on the economic strengths of their respective industries, governments, and labor organizations. While officially demonitized, the myth of gold as wealth still persisted and its value rose at times to $800 an ounce. With the high unemployment and idle industrial plant reminiscent of the prewar years, people still had faith in the one stable commodity, gold. While the governments failed to protect their workers and industries, and while their welfare systems became overwhelmed with the task of assisting those newly unemployed and in need, gold once again was sought after as a means of protection against the ravages of the troubled economic systems.

The Keynesian economic system, formulated to deal with the Great Depression, was no longer viable. After all, Keynesian economics provided the basis of all postwar activity, but in this crisis, fears of another severe recession leading to depression were expressed—and indeed, they were based on the reality of the time.

The Keynesian system tended to overemphasize the role of government at the expense of industry, and indeed, this approach provided the justification for the development of the arms industry, not only for the defense of the countries in which they flourished, but as serious export industries with the noneconomic consequences mentioned above.

During this period it was realized that the economic system, if it were to remain viable, required the working relationship of the industrial sector, the government, and labor in order to bring the economies out of the recession. With the heavy reliance on the welfare system the welfare utility function describes this relationship in the cyclical pattern of economic growth. As a country's ability to trade effectively depends on its domestic economic viability, the international utility function describes this external relationship.

With respect to domestic growth and economic trade—in contrast to noneconomic trading in arms—several important developments are occurring. First, there is the restructuring of the Eastern European trading countries and especially the Soviet Union which has made the ruble a convertible currency on the international markets. These countries are abolishing the central planning boards that had previously regulated their economies, and are establishing the welfare utility function, placing industry, government, and labor in viable working relationships. There is much change being undertaken in these countries, with each country seeking its own trading position in the world economic system, but requiring favorable trading status with the United States in order to open that market and other strong currency markets to their products. Trade is, however, a reciprocal relationship, and they are accepting Western goods and services, so that the international imitation effect is taking place, with the consequence that their domestic economies are becoming oriented to the dynamics of imitation, and this will lead to the establishment of innovation in which products unique to those countries will be exported. The stability of the Bretton Woods period is nonexistent, but a new dynamism is being generated, one that can bring these countries into the contemporary era, making them viable competitors with the established industrial economies.

There is another aspect of contemporary economics that is developing, this being the multinational corporations. These corporations were formed on the basis of production costs and logistics, with one alternating with the other with respect to priority. With respect to international economics, production costs are relative among the world's economies. They depend on the availability of necessary resources, the ease of obtaining them, and the availability of obtaining alternative resources. They also include labor's ability to manufacture, and for multinational corporations this includes the ability to manufacture on international standards, and the government's taxing policies and monetary policies as they affect the business sector of the economy, that is, the I of the welfare utility function. With respect to logistics, the issues are of potential markets and the ease of reaching them, of manufacturing goods and services at locations in which the productive capabilities of the management force and the labor force are competent for meeting the firm's standards in the potential markets. Transportation costs are also computed, together with the existence of an efficient commercial system for the transfer of funds internationally back to the home country's base of operations.

Moreover, multinational corporations are very diversified in several ways. They may be corporations manufacturing many products from foodstuffs to entering the entertainment fields, from motorcycles to musical instruments, from computer games to extremely highly technical equipment for research into artificial intelligence. They may also be single product corporations, such as hostelries, with each hotel providing the atmosphere of its host country, in which case the diversification is not with the product itself, but with its style. Multinational corporations may be based in foreign countries, but may supply their base country with the products manufactured in the host countries, as is the case with textile manufacturing for the base country's domestic markets. There are no rules, as it were, for multinational corporations for their operations within their host countries; as long as local laws are obeyed and taxes paid, the policies of each such corporation depends on the policies of the base country's corporation. On the basis of these policies, an acceptable trade-off is reached between costs of production and the strategy of location, so that the maximum utility of each of the corporation's businesses are achieving the highest profits and the lowest costs, given the host countries' cyclic positions and the plants' locations and market areas.

More than good business acumen is required for these plants. Their managers have to consider the political atmosphere as well as the economic conditions when entering into manufacturing. They have to muster the necessary domestic work force to comply with the base company's image, quality control, and desired output and marketing. In the sense that these corporations have plants on the scene, on location with an understanding of the market conditions, they have an advantage over domestic-based exporting. However, to compensate for the domestic based companies' flexibility—that is, their lack of initial heavy investment in plant, capital equipment, and supplying a viable labor force in their host countries—the multinationals have to utilize their on-location positions to expand further into other countries, to establish markets. Again, their strategies depend on the availability of labor, of the capital markets, and the political atmosphere, if they are to establish physical plants in these countries. If not, then their marketing operates in the same manner as a domestic firm exporting on the foreign markets.

There is another aspect of multinational production that has to be considered, and this is the establishment of plants in countries organized by customs unions. Customs unions are markets formed by countries in which their sovereignties are relinquished to a greater marketing board so that tariffs among the membership are either reduced or eliminated in order to encourage more trade among them. In the economic sense, they operate as a single country would, establishing tariffs against some countries while reducing tariffs for others in the trading process. For these unions to be effective, they have either to float their currencies freely against one another, or abolish their currencies entirely for a common currency for both internal and external trade.

As sovereignty is relinquished, customs unions are not strictly economic organizations, but also political. They are not evolved economic and political unions such as the United States, in which the states are both sovereign and part of the greater political federal body—although the comparison between these unions and the United States seems natural in understanding their workings. They are, rather, countries, each with its own traditions, histories, and cultures, that have formed together as political and economic bodies to compete effectively among each other and with those countries, those political and economic blocs, that are external to the union.

The role of the multinational corporation in the customs union is somewhat ambiguous, in the sense that corporations that were in countries prior to their forming into customs unions still remain in them after the unions are formed. Instead of taking advantage of the labor force, the government, and the marketing ability of each country, the multinational corporation finds that these distinctions, once so important, are diminishing, with an equaling of these factors throughout the union. In this situation, the corporations become as branches of the main company, with their importance being in location only. This location may, moreover, serve as the basis for moving into the markets of nonunion countries, and in this case, the situation with respect to location is the same as it was when no union existed.

One of the difficulties with the customs union is that while it may begin as a select group of countries trading among themselves with limited tariffs, other countries soon seek full or associate membership and are accepted because of their markets and abilities to contribute economically. The exclusiveness of the union is therefore diminished with increasing membership, and their reason for existence deviates from being a select group to a global trading bloc. However, with multinational corporations on their collective soil, with bases in countries that are their competitors, they are further weakened in their exclusiveness. They can, of course, establish multinational corporations in their competitors' countries, but by so doing, they weaken their positions still further by engaging in near-regular trading, as if they did not exist; this is because the profits go back to the country within the union in which the corporation is based, without the other members benefiting from the corporation.

Our political world is in a state of transition. If there are any tendencies in this transition, they are the abolition of the communist attachments and a seeking of national independent political and economic identities. This is certainly not easy, even though the national characteristics of these countries have been preserved in spite of their obeisance to the communist system. However, while these countries seek their national identities, they have to confront the duration and intensity that the communist system prevailed, and the deeply rooted influence that system has had. These countries strive toward a democratic system of government, but often wind up with different dictators—as with Romania—resulting in continuous grass-roots rebellion and the backlash of oppression.

These countries are also, together with the Soviet Union, seeking to establish market-oriented economies. They realize that the system of central economic planning is far from efficient, and while they have full employment, this employment is inefficient in production, and the central marketing and planning board has little or no real contact with the grass-roots factories and employees, increasing the inefficiency in planning and distribution, so that long consumer lines result, with the stocks in the stores limited. These countries seek economic systems based on those of the Western economies, and seek loans, grants, and favorable nation status in their trading relations with the advanced countries.

Communist China has also undergone modernization in its political system, but when the student body demanded greater freedom to be initiated at a faster pace, their protest was put down by the force of arms, resulting in death and defections by several student leaders. Too much freedom at too fast a pace posed a threat to that system, as its leaders did not know how to cope with the student movement, and as some politicians were viewed as exploiting this situation to further their own positions of power, there were recriminations and the loss of power as the hardliners took control, putting down the student movement and trying to establish a regime that bore a semblance to the previous dictatorship.

The changes sweeping the communist countries brought the realization that for their international commerce to be expanded and hard currencies earned, their internal economies had to be restructured so that they can become competitive internationally. This meant the hard realization that internal competition had to be developed and the hard doctrinaire communist policy of a central planning board had to be modified or abandoned for the economic system of the advanced economies, that of capitalism. They also realized that their welfare systems were somewhat efficient and able to assist those people who were too old or infirm to work, and provide state assistance to those firms that were undergoing the transition from strict central planning to a competitive position.

This assistance, however, had to be reoriented from complete aid to allowing these firms to become independent. Moreover, the labor movement was in place, nurtured by the communist system, so that unions similar to those in the Western countries could be formed during the transition. Hence, the sectors necessary for internal competition, those of industry, government, and labor, were already in place; the difficulty facing these countries and their leadership is how to work with these sectors to install a Westernized work ethos into their economies.

The Eastern bloc, China, and the Westernized countries face great challenges now. In 1992 the European Economic Community will be forged into a major customs union, with tremendous productive capacity and untapped market potential. With the easing of the Chinese markets and the restructuring of the Soviet and Eastern bloc economies, these countries serve as both potential markets for the European Community and for the other Westernized countries, as well as serving as markets for the reforming Eastern bloc and Soviet economy. Therefore, 1992 looks to be a year of great change. It is also the watershed year for the U.S. economy, as the Gramm-Rudman-Hollings Act of 1985 takes effect in 1993, by which time the budget for the United States is supposed to be in balance—this, in spite of the internal economic problems such as welfare payments and unemployment insurance, as well as medical assistance in the forms of Medicaid and Medicare—and with respect to the vast amounts of foreign aid and international military obligations.[3]

A problem common to the United States, the East European countries and the Soviet Union, the Asian countries including China, South America, and the Middle East countries is that of internal economy and international trading. This problem is manifested uniquely within each country, although the communist countries are experiencing a common situation of restructuring their economies to become competitive with the Western countries and be able to act as viable trading partners. The developing economies have the mutual problem of establishing viable infrastructures and governments that can allow for real economic growth to occur, providing industry and labor with opportunities for development and expansion. The emerging economies have in common the establishing of sound governments, not subject to revolutions, that will provide the basis for the establishment of industry and trained labor forces.

The objective for the emerging and developing countries is establishing a viable welfare utility function so that industry, government, and labor can work together to provide economic growth and development, bringing these countries into the business cycle pattern in which growth and economic expansion are the ultimate consequences. The objective of the developed economies is to establish sufficient confidence and opportunities to withdraw from the reliance on the welfare system and move into a system that encourages private enterprise. The Great Depression is over, and although the developed economies will continue to experience business cycles, industry, government, and labor can do much to use the cycles to remove the dependence on welfare. Indeed, welfare is a negative aspect of the Western economic system, one that was not meant to be and that had been introduced as an alternative to coping with the business cycle's recessions and depressions.

Trading requires economic strength as expressed by production and marketing. Hence, the ultimate objective of the world's economies is to become strong trading partners, with goods and services that can move with relative ease across international borders. The multinationals and customs unions are methods for encouraging trading, but ultimately it is the economies themselves that must have the strength to engage in trade. The multinationals must rely on their base country and the performances of their branches in their host countries, and this, in turn, depends on the strength of their hosts' economies. Customs unions must rely on the productive and marketing ability of their members, and this means the viability of the single member economies. And countries not relying on multinationals and customs unions—usually the emerging and developing economies—have to rely on their ability to generate growth through imitation and then innovation to be able to compete internally and externally. The promise of 1993 and beyond holds that the world will generate the highest levels of output and consumption in history; it also holds the premonition that, if not properly nurtured, the world's economies will be in chaos, emphasizing finance and paper profits and not genuine productivity and domestic and international commerce in the trading of goods and services. This premonition is based on a similar situation of the past era, that of the 1920s, with the consequence being the Great Depression. How multinationals, customs unions, and trading countries can handle the situation of our present time is the subject of the remaining chapters.

Chapter 9

CIRCA 1992:
MULTINATIONAL
CORPORATIONS

In a society that measures itself by the criteria of profits and product and
that believes in social regulation based on the fear of hunger and the love
of gain, the line between public and private will always be blurred, for the
functions of state and corporation overlap. The behavior of both is determined primarily by economic goals.

—Richard J. Barnett and Ronald E. Müller,
Global Reach

One of the lessons learned from the Industrial Revolution, and which holds
significant importance in our contemporary era, is that a society cannot be
measured—either by itself or by other societies—by the criteria of profits and
product alone. It is true that every society, regardless of its state of development, implements social regulation based on the fear of hunger and the love of
gain. Even societies torn by civil war seek to maintain the economic advantage
over hunger and stress to emphasize gain, either through their own productive
capacities, or through world aid. But even in these societies there is more than
just the economic and military struggles. Moreover, while the line between the
public and private sectors seems to be blurred, and while the functions of the
state and the corporations appear to overlap, there are clear and obvious distinctions between them. Corporations are in business to earn profits and governments must regulate the economies in which corporations exist. Where there

is overlapping, it exists because of the cycle's position, so that governments cool down the economies when they become overheated, that is, when prosperity slows down but consumer prices increase because of the constant demand and a reduction in production, and when the economies enter too deeply in recession, whereby governments trade off between increasing unemployment and burden on their welfare systems and applying monetary and fiscal policies to stimulate investment so that production can increase and unemployment decrease accordingly.

The behavior of both governments and corporations are determined primarily by economic goals, but these are most certainly not how societies are to be measured. There are other criteria for such measurement, such as artistic and scientific contributions. Moreover, these are necessary for industry to develop and expand. Art can be reinterpreted in packaging and in the very designs of products; science merges with industry in the form of technology—it was this merger that began the Industrial Revolution and maintains industrial development in our era. Science also merges with art in the designing of products, such as automobiles that are manufactured for their aesthetic appeal and for their styles that allow for efficient forms of transport.

To be correct, then, it must be stated that while the behavior of governments and corporations is determined primarily by economic goals, it does not mean that these are the goals by which societies measure themselves or are measured by others.

However, it is with respect to these economic goals that Richard J. Barnett and Ronald E. Müller wrote that the global corporation, that is, the multinational corporation, is "the first institution in human history dedicated to central planning on a world scale."[1] Because the primary purpose of the multinational corporation is to organize and integrate economic activity around the world in such a way to maximize global profits, Barnett and Müller maintain that the multinational as a global structure is expected to serve the whole. What the managers of the multinationals are seeking, then, is to challenge the concept of the nation-state by which national boundaries are drawn and in the process, transform it by transcending national borders.

In light of contemporary economics and the real challenges facing the modern world with respect to the changes that are occurring in the world markets and the formulation of the Common Market in Europe, some further thinking on multinationals must be undertaken. Any serious transformation of the world's economy will occur in 1992, in which Europe's nation-states will relinquish much of their economic and political sovereignty to a greater Europe, united by common economic interests. Indeed, the changes under way in the economies of the Soviet Union and Eastern Europe have, to a large extent, been undertaken in order to provide viable national competition to the European Economic Community, perhaps restructuring the Comecon when each economy is viable and productive, to provide an alternative for the world's markets. In this situation, multinationals that are European-based and with branches in other Common Market countries will be subjected to the economic regulations for the Community as a whole, so that those managers with the ambitions assigned to them by Barnett and Müller will not be able to realize them in the Community framework.

What is not in question is that the branches of the multinationals are there to serve the whole, for this is certainly the reason for the existence of the multinationals. They, like any other business, seek profits through sales, and their presence in different countries is because of the availability to obtain the benefits of on-the-spot location for international commerce. Also, the work force is sufficient to be employed, and the general economic conditions are such that placing a branch in the respective countries is profitable. These profits are returned to the head company through international banking transactions, but they are also susceptible to currency fluctuations. As Richard E. Caves has pointed out, exchange-rate fluctuations confront the multinationals with problems not only of market behavior, but also with their information systems, "how to assess and report changes in their asset values when exchange rates change."[2] He points out that this issue has greatly bothered corporate accountants for the reason that the correct analysis depends on forecasting what the present exchange rate portends for future exchange rates, as well as for local-currency prices abroad. The value of the foreign currencies earned from multinational activities, when translated into the base-country's currency determines to a large extent the profit rate achieved and contributes to the assessment of the branch companies' performances.

With respect to this, the domestic firm trading internationally is at an advantage because of its flexibility. Where markets are such that fluctuating exchange rates deem the trading nonprofitable, the process can be halted once all obligations are met. The multinational cannot exert this degree of flexibility because of the investment in fixed plant and production equipment for its lines of production. Obligations, once met, have to be considered with respect to other possibilities, and this requires either innovation, imitation, or both, according to the understanding of the managers in the field and with consent of the head office. In this sense, the multinational functions as both a domestic-based firm and as a multinational receiving permission for initiating programs by the home-based company.

What is in question is the political influence of the multinationals, their positions within their respective host countries, and the attitudes of some of their top managers. For example, consider this statement made by Barnett and Müller: "The central strategy of the global corporation is the creation of a global economic environment that will ensure stability, expansion, and high profits for the planetary enterprise."[3] This very strategy goes against the dynamics of contemporary economics, for disequilibrium prevents stability, the phasing out of entropic imitative products inhibits expansion in their respective markets, and profits are controlled by local and international competition. The managers of multinationals are well aware of these conditions, even though they, like the directorates of all businesses, try to override them.

As for their political influence, they have such influence in proportion to their economic strength, and this is with respect to each country in which they operate. But this is the same situation with every heavy industrial company. The image of the multinational paying off politicians for economic favors is not without question, for in those countries in which a corrupt atmosphere prevails, such paying off is "part of the game" and is not limited only to the multinationals.

As for the overall global strategy as stated by Barnett and Müller, multinationals seek to be global enterprises in the same manner that domestic industries seek to outperform their competitors and eventually close them down. Such globality, even when restricted to local markets, is unachievable, because of the nature of competition. A firm cannot be all things to all consumers all of the time, and competition makes up for this lack of universality. Moreover, competition provides incentives for innovation and imitation for the benefit of consumers, allowing them to allocate their liquidity according to their tastes and the possibilities on the markets. Seeking market domination, whether domestic or global, is certainly a force in economics, for this is, in fact, competition and the consumers benefit from its dynamics. To imply more from this globalistic competitive drive, such as the usurping of the local economics and converting them into branches of the multinationals, is to neglect the nature of the nation-state and its relationship to the multinationals.

The nation-state had its origins in the sixteenth century with the breaking down of the feudal system. With the migrations of peoples, however, the emphasis has been on the state, with the nation being subservient to the laws and political processes that have evolved. It is peoples, and not nations, that have become subjected to the state's rule. Michel Foucault pointed out that the state is continuously developing. He wrote:

But most of the time, the state is envisioned as a kind of political power which ignores individuals, looking only at the interests of the totality, or, I should say, of a class or a group among the citizens. That's quite true. But I'd like to underline the fact that the state's power (and that's one of the reasons for its strength) is both an individualizing and a totalizing form of power. Never, I think, in the history of human societies—even in the old Chinese society—has there been such a tricky combination in the same political structures of individualization techniques and totalization procedures.[4]

In other words, it is the state, or country, that has the authority to license the multinationals, and as they are strictly economic organizations without individualizing and totalizing forms of power, they are subservient to the authorities of the countries in which they operate. As the multinationals are competitors with the domestic industries, checks are placed on them from gaining the type of economic power that can influence political decision making; these checks being the very dynamics of competition with the domestic industries and with other multinationals that are in the same country.

The question must be asked about the reasons for the existence of the multinationals, if they function within a country in the same manner as other competitors. In other words, why should domestic industries spread out into other countries, and why should these countries accept them as competitors for their own industries? Moreover, can there be a conflict of interest between the host country and the multinational? Multinationals exist to facilitate the international commerce of the home industry. A firm engaged in trading must meet the receiving country's requirements of being able to compete effectively when tariffs are levied; they must also meet the shipping dates and quality control standards. The exporting company has to take into account the labor situation in its own country and must also register its profits from the exchange in terms of the foreign currencies received from its international transactions, and with the volatile fluctuations in currency exchange rates, profitability may be reduced.

Multinationals tend to lessen these difficulties. A firm engaged in competition is on location and does not have to worry about problems of labor and meeting due dates that other firms are freed from; all firms in the economy have the same type of problems. The multinational in the domestic economy does not have to determine its profits with respect to tariffs, nor does the issue of tariffs have any effect on its competitive position. With respect to the exchange rate differences, Richard E. Caves has written:

Exchange-rate variations confront the MNE [multinational enterprise] with problems not only of market behaviour but also of their information systems—how to assess and report changes in their asset values when exchange-rates change. This issue has already greatly bothered corporate accountants for the good reason that the right answer depends on forecasting on what today's change in exchange rates portends for future exchange rates as well as for future local-currency prices abroad.[5]

Accountants describe a corporate's standing with respect to the corporate's financial position; they also represent the corporate at the various government tax, national insurance, and where applicable, value tax offices. Neither accountants nor economists are prophets and hence have no real wisdom concerning future exchange rates in the home or base countries. What economists can do, however, is advise on how to secure the earnings in light of uncertainty of the direction the exchange rates may take. Various savings and investment programs with short- and long-term returns as well as arbitrage can protect the earnings, which can be transferred to the home corporation when the exchange rate is profitable. Finding the programs that provide the best interest without diminishing the corporation's liquidity in the host countries is a task for economists; they also have to determine the most opportune time to transfer the earnings to the home country, given the money invested and used in arbitrage transactions.

What must be dispelled is the myth that the multinationals seek to exploit their host economies. They are licensed to operate in the host economies on the basis of their competitive ability and their contributions in the way of output and employment to the host countries. There is no altruism here, and competition with the domestic companies prevents the multinationals from relying on the base country for support—the base country corporation has similar competition and its resources must also be utilized to obtain the maximum utility at the lowest possible cost.

This myth, however, is at its strongest in the emerging and developing countries where domestic competition is either weak or nonexistent and with the multinationals seen as "exploiting" the working classes and plundering the economy of its resources to serve the host country's ambitions. In the developing and emerging economies, these emotive terms cannot be dismissed lightly, especially with a multinational that becomes an important employer and manufacturer. Caves discussed three categories of multinationals operating in the developing and emerging countries. These are: the exporters of natural resources and resource-based products, the exporters of manufactured goods or components, and producers largely engaged in serving in the domestic markets of their host countries.[6] To this a fourth category has to be added, that being producers engaged in production in the markets of their host countries and using the host countries' locations to export to neighboring countries. The reasons for antagonism to the multinationals in the developing and emerging countries are important to consider, as they have a strong basis in the economic realities of these countries, and to some extent influence the future directions that are to be taken.

The reasons are threefold: First, there is the awareness that the industry to which people owe their livelihoods, is not really rooted in the country, but holds its allegiance to a corporative head office in another country, to which the profits derived from their labor will eventually flow. There is also the awareness that the level of development of the country bears directly on the level of political influence that the multinational has. Third, there is the awareness that the multinational is not theirs, that because of their economic circumstances they have to rely on the multinational for economic activity.

The first point is valid to the extent that the allegiance and the final flow of profits are possessed by the head corporation. It is not valid in the sense that the multinational's existence in the country depends on its ability to meet its production and marketing requirements, and this depends on its ability to employ workers and provide them with sufficient incentives to make their employment in the company worth their while. If the company profits, then so will its employees, and while the hostility may still exist, it is tempered by the personal economic benefits that it can provide, if successful.

The second point is valid to the extent that the multinational needs to be involved politically. In countries where political and economic influence are equated, opening up the company in this type of host country usually requires financial compensation to the country's rulers. This is calculated as an "operating cost" and the necessity to continuing these payments is certainly weighed against the advantages of going into the country. Moreover, should the decision be taken to move into the country, it is also undertaken with the awareness that in a situation where political and economic interests are equated, more than one politician may be able to support the corporation through payments, and that interests may be best suited by playing off one politician against the other.

These types of countries are usually unstable and subject to the periodic civil war. But, because of the multinational's political and economic interest and influence, and—more to the point—because of its impact on the economy in providing employment and stimulating market dynamics, it is usually unscathed in these recurring military dramas. In spite of this, though, multinationals seek more tranquil situations in which to operate, to the loss of the peoples in these countries.

The third point is certainly valid, and this, because of patriotism, results in antagonism. But the multinational is in the country because it serves its interests as well as the interests of its host, so that while patriotism cannot be ignored, it is to the benefit of the host and the multinational that it is there. Moreover, once the consequences of the multinational's economic position are realized, the antagonism may be somewhat cooled. The employment it provides, the liquidity it injects into the economy, and the auxiliary businesses that develop because of it, lead to the establishment of viable market economies that will eventually lift the economy from the emerging and developing levels to being full and equal competitors with the developed economies. Patriotism, in this situation, is best channeled into building up the domestic economy in light of the multinationals' presence and influences.

With respect to these presences and influences, Caves discussed two models of multinationals with respect to public policy, on the basis of five neoclassical welfare assumptions:

1. each government seeks to maximize the real income of its citizens;

2. decisions about income distribution are made separately from those concerning the maximization of income to be distributed;

3. each national enterprise is assumed to have an ambiguous national citizenship, so that its policies toward profits can be considered in terms of the national currency with the maximized profits as part of national income;

4. the multinationals have a downward-facing demand curve because of their unique assets, while the host countries have upward-facing supply curves;

5. each country makes its policy decisions on multinationals as either their sources or their hosts.

With these assumptions, Caves discussed the national preference model, which assumes a strong democratic system, in which elected officials seeking to maintain power propose packages of measures expected to appeal to the voting majority. The voters as producers may hold various shares in factor services they supply, but it is assumed that the factor services yielded by the multinationals do not reach domestic voters. As foreign workers in the multinationals cannot vote, redistributing the income gained from multinational enterprises will reduce the burden on the citizens and impose it to the equal extent on the multinationals, which have no say in the matter.

The second model, that of government policy, shifts the emphasis from the utility-maximizing electoral behavior to the utility of a coalition of officials who pursue numerous policies but lack the policy instruments sufficient to attain them. Perhaps powerful interest groups restrict the attainment of these policies; perhaps they are restricted by the norm of convention or by constitutional considerations. The government tries periodically to change the economic allocation resulting from market transactions, often lacking the ability to carry these changes out, but if multinationals enjoy better economic allocation than the nationals, they draw attention of the government and their lack of national status makes them fair game for conducting economic reallocation through taxation, with the whip of restricting their practices if opposition is expressed. In each model, the lack of national status makes the multinational in the host country a prime target for the redistribution of their income.[7]

Caves's argument with respect to public policy is valid if his five welfare assumptions are accepted. It is held here, however, that these assumptions are highly questionable. First, individuals try to maximize their incomes through bargaining and through being represented in labor organizations; the role of government in the welfare situation is to maintain a viable economic atmosphere, relating industry and labor into a working coalition. Second, government decisions about income distribution, either through taxation or through investing in local infrastructure, influence both income distribution and the ability of the recipients to maximize their incomes. The third point is accepted, with the reservation that enterprises engaged in foreign trade—either domestic or multinational—deal primarily with the country's currency in which they reside. Fourth, both multinationals and domestic enterprises have the same type of supply and demand curves, for a multinational that is not economically profitable in a host country will be closed down. The shifting of resources depends on the multinational's ability to maintain a competitive and profitable position with respect to both domestic and foreign competitors. The fifth point is accepted with the reservation that while countries make their policies concerning multinationals as either hosts or their sources, the prime requirement that is to be met by the multinationals is the benefits in terms of employment, revenue, and output the multinationals can supply.

Hence, Caves's treatment of multinationals as prey for governments in taxation and income redistribution has to be modified. They exist in countries because it is to their mutual advantage, and if multinationals are overly exploited, they can relocate in countries more hospitable.

Multinationals serve in public policy the way that domestic firms serve. They are incorporated into the economy and are therefore classified within the *I* sector of the welfare utility function. In this sense they contribute to the economy in competition and as innovators and imitators, subject to the same dynamics of the economy's business cycle and the same types of choices of opting for liquidity or production. Agreement is reached between the branch company and its head office on policies when the head office understands the local market situation and the stage of the economy's cycle, as well as the company's profit position. This operates in the same way as those companies in the domestic market; the only difference is the location of the head office.

Multinationals are thus to be represented in a country's international utility function, because they operate within the country, are subject to its rules and laws, and contribute and respond to the economy's market dynamics. Like domestic firms, they base their business practices not on altruism but on the profit motive. They may move into an area of a country where markets are nonexistent and build them up, providing employment and liquidity in the area, or they may locate in a highly industrialized area to take advantage of its amenities; the final decisions are taken by the home office. Market research is undertaken as with the domestic firms, and the multinational's ability to manufacture, given the domestic conditions, is also considered. This is sound policy and is incorporated into the multinational's information system and provides part of the basis of the firm's operations—the other part being the dynamics that are generated because of the operation and the information system's ability to allow changes to be incorporated. Flexibility here is just as important as with the domestic firms, and it may be somewhat restricted because of the flow of information from the host to the head office. The difficulties of information flow can be overcome through modern technology and accurate detailing.

Multinationals are not new; they are a product of the Industrial Revolution and existed when oil companies established firms in different countries. Since then they have expanded, with many multinationals now existing, each remaining in its host country on the basis of profitability and its socioeconomic contribution. If there is resentment in seeing a Japanese firm in an American city, or a French company on German soil, it is due to the irrationality of nationalism, inbred in the world's cultures since the forming of the nation-states. Multinationals are effective in producing and marketing goods and services and they survive only if they are competitive. In our era of knowledge, however, irrationality still exists and often conflicts with reason, and arguments against multinationals are based on nationalism and not on sound economic thinking.

Chapter 10

CIRCA 1992:
CUSTOMS UNIONS

One consequence of the reluctance of nations to move toward full integration of capital markets is a tendency to seek solutions for payments pressures in enlarged international reserves.

—J. C. Ingram,
"Some Implications of Puerto Rican Experience"[1]

The year 1992 is that given for the European Economic Community to consol-
idate into a full customs union. Hence, the dream of conquerors throughout the
continent's history will be realized, with the final consummation of European
unity.

The question as to why such consolidation will occur in 1992, when the best
armies in Europe could not impose such unity, is related to another question,
that being why the EEC has been so successful, while the Eastern bloc customs
union, the Comecon, has not.

The answer to these questions is, in fact, twofold: Conquerors offer nothing
to the conquered except their existence; apart from this, the motivation to work
for the conqueror is lacking. The wars of conquest, from the ancient Roman
Empire to the slaughter of World War II, were conducted on the principle of
unification and domination. This is certainly not the basis for forming a viable
economic structure capable of high quality production and rigorous competition
with the industrialized nonunion countries. Hence, the failure of the Comecon

to compete effectively with the European Community because the Comecon was dominated by the Soviet Union, and the union was forged into existence to primarily serve Soviet interests.

The inability to force unification through domination is one reason, therefore, that the dream of conquerors of a unified Europe never materialized. Indeed, through the consummation of a solid economic agreement, the centuries of nationalism and mistrust are being placed aside, with nations relinquishing their economic sovereignty to some extent to the greater entity of a united Europe.

The second reason that more nations do not form customs unions is expressed to some extent by the opening quote by Ingram. Customs unions require the integration of capital markets, unifying them ultimately into a single-currency market. Nations are reluctant to merge their capital markets because they seek to obtain foreign currencies through trading, to maintain a mercantilistic favorable balance of trade. Through the merger of capital markets, these countries lose their leverage as the markets of those countries they have merged with operate with a common currency so that trading among the partners does not enrich the foreign currency holdings with respect to the partners. By merging the capital markets, there is a resignation of national independence to the greater body of the union; countries that do not join such unions seek to maintain their economic and political independence and to control their own destinies.

The arguments for customs unions are very convincing, especially in our era of knowledge, when high technology is extremely competitive and the duplication of products tends to be wasteful. But for Europe, there is the reason that after centuries of national animosity and war, and especially after the two world wars in which the slaughter and devastation were unacceptable by the combatants, it was realized that while nationalism would not be diminished, it could be rechanneled into a greater Europe that could be competitive with the United States and China, should the latter be aroused from its domestic slumber and become a viable economic force.

Charles Kindleberger explains that a customs union differs from a free-trade area in that the customs union "adopts a single common external tariff, while the free-trade area countries all retain their individual tariff walls vis-à-vis the outside world but remove tariffs among themselves."[2] Customs unions may adopt associate trading countries, reducing the tariffs on their products in exchange with a mutual reduction by the associate, to facilitate commerce between the two. For developing and emerging countries this is important because it enables their economies to organize for trading with the unions; in doing so, however, revenues from the absence of taxation are lost. The governments of the emerging and developing countries have to decide which is more valuable for their economies, and wise administrators will certainly decide for the associate status, providing that they have products that are wanted by the union members and that trading will not affect more than marginally the competitive positions of the member countries, so that some resources are released for production elsewhere.

There is another issue for consideration by the emerging and developing countries. The customs unions are formidable markets capable of producing at highly competitive rates. To supply them with products that they already produce can be seen as an act of "charity" on their part, because to accept in trade products that they already have or that are of only marginal utility is to assist the developing and emerging countries' industries. However, it also provides the psychological reenforcement of these industries, which might be advantageous to the long-run development of these countries' industrial growth. They too seek diversification in production through the establishment of business cycle patterns and the stimulation of innovation and imitation. One consequence of this is the tendency for these countries to merge into a customs union to compete with Europe and the United States. While such difficulties as geographical location and political differences have to be considered, the economic advantages may make such a move worth the while as their industries develop internally and become competitive. In their situation national pride has not developed over centuries and the newness of their countries may allow them to break down any political barriers that may exist. Europe can indeed be an example, even though in the best of situations the geographical conditions present a formidable obstacle.

Customs unions are not evolved political and economic entities, as is the United States, for example, but are formed through agreements among the members as to their respective economic relationships, with the political considerations being formed and—with the success of the economic relationships—indeed evolving in the process. There are important internal problems that have to be overcome, however, for the union to become a viable trading bloc. These problems pertain to the economics of each member in its relationship with the entire union. Consider the European Community, for example. While their membership has, for most of the countries, been of long standing, the union is to be finalized in 1992 as both an economic and a political entity. Great Britain and France have their own unique economic conditions, and the unification of the two Germanies and their difficulties in overcoming the differences in their economies and work ethics, pose difficulties for the union. Great rivalries, too often manifested on the fields of battle and now in economic competition, have to be quelled for the mutual benefit of the members. This can be done somewhat with the establishment of tariffs acceptable to all and with the issuance of a currency common to each of the members. The real difficulty, however, lies within the internal dynamics of each country.

It must be understood that within a customs union, even a single currency acceptable to all its members is subject to regulation within each country. The variations of the U.S. dollar's value, with respect to its purchasing power and interest rates within that country, were resolved by the formation of the Federal Reserve Board with its twelve districts, and each regulated by a representative

Federal Reserve Bank. Europe does not have such a banking system, so each economy operates on its own production schedules with output accorded to projected demand. This may be fine for an independent country that seeks export markets, but quota systems and traditional production motivation will just not work smoothly. Hence, when British farm produce exceeds what the French farmers consider the limit allowed by agreements, dumping of British produce by angry French farmers occurs. In other words, agreements cannot determine markets, but market dynamics can. The problem is that the British economy operates on its own terms, and so does the French, German, and those of the other members. Just as within the United States there are differences in regional output, with goods and services flowing to where they are most in demand, the internal economies of the union members operate similarly. They do not operate as to allow the flow of goods and services freely across national boundaries as they do within the United States.

Quotas are established on the basis of politics, while output is based on the utility perceived from output. Even in agriculture, farmers have destroyed their crops if their remuneration was not sufficient, and animals have been slaughtered if their prices were too low. The point is that, quotas withstanding, countries—industries within each country—will produce according to the understanding of the utilities of production as expressed in their information systems. Customs unions may try to impose quotas, but they have to consider the value of the currency within each country, as the finance ministers regulate the interest rates to insure the highest investment, the best interest, and the best conditions for trading. Quotas will yield to the economics of each situation and while, in the esprit of cooperation they may be upheld, the demands of economic conditions, each country's international utility function, will bring about independent responses according to the situation.

This does not mean that the customs union as a near-ideal market situation is inherently economically unsound. On the contrary, its idealism stems from the fact that the customs union is the second-best situation to free trade. Quotas may exist, but they do not prohibit the flows of goods and services within the quotas' limits. Nor do they restrict the movement of labor across national boundaries as jobs are sought and skilled people employed. Moreover, the unrestricted flow of resources across national boundaries, without tariffs or other restrictions, is to the benefit of the union as a whole. For while enriching the industries in one country through the uses of these resources, the entire union benefits. Importing goods and services from nonmember countries will allow these imports to flow to the regions most in need. And where competition among the countries does exist, the industries will regulate their output to the free markets of the union as understood through market research and the de facto demand for their products. For markets in imitation this is fine. Their unity allows for internal development and the common currency provides for the ease of purchasing among all the union's citizenry.

There are, however, more considerations in the customs union than these.

For while the union is a near free-trade area within, it is subject to the rigors of international competition, as well as to the dynamics of innovation and imitation within, with each country operating according to its own unique international utility function. Moreover, the unrestricted movement of labor and resources aids each country, each region of the union, as its sectors undergo the process of innovation and imitation.

Nevertheless, with each member country having its own rich history and economic position, each country will experience its own economic dynamics with innovation and imitation occurring primarily for the domestic markets and with exports first to the other members and then to foreign countries not in the union. While the absence of import restrictions and the abolition of tariffs make the importing of innovations among the union members easy, once imitation sets in among the members import quotas will be established; the consequence is that the member countries have to look outside the union to export surplus imitative products. In this sense, internal competition is restricted, and with many imitators, resources are used inefficiently. Hence, protection of domestic markets from union competitors, through the political process of establishing quotas, certainly hinders the functioning of the second-best alternative to free trade. This restriction on competition protects those industries that are unable to compete effectively within the union and are thus restricted in their competition outside the union in the arena of international trade. Under nonunion conditions such industries would be protected and therefore not worry about their inability to compete successfully, or if unprotected they would shift their market orientation into production lines that would yield profits, instead of continuing producing at lower profits or at a loss.[3]

The historical differences and conflicts are always difficult to overcome, to be placed aside for the benefit of the greater union. However, even when this is accomplished there are other difficulties that have to be considered. One is the unique cycle of each member country, developed over the years of economic independence and the effects these cycles have on each member country. This is not like the United States which may have one depressed regional area while others are in various phases of cyclical dynamics. Indeed, with respect to this, the U.S. government, given its welfare utility function, can invest in the depressed area, while industry may find the pool of skilled workers and low wage acceptance to its benefit to enter into the area. No such mobility exists within common markets, as they are unions of sovereign countries and they will not allow a central economic body or foreign industry to move into their countries with the ease that exists in the United States. National pride and the weight of history tell against this freedom of movement. How common markets evolve will be known as their futures unravel through time. But their present difficulties are certainly real and overcoming them will take more than an act of political decision making.

Countries joined in union but experiencing different cyclical phases affect the intensity of aggregate union output and demand. A unified Germany, for example, may be producing far more than Great Britain, while the French may not want to purchase too much of either country's products because of recession. With the French markets in recession, Germany's sales are reduced, even to the other members as their sales to Great Britain and France are likewise affected, regardless of their cyclical positions. Of course, the solution to this difficulty is to export outside the union, but this may raise other difficulties.

One such difficulty is the competition with imitative industries of the union as they seek sales for the same reason. Instead of the harmony of the second-best to free trade, union members will be competing rigorously among themselves in the nonunion exporting markets, while maintaining a harmonic relationship within the union. The difficulty here is in the political arrangement, in other words, in the procedures that have been established that prevent the breakup of the union over situations such as this. Again, the weight of history and of nationalism may be too great for the political arrangements to bear and the union may collapse.

This is not like competing industries in the United States seeking to export to the same countries. The difference is that the mobility of these industries and their information systems can bring about shifts in market orientation and that competing is not a matter of national pride for each industry. Economic ego plays a role, of course, and where competition is not successful, markets can be shifted. National ego, however, is another matter, so that the industries of one country not in a customs union will result in a reorientation of priorities, while competition among union members may result in patriotic calls for succession and the economic unfurling of the flag. This is a serious situation and one that can be of potential crisis. The economic and political leaders of the customs union have to deal with this, considering its various scenarios with astuteness and wisdom.

Another such difficulty is the matter of currency for the customs union. Again, nationalism enters into this situation, and for the betterment of the union, nationalism, which has been nurtured over the generations, in which the praises of the nation have been inculcated into the historical mythos and conscience and the attributes of other countries placed in negative and highly exaggerated contexts, has to be repressed for the greater good. This, of course, was the main reason for the debate among the British subjects about entering the common union with Europe; Great Britain's geographical isolation has kept it apart from Europe, even though it was involved in much of Europe's strife and development. Compromising this nationalism for the greater European union thus brought heated debates in the news media, in the Parliament, and in the streets.

To alter a country's currency for the greater good of a customs union is a psychological factor that the economic and political leaders of a customs union have to consider. For the French to abolish their paper currency, with its great writers and artists on its notes, and for the British to forego their currency with the monarch's picture for a paper currency not reflecting the British uniqueness, require great nationalist sacrifices on the part of these people—it was enough for the British to reject its system of the shilling at 12 pence with 20 shillings to the pound for the metric standard, with the pound at 100 new pence. But the current British peg of the pound sterling to the German deutsche mark with a 6 percent float either way, is insufficient for a genuine unification of the customs union. The separate currencies of the members are incorporated into their international utility functions; as long as these currencies remain unique to their countries, their I_ts will also be individual and unique. In other words, the unification necessary for such a union to perform according to its requirements will be chimerical and unattainable—with the British currency pegged to the German currency, to what is the deutsche mark pegged?

A country's economic position with respect to trade is based on its international utility function; as this function is composed of the welfare utility function and the country's currency, countries united in a customs union cannot have a national currency for the union to be economically viable as a trading bloc. Using the analogy of the United States again, it is as if each state in the union had its own currency and control over it. The United States would lose its position as a world-trading country as each state would conduct its own trading policies, with its own tariffs and currency regulations. The country as a united political and economic entity would not last for long and would be fractured into its states' borders, with treaties being conducted and the threat of war persistent as the balance of economic power shifted from state to state.

As a country holds control over its own currency, its issuance, its inflation, banking policies, and investment climate, it determines its currency pegging, its timing and rate of devaluation, its tariff policies and trade agreements. The idea of the customs union is to abolish the differences of these policies among the members so that a common trading policy can be formulated both within the union and with respect to nonunion countries and other trading blocs. For these common policies can take hold only when there is a single currency representing the union's countries. Each country has its own cyclical movement, and the closer economically countries become there is a tendency for the cycles to be in phase. Economic closeness requires more than the free movement of labor and resources and the removal of trade barriers, even though quotas may be agreed upon. It requires a common currency for such union, for the cooperation necessary for the union to work. With a common currency the union's economic and political leaders can establish the union's policies without the interference of currency fluctuations and unilateral actions to alter currency parities and floats. The only arbitrage that would occur is the movement of a common currency in regions of the union offering the highest interest rates and the best investment conditions. This will generate internal competition—such as exists within the geographical areas of the United States—and thereby increasing monetary utility and efficiency will benefit the citizens of the union. Hence, instead of as many currencies as there are countries in the union, each with its own exchange rate and pegged to a float on whatever currency is decided upon, there will be a single currency, whose strength is dependent on the economic output and potential of the union.

With this condition, then, the member countries will find their cycles coming together in phase, operating as a single country. With resources and labor being mobile, without the restrictions of borders, they will move into regions that provide the best conditions, thereby easing regions in which economic difficulties become apparent. The members' I_is will then move into phase and form a single international utility function that can be approached with respect to industry, government, and labor—the sectors of the welfare utility function—and to the common currency, regulating the economy as best as possible to reduce unemployment, increase industrial efficiency through internal and foreign competition, and provide a strong basis for labor participation in building the economies of the member countries.

With the various cultures and the different industries represented by a customs union there is a unique strength in their diversity. This strength is manifested in their unity, with the benefits of near-free trade among the members and the economic power generated within and by the quality, quantity, and terms of trade with the rest of the world. The reluctance that Ingram wrote of would then be overcome by the single currency in the union that is traded for the remaining currencies in the world. Moreover, through trading, the transactions take place in the currencies of the trading partners, so that the union countries will obtain foreign reserves, while the trading partners will obtain the common union currency, it too serving as foreign reserves to the trading countries.

There are many difficulties in the forming of a customs union. These difficulties are both economic and administrative: how the union will be regulated, what terms of trade are to be given by the union's trading partners, under what conditions will new members and associate members be accepted into the union, and from which countries and under what conditions of rotation are terms of administration to be established. While unions evolve into political entities, their reasons for coming into existence are strictly economic and their functioning remains primarily on the economic foundations. Moreover, customs unions are formed usually on the basis of geography—the British Commonwealth, a form of customs union, is the exception—and the geographical factor is important in uniting countries in a common economic bond, providing that political animosity does not prevent this. Customs unions are perhaps the direction to be taken as resources in the new industrial concepts become esoteric. Profits are more easily obtainable in this calculation, if internal trade is free while external trade remains highly competitive. Customs unions may, therefore, be the trend of the future in international trade.

There are many political trends in our contemporary era. There is the formation of the European Community, the questionable status of Comecon, the thawing of Eastern Europe, the development of many of the Asian countries with the possibility of a future customs union forming there, and this with the occasional awakening of the great Chinese people to their economic potential. There are the conflicts in Africa and the development difficulties that seem to be pernicious in the South American continent. The Middle East is a special situation, one of great economic potential but with conflicts whose roots go back to prehistory and the ancient Bible. With the development of knowledge systems and industrial output, among all the international confusion there seems to be an overriding trend of a world slowly moving into a unifying pattern, one where the economics of international trade are bringing countries with common interests to the point of overcoming their conflict and working together in an economic relationship. This is happening in Europe, where the last great war served as a major battleground, and because of the strength of the European Community, the rest of the world is watching to see the lessons to be learned and to understand how they too can benefit from trading with the Community and perhaps form their own customs unions. In this sense, the year 1992 represents a watershed for the world's countries as the European Community will be a trading force of great importance, setting the example for all other geographical regions willing to enter into such beneficial economic arrangements.

Chapter 11

TRADE FOR A
DEVELOPED ECONOMY

The more developed an economy, the greater the integration among its industrial, governmental, and labor sectors. This integration is expressed in the dynamics of the welfare utility function. However, this integration differs from that of the former Eastern bloc countries with their centralized planning boards and quotas from each industry in terms of output. Certainly there was full integration in these countries, but it was not the kind conducive to economic growth. This integration did not allow for innovation and imitation to be initiated by the various industries' directorates, and hence they did not generate the shifts in consumer liquidity and in the stimulation for new and better products. They did not stimulate demand competition for liquidity. Indeed, in this type of integration, demand was planned by the respective authorities, as well as the amounts of goods and services produced to meet this demand. This "Say-like" situation was justified by the reason that the business cycle would not exist and unemployment would therefore be a condition of the Western countries.

The drive to eliminate the unemployment situation inherent with the business cycle's downward motion is certainly noble. Unemployment is one of the worst blights on the contemporary economy, one that not only results in the reduction of consumption, but also of personal self-esteem for those so affected by the cycle's downward motion.

The different approach to unemployment taken by the Eastern bloc and the Western countries (Japan is included in this category) account for the different results in the systems' performances. In our present time the Eastern bloc countries are abandoning their system for one of a less restricted economy, one in which the market forces are allowed to operate. This requires the reduction of planning by central authorities and the placing of the responsibility for production in the decision-making processes of the various firms' directorates. Hence, with the changing system, innovation, imitation, and trade on a private basis are coming into these economies.

Unemployment was restricted to frictional unemployment, for those who were relocating or were unable to work because of illness. The consequence was that quotas were indeed met, but black markets existed for people to purchase products of quality. Queues were the common shopping situation, with people arriving at the serving counter only to find that the goods and services were sold out. Production was not geared to compete for consumer liquidity, but to meet the requirements of output as directed by planning authorities.

With the European Community finally coming together as a viable customs union in 1992, the leadership in the Soviet Union sought to make their country competitive and able to trade with the Community. This required a complete revision of the planning system, breaking with a torturous past established by Josef Stalin, instilling private enterprises within the system. This was undertaken with the assumption that this enterprise built the Western countries into strong economic competitors, and if properly implemented it will eliminate the diseconomies of the Soviet Union as well, establishing powerful industries to compete effectively with the European Community in 1992 and beyond.[1] In spite of their system of unemployment and welfare, the Soviet Union and its Eastern bloc satellite countries were behind the capitalist Western and Western-oriented countries in economic growth and development.

Of course, in the Western capitalist countries, it was the market that determined production in quantity and quality. Throughout the development of the Industrial Revolution the economic system underwent changes, while remaining loyal to its market-system orientation. The development of industries made obsolete Smith's "invisible hand" regulator, and consumer fickleness in response to the various products available due to industrial expansion rendered Say's Law of Markets invalid, although it still retained its attraction in economic theory and is still incorporated in the body of economics concerned with static and dynamic equilibrium.

Unemployment became a function of the business cycle, and while it was always a blight whenever it occurred, it was only during the Great Depression that its impact became branded indelibly into the body of economic and political theory, never to be allowed to occur again in such intensity. The welfare systems in the Western countries were always present in their various forms according to the societies' social, political, and economic development. But only during the Great Depression did the paradox of unemployment exist, with massive productive capital and a strong and skilled labor force in the capitalist countries being idle, side by side. This brought about a revaluation of welfare, leading to social security (national insurance), and in Great Britain and France, an attempt to provide for socialized medicine.[2]

In the aftermath of World War II, when efforts were made to revive the world's economies, it was clearly understood that trade had obtained a major significance in world economic development. The beggar-thy-neighbor policies enacted during the depression attested to this, and the Bretton Woods Conference, the International Monetary Fund, and the World Bank were established to rectify the distortions taken in the world markets under the sincere but false pretext of protecting national industries and employment.

While the Eastern bloc countries maintained their welfare systems with full employment and accompanying social services, the Western countries still maintained their market systems while their national and local governing bodies were required by the social ethos to provide welfare services. They were considered as a negative aspect of the economic systems, to be used only when necessary. The positive aspect was for employment to be obtained, where people can earn their own livelihoods and contribute to the market system through their purchases. Moreover, through employment, industries produced sufficiently for those specific industries interested in trade to take their risks in foreign markets as well.

The concern for social welfare and for strong industry and a viable and up-dated work force led to the formulation of the welfare utility function, a concept that had existed in operation since the end of the war, but achieved its present form in response to the noncyclical recession brought about by the energy crisis following the Yom Kippur war.[3] By assuring strong industries, a government able to respond to the economy's requirements without impinging on individual liberties, and a labor force receiving benefits for its work and willing to adapt to changing production requirements, the welfare systems have been incorporated into the economies with the intention of reducing welfare and increasing employment and industrial output as consequences.

The extent of a country's economic development is determined by the extent of the working relationships among the industrial, governmental, and labor sectors of its economy. The close relationships among these sectors allow for industry to innovate and imitate, for labor to work according to its acceptance of industry's terms, and for government to act as the economic regulator, smoothing out the excesses of the business cycle. These relationships can function only in a market system, and the extent of the market's ability to absorb new products and to cast aside those for which consumption has declined significantly, indicates its strength and ability to produce and for its products to be consumed. The international utility function expresses this with the welfare utility function and the country's currency.

The value of currency is determined by the country's inflation rate and by the ability—actual and potential—for producing. The rate of inflation is regulated according to the welfare utility function. Industry that is efficient—and in competitive markets inefficient industry has a very short life-span—will produce for profit and sell competitively, thereby acting as a brake on inflation. Labor will bargain according to the pressures of its membership and its understanding of industry's ability to pay. Government will adapt monetary and establish fiscal policies that it considers will assist both industry and labor in the production processes.

The currency's value as determined by its actual and potential ability to produce is strictly for international commerce. A country with relative low output and internal scarcity will have a currency that is soft, not wanted in foreign transactions; its international commerce will have to be conducted in a currency of a country with strong industry and plenty in its markets.

Viable international utility functions are now being sought by the Eastern bloc countries. Their welfare utility functions did not allow for sound working relationships among the sectors, for all was established by central planning boards. There were no market mechanisms that indicated the need for innovation or that certain products were no longer profitable for continued production. Labor was employed, but the work produced lacked sufficient utility to maintain quality production; the goal was to meet the quantitive quotas established by the planning boards. Consumers could not exercise their rights of preference according to their personal utility orderings because the markets provided very little difference in the products, in their quantity and quality available—the long queues and insufficient supplies attested to this.

Their currencies were not used when trading with non-Comecon countries, because they were soft and had little or no value in the international markets. The exchange rate of the Soviet ruble was certainly exaggerated with respect to the dollar, but this was for the official exchange within the Soviet Union, for tourists who nevertheless sought the black market rate. The recent monetization of the ruble for international transactions, at rates both realistic and flexible, indicates the new confidence being gained because of the revitalization of the Soviet economy being undertaken with the inducements being provided for private enterprise. This is to alter the government's role in economic activity, changing it from being a planning board to one that regulates the dynamics of industrial production. This is to bring the industry and labor in line with the Western systems, that is, to establish a viable welfare utility function, so that an international utility function can be formed with the currency's status changing from not wanted to hard currency representing the potential of the industry that will be translated into actual competitive production for both the domestic and international markets.

The establishment of working welfare utility functions can be translated into international utility functions once their currencies are acceptable in foreign transactions. Hence, these countries must establish working relationships with the government, industry, and labor sectors that allow for innovation, imitation, and for labor being able to bargain for its wages. The Eastern bloc countries are thus undergoing great changes, diminishing the central planning authorities of their decision-making powers, and placing the emphasis on industry and the labor force to produce and compete. The changes are radical, given the context in which they are occurring. Their encouragement is due to the fact that the economies, as they were, certainly could not continue operating. The long queues for consumer goods and services, the loss of work time to purchase, the poor quality of merchandise compared to Western standards, and the awareness of the deficiencies due to travel as the world's political Cold War began its thaw, certainly resulted in dissatisfaction and the call for changes.

The second fact that brought about these changes is that the world's economic system itself is changing and without the ability to compete successfully, those countries operating on the premises of a system that never functioned well in any case will certainly lose out and be subject to internal dissension and perhaps revolution. There is the increasing need for strong foreign currency, for example, so that trade can be engaged in and the countries' own currencies can be protected with the backing of foreign reserves. There is also the possibility for foreign investment in the form of multinationals that can provide different emphases on the production processes and provide greater skills for the domestic labor force that can be transferred to other industries. Moreover, with the formation of the European Community in 1992 there will exist markets of great potential, for both importing and exporting. Not only will the internal movement of resources insure increased production, but there will also be the movement of imported goods and services, freely across national boundaries, once the initial tariffs are met. The Eastern bloc countries must undergo the necessary changes in order to compete within the European Community and to have its goods and services exported to the Eastern countries.

The changes they are undergoing will thus raise their economic positions, from being within a trading bloc that was inefficient and subservient to the demands of the greater trading partner, the Soviet Union, to being countries with strong and developed economies which, together with the Soviet Union if they so agree, can form an Eastern customs union that can compete viably with the European Community and the United States. The aim of these countries, and the other countries in various stages of economic development, is to reach the status and economic power of being developed countries. The only way this can be achieved—regardless of the differences in histories and cultures— is to establish viable and working welfare utility functions that can then transform their currencies into tradeable money. This will then be expressed within their established international utility functions on the basis of which trade will be conducted accordingly. But they will have economies capable of producing competitively and will have the goods and services with which to trade, as well as currencies that can be used for conducting the transactions.

COMMENTS ON THE UNITED STATES

The position of the United States in world trade is somewhat complex. If taken in its geopolitical boundaries and considered in strict economic terms, the United States can be conceived as a customs union consisting of forty-nine land-bound countries, or states in this case, each with its own constitution and political system, yet sharing with each other a common federal government that oversees their working with each other and their abilities to contribute to the common welfare of their citizens and to the union as a whole. With Alaska and Hawaii included, and with Puerto Rico having dominion status that might one day be translated into statehood, this economic and political body is a union of vast resources. Populated by both native Americans and immigrants and their descendants, the labor force is vast; due to its diversified population, it is also dynamic and productive. Its attraction has not waned and people continue to migrate to the country, to seek better political and economic circumstances.

Hence, its unique strengths have placed it in the center of world trade. Since the end of World War II it has operated largely on a help-thy-neighbor-there-fore-help-thyself policy, dictated by the circumstances of the Cold War. Its policies of aid have been dictated by both economic and political circum-stances, in competition with its Cold War enemies, the Soviet Union and Com-munist China. The United States has therefore allowed itself to be "used" by other countries to gain trading and aid concessions for their development—covertly or explicitly—when the communist countries were able and willing to be surrogates when the U.S. government did not respond appropriately.

With the Cold War coming to an end, and with the Soviet Union and Com-munist China opening up their countries for trade and seeking special trading terms with the United States, the situation is now different. The Cold War thaw has stimulated dynamics in politics and economics, the direction of which is somewhat uncertain. Romania and Hungary are trying to avoid hostilities, the African continent is uncertain of the systems its countries want while South Africa is slowly breaking from the apartheid that has hindered its economic development and made it a castaway in international politics, and moving re-luctantly and cautiously into the new era. There are certainly great changes occurring, and the focus for stability is on the United States and its powerful economy to provide aid and trade during these unstable times.

Trade is a result of industry seeking new markets. Where industry is re-strained by the economy's internal circumstances, trade is also restricted. Busi-nesses seek to have a degree of liquidity at their disposal after meeting costs. This liquidity is to provide the opportunity to maneuver between investing in new projects or holding liquidity in light of uncertainty or the consideration of further decisions. Liquidity held without earning interest or making a profit is liquidity whose value declines in light of profits earned from alternative uses. The interest received therefore depends on the utility of money. During reces-sions, when investment money is in demand, the interest received is relatively high; during prosperity, when in its early stages investments approach saturation given the existing possibilities, interest declines accordingly. However, given periods of global instability such as the world's nations are now experiencing, uncertainty is reflected in interest rates, high for loans and low for investments, reflecting the uncertainty in each of these markets.

As well as the changes occurring in the Eastern bloc and the forming of a new giant competitor of the European Community, there is the continuing instability in the Middle East, with its vast surplus of oil. These are directly affecting the value of the U.S. dollar, reducing its value in comparison with other strong world currencies.

As was argued throughout this work, a country's $\bar{I}_t$ is determined by its welfare utility function and its currency value with respect to trade. Its currency's value is determined by the efficiency of industry, government, and labor in maintaining the economy on a growth pattern, and by the demand for the currency for both speculation and for transactions and reserve holdings by other countries.

The U.S. position in the world economy is certainly unique to our era. In the present social time[4] its currency value is low internationally, while its economic strength and production potential still are unmatched by any other country. It has a massive trade deficit, yet supports much of the world's economies through overt and covert financial assistance, and the developing economies are seeking favored nation status in their trade relations.

A closer examination of the U.S. economy reveals an economic system, extremely dynamic and innovative, with imitative industries ready to enter into profitable markets. The government sector, however, is still haunted by the Great Depression, the ghost of which appears during every recession. Its welfare system stands within two dynamic and often opposing concepts. There is the socialization concept as expressed by Medicare and Medicaid, and by the sponsoring of programs for assisting small businesses such as the Small Business Act of 1953, and the Minority Business Development Agency, founded in 1979, to assist minority businesses. The other concept is the strict Jeffersonian tradition of the government that governs least, governs best and the laissez-faire philosophy that developed from the writings of Adam Smith, J.B. Say, and the other early modern economists. Every consideration toward welfare has been taken with respect to the socialization and the Jeffersonian laissez-faire traditions. It was during the Great Depression, however, when it was understood that the U.S. economy had become highly complex, far removed from the simple economy that existed during the early years of the country. There was a need, therefore, to serve the welfare of the people, without overstepping the bounds of a liberal economic system. Government had to become active, but not at the expense of curtailing individual liberties. This situation exists today and is responsible for the working of the three sectors in the economy. The government's role is to maintain the economy and its welfare without infringing on individual liberties. In the area of social welfare, this is crucial.

The United States has an internal debt, but its welfare system is evolving to assist those who are in need. During the energy crisis following the Yom Kippur war, the welfare system was thrown into disarray. Overlapping agencies, uncoordinated programs with gaps, cross-purposes, and other deficiencies became glaring as the government struggled with the unemployment that the energy crisis generated. Money had to be allocated to these programs and with unemployment up and production slacking, inflation was the result. Interest rates were raised to curtail borrowing and encourage investing, but liquidity was short due to unemployment, and inflation continued to rise. With the energy crisis eventually under control, the economy began producing once again and its inflation rate declined and unemployment dropped accordingly. The welfare system was still intact and the government's goal was to reduce significantly the number of recipients of its generosity. The Reagan administration sought to streamline the welfare system by cutting the programs that benefited the poor and to place greater responsibility on industry for retraining these needy people and absorbing them into the production process—another example of genuine social concern and the Jeffersonian laissez-faire concepts. In this manner the reliance and burden on the welfare system were to be reduced and production increased accordingly because of the newly employed.

Industry, however, is not altruistic when employing people it does not require. The recession of the 1970s had certainly prevented economic expansion, and the cycle began to swing upward when the Reagan administration began its first term in 1981. Then industry was willing to employ more people as suited its position, but not because of government encouragement. By 1988 the cycle had moved upward sufficiently that in the Economic Report of the President in February 1988 it was stated that "the investment in formal worker-sponsored training has been estimated to be about 60 billion per year and has been rising."[5] But this has resulted in reduced aggregate wages for the trainees and reliance on the welfare system for additional compensation during the training periods and for family support in general. Moreover, this retraining is a result of the cycle's upward movement, in which a better economic climate for expansion exists than with the administration's program of streamlining the welfare system, reducing its role in society and replacing it to a large extent with industrial employment for a continuously expanding market-oriented economy.

A continuously expanding market-oriented economy is dynamic and also export-oriented. The U.S. economy is so oriented, and has direct exports and multinational companies in many parts of the world. The economy's strength is so important for the rest of the world that countries once hostile in the Cold War environment are seeking favored nation trade status with reduced tariffs and the opportunities for economic development through trading.

Still, the United States has a severe balance of trade deficit that is worrying. This is not, however, because of losses made on trading agreements by the country's industries and businesses. It is because of its vast aid programs, in part necessary to support allegiances made in the chill of the Cold War, such as NATO (North Atlantic Treaty Organization) and the allies in the Middle East, such as Israel and, since Anwar Sadat's trip to Jerusalem, Egypt.

While NATO's significance is being reduced due to the new global political situation, with a co-measured reduction of its opposition, the Warsaw Pact, the Middle East still remains a source for vast amounts of U.S. aid. The situation in Asia, with the overtures being made by Vietnam, Cambodia, and other countries that were once areas of great hostility and bloodshed in war, also require aid and to some extent trade. While the money invested in these areas is registered as a deficit in the accounting procedures in the budget, the investments are made within a "short-term" loss, in order to establish the economies of these countries on a basis of growth and genuine trade, for their future industries and U.S. industries alike. Until this happens, there is the deficit due to these countries and it will most likely grow.

The Middle East is, perhaps, the most sensitive region. Its continuing drive toward fundamentalism on the one hand and modernization on the other is sufficient enough for concern and for attempting to invest in these countries to bring their economies, in all aspects, in line with the major economies of the West. With its heavy investments in oil, and the crucial role that oil has played in the world's economies since 1973, tremendous amounts of money and infrastructure have been invested just to protect the energy sources. This has also contributed to the deficit in the balance of payments, and its reward is the purchase of oil at reasonable prices and the guarantee of its flow. Granted that this heavy investment in protection was undertaken originally in the Cold War to keep the Soviet Union and its allies away from the crucial product; but now, with the Cold War fading into history, this protection is still needed to keep the oil producing countries secure among themselves.[6] The Middle East is still highly unstable, and with the Iran-Iraq war over and the heavy costs that have to be paid for that war, each country is seeking funds from other sources. The United States is supporting Iran to some extent in the revitalization of its war-torn economy, and was also assisting Iraq. But in the balance of power that prevails in that region, enemies soon become friends and friends are invaded as blood enemies. The investments made in protection have been to maintain a degree of stability, but these investments have added to the balance of payments deficit. Accounting describes the situation, but policy determines the reality of the situation.

Considering its $\bar{I}_t$, the U.S. currency is low with respect to the other hard currencies. The Japanese, for example, deal extensively in trade, but their international political commitments are nil compared to the United States, so that their activities are commercial and receive the value of their bargaining. The Germans are currently engaged in reunification, and their political contribution lies in assisting the Soviet economy—a payoff for allowing reunification. Both the French and the British have forces in other parts of the world—the Middle East, for example, and this places a strain on their economies. Their commitments, however, are nowhere near the same proportion as those of the U.S. economy. The point is that the world demand for the dollar has diminished due to the international lack of confidence in the U.S. economy to both meet its international commitments and maintain growth and active innovation and imitation. The reliance on the welfare system is an indicator for these countries, although their own welfare systems are extensive and contain inefficiencies.

To project into the future would be foolish, but to consider the future with respect to the present can provide possible guidelines as to what the future may bring and how to prepare for it. The business cycle is built into our system, and this system is now being adopted by the world's economies. The stronger the economy, the better it can adapt to the cycle's changes. The U.S. economy is certainly strong enough to survive all crises economically caused, because unlike its competitors, it has the ethos of the Jeffersonian dictum and of laissez-faire combined with a social awareness brought about by the Great Depression. Its economy remains vital and dynamic and will ride out internal difficulties. It has international competitors: the Japanese and German economies are strong, and the British and French economies provide challenges. Moreover, with the European Community coming together in 1992, and with the dictates of the United States restraints on its budget, difficult times are ahead for the country. But it was a country that thrived on competition and will continue to do so. It will continue to be a major force in international finance and its diverse population will require its citizens to sharpen their wits in business. Its currency may be valued low with respect to other hard currencies, but its international utility function includes its welfare utility function; its industries, its government, and its labor are strong working forces and their continuing to be so guarantees the United States the central position in the world's political and economic markets.

Chapter 12

CONCLUDING COMMENTS

Practical men, who believe themselves to be quite exempt from any intellectual influences, are usually the slaves of some defunct economist. Madmen in authority, who hear voices in the air, are distilling their frenzy from some academic scribbler of a few years back. I am sure that the power of vested interests is vastly exaggerated compared with the gradual encroachment of ideas. Not, indeed, immediately, but after a certain interval; for in the field of economic and political philosophy there are not many who are influenced by new theories after they are twenty-five or thirty years of age, so that the ideas which civil servants and politicians and even agitators apply to current events are not likely to be the newest. But soon or late, it is ideas, not vested interests, which are dangerous for good or evil.

—John Maynard Keynes,
The General Theory of Employment Interest and Money[1]

We have works of historians who have recorded for posterity the attitudes and policies of history's madmen who held political authority throughout the eras of social and political development. However, it is in our century, when the countries of Europe and Asia and of South America have been drawn together politically and economically, that the destruction has been the most horrendous and devastating. Even our era is characterized by the turmoil in Africa and the Middle East, and by the lack of direction being experienced by those countries in the Eastern bloc that are now in the centrifugal storm brewing in the Soviet

Union. Madmen and sane men have confronted one another with the power of their armies and have destroyed the lives of nations. The deaths in World War I were not enough for the madmen who sought vengeance and initiated World War II. The conflict of ideologies that followed has been responsible for the nations' wealth, in human lives and in resources, to be channeled into the means of war. Our era of knowledge has led to the increase in science and technology for the improvement of mankind; science and technology are also being used to hone instruments of destruction and war and to "improve" on their means of application.

The distrust of the foreigner has always been a motivating factor for the madmen in authority to muster their peoples into battle. The unification of Europe, for example, has always been an ideal among its leaders. But Europe contains "foreigners" and therefore such unification can be valid only when imposed by a superior race or country or nation who can keep the foreigners in their place. This is why such unification, until now, has always failed. It will succeed in 1992 because the representatives of the member countries meet with and deal with each other as equals in a grand and exciting program.[2]

International trade is, by definition, commerce among foreigners, and because it is commerce, there is mutual respect in the realm of economics among the trading partners. Aid, however, is not provided by the motivation of respect, but from a superior attitude of wanting to help, or of having to help for international political reasons. These are vested interests, such as Keynes mentioned. But the idea, promulgated after World War II, that trade must be encouraged and able to flow with minimum constraints, was the impetus for the creation of the International Monetary Fund, GATT, and the World Bank, established to provide the necessary economic and political means for moving the nations of the world into the direction of such trade.

Our world is still indecisive in this endeavor. There are still boycotts, embargoes, and absence of trading due to the lack of diplomatic relations. Again, the "foreigner" is suspect. Either religion or race or political orientation are involved, and these are always alien and hence unacceptable.

But the idea of a world at peace is still penetrating these barriers. Multinationals and customs unions break the walls of suspicion of foreigners. Indeed, any industry that has the resources and the goods and services demanded by the world's countries can be a multinational. The European Community is uniting countries that were historically bitter enemies in the necessity of trade among equals, and other countries are restructuring their economies to take advantage of this market potential.

Vested interests have kept the walls up that have separated countries. Religion, race, political differences—the distrust of the foreigner—have been exploited by the madmen in authority to keep their power. But the idea of world union through diversification, of different cultures, religions, races working together and exploiting their unique qualities, manifested in their cultures is now prevailing. There are world tensions but these are offset by the ability for coexistence among the many nations. But nations must meet one another as equals for peace to prevail, and one certain way that this has been achieved is with nations meeting in the arena of international trade, with commerce being conducted for the benefit of producers and consumers alike.

NOTES

CHAPTER 1

1. Jacob Viner, *Studies in the Theory of International Trade* (London: Allen and Unwin, 1937), p. 291.

2. See John Maynard Keynes, *The General Theory of Employment Interest and Money* (London: Macmillan and Co., 1947).

3. See Adam Smith, *An Inquiry into the Nature and Causes of the Wealth of Nations,* ed. Edwin Cannan (New York: Modern Library, 1937), esp. pp. 420–55.

4. See this writer's discussion and critique of Say's Law of Markets in *Contemporary Economics: A Unifying Approach* (New York: Praeger, 1986), pp. 5–25. Say's Law is one of the most important laws of economics and is based on Smith's "invisible hand." It has been repudiated by such economists as Malthus in his Letters, and Keynes in the *General Theory;* yet, it is the basis for equilibrium theory in economics.

5. See David Ricardo, *Principles of Political Economy and Taxation* (New York: Dutton, Everyman, 1911), esp. Chap. 7, for his treatment of comparative costs.

6. A consequence of this Ricardian argument is that the mechanism for clearing the domestic markets also affects the foreign markets. As exports stem from domestic production and are surpluses transferred for imports and/or coin, then products that are in demand internationally but have little domestic appeal, will have to be phased out. Ricardo did not develop this aspect of foreign trade sufficiently, but perhaps this was due to the fact that the Industrial Revolution was still in its early stages, and the concept of producing for exports primarily was not relevant.

7. Hume's emphasis was not, therefore, placed primarily on money or gold, as was for the mercantilists. He emphasized production, with supply and demand being regulated by money. In this sense Hume was not primarily a monetary theorist, but—like

Adam Smith after him—a true forerunner to Keynes. However, with money serving to clear the international markets among trading countries, Hume can be seen as a precursor to Say, who focused on the domestic markets. Indeed, Hume's Law can be understood as an international version of Say's Law. It appears, then, that an "invisible hand" has lurked in economic theory in several forms, both pre- and post-Smith.

8. See David Hume, *Writings on Economics,* Eugene Rotwein, ed. (Salem, NH: Ayer Co., Publishers, 1955). See also, Hume's *Political Discourses* (Edinburgh, 1752). Two essays from this work are reprinted in *Readings in Economics,* ed. K. William Kapp and Lore L. Kapp (New York: Barnes and Noble, 1953). The essays are: "Of Money," and "Of the Balance of Trade," pp. 82–96.

9. See John Stuart Mill, *Essays on Some Unsettled Questions in Political Economy,* reprint of the 2d ed. (New York: Augustus Kelley, 1978). See also, *Principles of Political Economy,* Introduction by William Ashley (New York: Augustus Kelley, 1987); see also, *The Influence of the State in the Economic Growth of Nations* (Albuquerque, NM: Found Class Reprint of 1923 ed.)

10. W. Arthur Lewis, *Theory of Economic Growth* (London: Unwin University Books, 1965), p. 340.

11. For example, President Jimmy Carter's sanctions against the Soviet Union because of the Soviet invasion of Afghanistan, the boycott of South Africa because of that country's policy of apartheid, and the Arab League's boycott of Israel because that country exists.

CHAPTER 2

1. Milton Friedman, "The Case for Flexible Exchange Rates," in *Essays in Positive Economics* (Chicago: Chicago University Press, 1966), p. 164. See also Ronald MacDonald, "Introduction: The Case for Flexible Exchange Rates and Some Stylized Facts from the Recent Experience With Floating Exchange Rates," in *Floating Exchange Rates: Theories and Evidence* (London: Unwin Hyman Ltd., 1988), pp. 1–37.

2. Friedman, "Case for Flexible Exchange Rates," pp. 162–63.

3. For a discussion on this new era and its actual and potential ramifications, see David Z. Rich, *The Dynamics of Knowledge: A Contemporary View* (Westport, CT: Greenwood Press, 1988).

4. The IMF originally represented largely the conception of H. D. White of the United States Treasury, rather than Keynes's approach that he had formulated in opposition to White's plan. See *Review of the Executive Directors and Summary Proceedings,* First Annual Meeting of the Board of Governors, International Monetary Fund (November 1948).

5. Of course, the goal was the elimination of tariffs after the countries established sufficiently strong foundations to be able to compete effectively. Thus, the tariffs that were erected were tolerated, although in several countries, Japan being one, they did not come down to any extent, relative to the other countries.

6. For a discussion on this point, see David Z. Rich, "Introductory Comments on the Cycle," in *Contemporary Economics: A Unifying Approach* (New York: Praeger, 1986), pp. 111–19.

7. See, for example, Arthur C. Pigou, *The Economics of Welfare* (London: Macmillan, 1920), and J. M. Keynes's critique of Pigou's argument in *The General Theory of Employment Interest and Money* (London: Macmillan, 1947), pp. 272–79. See also my

work, *The Economics of Welfare: A Contemporary Analysis* (New York: Praeger, 1989), pp. 102–48, for the discussion on the welfare utility function. Keynes's critique of Pigou is based on his argument against the neoclassical Pigovian assumption of full employment. In my work, employment is one function on the business cycle, and can be treated with respect to the cycle's position.

8. Japan was able to wage a prolonged war in China and then against the Allied forces because it had a disciplined work force and a potentially strong industrial base that was converted from peacetime to wartime production. Having received extensive assistance from the United States after the war, its reconstruction was successful and its industry is now among the most productive and influential in the world.

9. Hence, for Japan to maintain its level of production and indeed expand it, it acquiesced to the Arab countries' demand that it accept the United Nations resolution that Zionism is a racist movement.

CHAPTER 3

1. Arthur I. Bloomfield and Wilfred Ethier, "Developments in International Economics," in *Modern Economic Thought,* ed. Sidney Weintraub (Philadelphia: University of Pennsylvania Press, 1977), Essay 26, p. 517.

2. See James Tobin, *Asset Accumulation and Economic Activity* (Chicago: Chicago University Press, 1980), p. 95.

3. The lack of viable substitutes pegs demand to the supply of these products, but cyclical changes influence the quantity of demand, even in the two-country two-product model. Demand may decline, reducing supply, but when stability is reached, with demand equalling supply, the elasticities will not be tending toward infinity, as the supply curves slope downward and the demand curves upward. Elasticities will always tend to 1.

See Abba P. Lerner, *The Economics of Control* (London: Macmillan, 1944), and Alfred Marshall, *Money, Credit and Commerce* (London: Macmillan, 1923).

4. See Paul A. Samuelson, "International Trade and the Equalization of Factor Prices," *Economic Journal* 58 (1948): 163–84.

5. See Paul A. Samuelson, "International Factor Price Equalization," *Economic Journal* 59 (1949), and Wolfgang F. Stopler and Paul A. Samuelson, "Protection and Real Wages," *Review of Economic Studies* 9 (1941): 58–73.

6. See T. M. Rybczynski's article, "Factor Endowment and Relative Commodity Prices," *Economica* 22 (1955): 336–41.

7. Wassily Leontief's article "Domestic Production and Foreign Trade: The American Capital Position Re-Examined," *Economica Internazionale,* 7 (1954): 3–32, discusses this argument. Moreover, see his "Explanatory Power of the Contemporary Cost Theory of International Trade and its Limits," in his *Essays in Economics* (New Brunswick: Transaction Books, 1985), pp. 373–80. This essay was published previously in *Economic Structure and Development* (Amsterdam: North Holland Publishing Co., and New York: American Elsevier Publishing Co., 1973), pp. 153–60.

8. Richard J. Barnet and Ronald E. Müller, *Global Reach* (New York: Simon & Schuster, 1974), p. 260.

9. J. Marcus Fleming, "Domestic Financial Policies Under Fixed and Under Floating Exchange Rates," in *International Finance* ed. R. N. Cooper (Baltimore: Penguin Books, 1972), p. 299. Reprinted from *International Monetary Fund Staff Papers* 9, 3, (1962).

See also, R. A. Mundell, "Capital Mobility and Stabilization Policy Under Fixed and Flexible Exchange Rates," *Canadian Journal of Economics* (November 1963): 475–85. Also, see the discussion on the Mundell-Fleming model in Ronald MacDonald, *Floating Exchange Rates: Theories and Evidence* (London: Unwin Hyman, 1988), pp. 41–58, and the bibliographical listings for the works of these men.

10. See Gustav Cassel, *Money and Foreign Exchange After 1914* (New York: Macmillan Co., 1923) and L. A. Metzler's review of Cassel's work, "Exchange Rates and the International Monetary Fund," in *International Monetary Policies* (Washington, DC: Federal Reserve System, October 1947).

11. Bela Balassa, "The Purchasing-Power Parity Doctrine: A Reprisal," *Journal of Political Economy* 72 (1964): 584–96. Quoted here in *International Finance,* ed. R. N. Cooper, p. 205.

12. For uncertainty in the physical sciences, see Werner Heisenberg, *The Physical Principles of the Quantum Theory,* trans. Carl Eckart and Frank C. Hoyt (New York: Dover Publications, n.d.). In this work, Heisenberg elaborates on his famous uncertainty principle, in which both the position and the velocity of a sub-atomic particle cannot be known at the same time. The knowledge of one is on account of the knowledge of the other, as the observer interacts with the observed and exerts an unwilling influence.

Uncertainty in mathematics is found with Gödel's Proof and with the attempts prior to Gödel and since to axiomatize mathematics. Moreover, with the new nonstandard analysis, a system of mathematics is being developed, with its direction and consequences still not clear. See Kurt Gödel, "On Formally Undecidable Propositions," in *"Principia Mathematica" and Related Systems,* trans. Bernard Meltzer. Introduction by R. B. Braithwaite (New York: Basic Books, 1962). Also see Morris Kline, *Mathematics: The Loss of Certainty* (New York: Oxford University Press, 1982), esp. chaps. 12–15. Also, see Edna Kramer, *The Nature and Growth of Modern Mathematics* (Princeton: Princeton University Press, 1982), esp. chaps. 27–30.

13. Indeed, such a derivation can be found in David Z. Rich, *Contemporary Economics: A Unifying Approach* (New York: Praeger, 1986), pp. 8–12.

CHAPTER 4

1. Guy Routh, *The Origin of Economic Ideas* (New York: Vintage Books, 1977), pp. 301–2.

2. See David Z. Rich, *The Dynamics of Knowledge* (Westport, CT: Greenwood, 1988), especially Part III, "The Dynamics of Our Era of Knowledge," pp. 131–202.

3. See J.-C.-L. Simonde de Sismondi, *Nouveaux Principles d'Economie Politique* (Paris: Galmann-Lévy, 1971); and James Mill's article, "The Article on Government," Supplement to 1829 ed. of *Encyclopaedia Britannica.* With respect to Mill the elder, his economics and political philosophy are considered to be the cut-off point in the history of the disciplines, separating classical from neoclassical economic thinking, with Marx as the watershed. Marx wrote *Capital* while in London, and he was certainly influenced by Ricardo's and Mill's works. While Ricardo emphasized the economics, Mill emphasized the political aspects of economic theory. Marx synthesized these differing approaches into a unified theory of political economy.

See Alfred Marshall, *Principles of Economics,* 9th ed. (London: Macmillan, for the Royal Economic Society, 1961); Joseph A. Schumpeter, *The Theory of Economic De-*

velopment, trans. Redvers Opie, (New York: Oxford University Press, 1969), and the discussion on Schumpeter's theory in David Z. Rich, *Contemporary Economics: A Unifying Approach* (New York: Praeger, 1986), pp. 103, 105–7; Vilfredo Pareto, *Manual of Political Economy,* trans. Ann Schwier and Alfred Page, (New York: Augustus M. Kelley, 1971), the discussion on Pareto's economics in David Z. Rich, *The Economics of Welfare: A Contemporary Analysis* (New York: Praeger, 1989), pp. 18, 19, 24, and James Burnham's discussion on Pareto in *The Machiavellians* (Chicago: Gateway Edition, 1963), pp. 191–248.

CHAPTER 5

1. Gottfried Haberler, "The Market for Foreign Exchange and the Stability of the Balance of Payments: A Theoretical Analysis," *Kyklos* 3 (1949): 193–218. Quoted here from *International Finance,* ed. R. N. Cooper (Baltimore: Penguin Books, 1972), pp. 132–33.

2. See John Maynard Keynes, *The General Theory of Employment Interest and Money* (London: Macmillan and Co., Ltd, 1947), pp. 135–46.

3. Keynes, *The General Theory,* p. 141.

4. The concepts of innovation and imitation with respect to economics were explored and developed in my work, *Contemporary Economics: A Unifying Approach* (New York: Praeger, 1986), pp. 90–143.

5. Robin Marris, *The Economic Theory of "Managerial" Capitalism* (London: Macmillan and Co. Ltd, 1967), p. 108.

6. Herbert A. Simon, "Theories of Decision-Making in Economics and Behavioral Science," *American Economic Review 49* (1959):253–83. Quoted here from *Managerial Economics,* ed. G. P. E. Clarkson (Baltimore: Penguin Books, 1968), p. 26.

7. Simon, "Theories of Decision-Making in Economics," p. 28.

8. See, for example, the discussion on the U.S. welfare system in David Rich, *The Economics of Welfare: A Contemporary Analysis* (New York: Praeger, 1989), Chap. 12, pp. 151–73.

CHAPTER 6

1. Jacob T. Schwartz, "Mathematics as a Tool for Economic Reasoning," in *Mathematics Today,* ed. Lynn Arthur Steen (New York: Vantage Books, 1980), p. 285.

2. An economy in constant equilibrium can be considered a strict welfare economy, as innovations and imitations are nonexistent and the government therefore controls the means of production and distribution. To maintain its position, the government must demonstrate a degree of benevolence in the distribution of the goods and services; otherwise, it will be overthrown and a more dynamic economy instituted—as recent events in Eastern Europe have attested.

3. The terms *innovation* and *imitation* were developed rigorously in my work, *Contemporary Economics: A Unifying Approach* (New York: Praeger, 1986), pp. 92–107.

See also, Eugin E. Slutsky's "On the Theory of the Budget of the Consumer," in *Readings in Price Theory* (London: Allen and Unwin, 1953), and my critique of Slutsky's theory in *The Economics of Welfare: A Contemporary Analysis,* (New York: Praeger, 1989), pp. 23–26.

4. For a discussion of "sheeplike behavior," see Robin Marris, *The Economic Theory of 'Managerial' Capitalism* (London: Macmillan, 1967), pp. 142–45.

5. Emmanuel Farjoun and Moshe Machover, *Laws of Chaos* (London: Verso Editions, 1983), p. 33.

6. See Arthur C. Pigou's *Economics of Welfare* (London: Macmillan, 1920), and Keynes's critique in *The General Theory of Employment Interest and Money* (London: Macmillan, 1947), pp. 272–79. The work to which Keynes refers is the 4th ed., 1932, when the Great Depression was making its full impact.

7. See J. A. Schumpeter, *The Theory of Economic Development*, trans. Redvers Opie (New York: Oxford University Press, 1969): see also my critique of Schumpeter in *Contemporary Economics*, pp. 90–99.

8. See *Sir Isaac Newton's Mathematical Principles of Natural Philosophy* Florian Casori's revision of the 1979 translation, ed. Andrew Motte (Berkeley: University of California Press, 1947).

9. See Alfred Marshall's classic, *Principles of Economics*, 8th ed. (London: Macmillan, 1890), and *Money, Credit and Commerce* (London: Macmillan, 1923).

10. For an interesting but somewhat Marxist-oriented discussion on the development of industrialization, see Immanuel Wallerstein's collected essays in his book *The Capitalist World-Economy* (New York: Cambridge University Press, 1987), especially his chapter "The Rise and Future Demise of the Capitalist System: Concepts for Comparative Analysis," pp. 1–36.

11. The labor movement is as old as the guild associations. But during the Great Depression when labor was confronted with high unemployment, unions grew in strength and in influence to protect the rights of those workers still employed and to insure fair wages and decent working conditions for those who would find employment when the Depression ended. The general sympathy for the plight of the workers during that troubled period certainly provided the conditions in which the labor movement could advance.

12. See Alan Turing's essay, "Computing Machinery and Intelligence," reprinted in *Minds and Machines,* ed. Alan Ross Anderson (Englewood Cliffs, NJ: Prentice-Hall, 1964).

13. How far back in history the notion of the atom goes is far from certain. But the Greek Democritus (c. 460–c. 370 B.C.) and later, the Roman Lucretius (c. 96–c. 55 B.C.) were instrumental in the development of this concept.

14. Even matters of defense can be directly related to welfare, because the decision to establish a defense-based industry or to close one in a region affects business in that region when implemented, thereby influencing the employment situation and regional development.

15. There is another sector of society that cannot be dealt with here. This is the sector of the economically (and hence socially) disenfranchised; those people who are poor or indigent and without assistance other than welfare, and those people who are homeless and must beg for their livelihoods. See Rich, *The Economics of Welfare,* pp. 109, 110, and Chaps. 10 and 11, pp. 111–48, for a discussion of the business cycle and poverty.

16. For discussions on this point, see Rich, *Contemporary Economics,* Chap. 8, pp. 120–43; and Rich, *The Economics of Welfare,* Chap. 7, pp. 62–96.

CHAPTER 7

1. David Hume, "Of the Balance of Trade," from *Essays, Moral, Political and Literary*, vol. 1. (London: Longmans Green, 1898). Quoted here from *International Finance*, ed. R. N. Cooper (Baltimore, MD: Penguin Books, 1972), p. 33.

2. For a discussion on this, see David Z. Rich, *The Economics of Welfare: A Contemporary Analysis* (New York: Praeger, 1989), Chap. 12, pp. 151–71.

3. See the discussion on this point in David Z. Rich, *Contemporary Economics: A Unifying Approach* (New York: Praeger, 1986), Chap. 8, pp. 120–43, and Rich, *The Economics of Welfare*, Chap. 7, pp. 63–96.

4. For a discussion on liquidity, money, consumption, and disposable income, see Rich, *The Economics of Welfare*, Chap. 7, pp. 63–74.

5. The variables y_c and y_d are interchangeable when $y_c > y_d$, so that savings and investments are reduced and consumption increased.

6. This was the objective with my *Contemporary Economics* concerning the theoretical and practical concepts and applications of contemporary economics; it was also the objective in my *Economics of Welfare* with respect to welfare economics and micro and macroeconomic dynamics. It is also the objective of this present work concerning international economics, and for this reason the welfare utility function has been extended into an international utility function.

7. For example, the costs of alternative resources will be reduced due to competition, as close alternative resources compete for uses. Also, alternative production methods will lead to the most efficient method at the lowest costs of production.

8. See Rich, *The Economics of Welfare*, pp. 141–43, for further comments on these points.

9. See Immanuel Wallerstein's chapters, "An Historical Perspective on the Emergence of the New International Order: Economic, Political, Cultural Aspects," and "Class Conflict in the Capitalist World-Economy," in *The Capitalist World-Economy* (New York: Cambridge University Press, 1987), pp. 269–83.

10. Charles P. Kindleberger, *International Economics* (Homewood, IL: Richard D. Irwin, 1963), p. 132. With respect to the demonstration effect, Kindleberger refers to Rangar Nurske but does not provide a source.

11. The economics of the underdeveloped countries will be treated in a later work. These economics have nineteenth-century economic circumstances and are trying to compete with the developed countries, to achieve their living standards, their levels of education, and certainly acquire their technologies. Their economic development is hindered by their frequent political and military conflicts with their neighbors, or as surrogates during periods of military tension. They are thus in the late twentieth-century paradox of maintaining their historical identities which keeps them in a nineteenth-century economic situation, and acquire the benefits of the developed economies, which they cannot afford. But, as was said, this will have to wait.

12. The Hecksher-Ohlin model of factor endowments and trade has become standard in the textbooks on trade. Its advantage is that it concentrates on the interrelationship between a nation's pattern of international trade and its endowment factors of production, including capital. See Kindleberger, *International Economics*, p. 246.

See also J. M. Keynes's discussion on E. Hechscher's work, *Mercantilism*, in *The General Theory of Employment Interest and Money* (London: Macmillan, 1947), pp.

341–50, 358; and Bertil Ohlin's classic work, *Interregional and International Trade* (Cambridge MA: Harvard University Press, 1933).

CHAPTER 8

1. Developing countries such as Brazil, China, and Chile direct enormous resources into the armaments industries in order to gain windfall profits from the demand for arms. But this is done at the expense of channeling resources into the development of viable economic industries that can compete successfully in the international markets for consumer goods and services.

2. See Tim Congdon, *The Debt Threat* (New York: Basil Blackwell, 1988), especially Chaps. 2 and 5. This is an important work, one that should be read by economists concerned with domestic and international economics.

3. See David Z. Rich, *The Economics of Welfare: A Contemporary Analysis* (New York: Praeger, 1989), Chap. 12, pp. 151–71 for a discussion on and possible solutions to this problem.

CHAPTER 9

1. Richard J. Barnett and Ronald E. Müller, *Global Reach* (New York: Simon and Schuster, 1974), p. 14.

2. Richard E. Caves, *Multinational Enterprises and Economic Analysis* (New York: Cambridge University Press, 1985), p. 194.

3. Barnett and Müller, *Global Reach*, p. 152.

4. Michel Foucault, *Foucault Reader*, ed. Paul Rainbow (New York: Pantheon Books, 1984), p. 14.

5. Caves, *Multinational Enterprises*, p. 194.

6. Ibid., p. 253.

7. Ibid., Chap. 10, pp. 279–99.

CHAPTER 10

1. J. C. Ingram, "Some Implications of Puerto Rican Experience," in *International Finance*, ed. R. N. Cooper (Baltimore, MD: Penguin Books, 1969), p. 97. From *Regional Payments Mechanism: The Case of Puerto Rico* (Chapel Hill: University of North Carolina Press, 1962), pp. 113–33.

2. Charles P. Kindleberger, *International Economics* (Homewood, IL: Richard D. Irwin, 1963), p. 321.

3. Even though these losses can be used as tax write-offs, the difficulties of obtaining resources and alternative resources in production makes profits a better position than losses for tax benefits. Production is based on utility, and losses, even for taxes, place industries in entropic positions, reducing their chances at liquidity and the maneuverability liquidity provides.

CHAPTER 11

1. Had the situation in the European Economic Community remained unchanged, that is, without the final coming together and merging into a powerful customs union, the

Cold War would have thawed but at a slower pace. Moreover, the Soviet economy would have changed gradually. But Mikhail Gorbachev's astute awareness of the situation that would exist once the Community was finally formed, brought him to the point that economic changes would have to be rapid and painful, introducing into the Soviet economy concepts that had been alien for so long. Gorbachev's political and economic acumen have made him into a great world leader.

2. The Medicare Act of 1965, and later Medicaid, were programs initiated by the U.S. government. The cry of socialized medicine was raised by their opponents, but the programs have provided the basis for treatment for people who could not afford it and would have otherwise had to go without.

3. The current energy crisis brought about by the confrontation with Iraq has not had the psychological effect as did the energy crisis following the Yom Kippur war. This is due to a wiser public and better prepared energy systems and oil stocks held in reserve.

4. In *The Dynamics of Knowledge: A Contemporary View* (Westport, CT: Greenwood Press, 1988, p. 29) social time was stated as being delineated by the specific universal contributions made in the era. Perhaps historians will call our social time as the decline of the Cold War and the search for a new political order, see, however, Chap. 2, pp. 19–38.

5. From the Economic Report of the President "Human Capital" section, (Washington, DC: U.S. Government Printing Office, 1988), pp. 165–77; quoted here from page 171.

6. The current crisis with Iraq indeed expresses this, as oil producers such as Iraq and Saudi Arabia face one another in preparation for battle. Oil producers such as Egypt for the Arabs and the United States and Great Britain for the Western countries, are also involved. At the time of this writing, the problem has not yet been resolved. Diplomacy and the military posturing are being used to defuse the situation and it is hoped that it will be resolved without bloodshed; the gains achieved from its resolution will, moreover, set the policies for energy procurement for the next decades.

CHAPTER 12

1. John Maynard Keynes, *The General Theory of Employment Interest and Money* (London: Macmillan, 1947), pp. 383–84.

2. The Indian subcontinent could establish a customs union, as the histories of the peoples certainly unites them, especially after World War II. Here, it is religion that keeps up the barrier. In Africa, it is tribal distinctions. But these barriers will fall under the impact of the current world dynamics and the necessity for their countries to be economically strong through trade.

SELECTED BIBLIOGRAPHY

Three books cited in this work include extensive bibliographies and should be referred to for the relevant topic.

For general international trade theory, in which classical, neoclassical, and middle-period Keynesian theories are discussed, see Charles P. Kindleberger, *International Economics,* 3d ed. (Homewood, IL: Richard D. Irwin, 1963). For a discussion on exchange rates, see Ronald MacDonald, *Floating Exchange Rates: Theories and Evidence* (London: Unwin Hyman, 1988). For a discussion on multinational enterprises, see Richard E. Caves, *Multinational Enterprise and Economic Analysis* (New York: Cambridge University Press, 1985).

Arendt, Sven W., Richard J. Sweeney, and Thomas D. Willett. *Exchange Rates, Trade and the U.S. Economy.* Cambridge, MA: American Enterprise Institute/Ballinger Publications, 1985.

Bauer, Peter T. "Background to Aid." In *Equality, the Third World, and Economic Delusion,* ed. Peter T. Bauer, pp. 138–50. Cambridge, MA: Harvard University Press, 1981.

Bigman, David, and Teizo Taya. *Exchange Rate and Trade Instability.* Cambridge, MA: Ballinger Publications, 1983.

Blackhurst, Richard and Joan Tumlir. *Trade Relations under Flexible Exchange Rates.* Geneva: GATT Studies in International Trade, 1980.

Blaug, Mark. *Economic Theory in Retrospect.* Revised ed. Homewood, IL: Richard D. Irwin, 1968.

Brandt, Willie, *North-South: A Program for Survival.* Cambridge, MA: MIT Press, 1980.

Cline, William R. *International Debt*. Washington, DC: Institute for International Economics. Cambridge, MA: MIT Press, 1984.

Cohen, Benjamin J. *In Whose Interest?* New Haven, CT: Council on Foreign Relations, Yale University Press, 1986.

Corden, W. Max. *Trade Policy and Economic Welfare*. Oxford: Oxford University Press, 1974.

Culberston, John M. *The Trade Threat*. Madison, WI: Twenty-first Century Press, 1989.

Dornbusch, Rudiger. *Exchange Rates and Inflation*. Cambridge, MA: MIT Press, 1989.

Dreyer, Jacob J., Gottfried Harbeler, and Thomas Willett. *The International Monetary System in Time of Turbulence*. Washington, DC: American Enterprise Institute for Public Policy Research, 1982.

Drucker, Peter F. ''Behind Japan's Success.'' In *Toward the Next Economics,* ed. P. F. Drucker, pp. 164–80. New York: Harper and Row, 1981.

Ferris, Paul. *The Master Bankers*. New York: William Morrow, 1984.

Fieleke, Norman S. *The International Economy Under Stress*. Cambridge, MA: Ballinger Publications, 1988.

Gereffi, Gary. ''Development Strategies and the Global Factor.'' *Economic Impact*. Washington, DC: U.S.I.S., 1991, pp. 51–57.

Griffin, K., and A. R. Kahn. ''Poverty in the Third World: Ugly Facts and Fancy Models.'' *World Development* (March 1978): 295–304.

Hogan, Michael J. *The Marshall Plan*. New York: Cambridge University Press, 1987.

Hollinger, Steven, Douglas Hollinger, and Fred M. O'Regan. *Aid For Just Development*. Boulder, CO: Lynne Reiner Publishers, 1988.

International Herald Tribune. Advertisement. ''The Oil Industry.'' Frankfurt, October 16, 1990, pp. 17–19.

———. Advertisement. ''Commercial Real Estate.'' Frankfurt, October 25, 1990, pp. 9, 10.

Kahn, Herman, with the Hudson Institute. *World Economic Development*. New York: Morrow Quill, 1979.

Keohane, Robert O. *After Hegemony*. Princeton, NJ: Princeton University Press, 1984.

Kilby, P. *Entrepreneurship and Economic Development*. New York: Free Press, 1971.

Kissinger, Henry. *A World Restored*. Boston: Houghton Mifflin Co., 1973.

Makin, John H. *The Global Debt Crisis*. New York: Basic Books, 1984.

Mason, Edward S., and R. E. Asher. *The World Bank Since Bretton Woods*. Washington, DC: Brookings Institution, 1973.

Meller, P., and A. Mizala. ''U.S. Multinationals and Latin American Manufacturing Employment Absorption.'' *World Development* (February 1982): 115–26.

Mende, Tibor. *From Aid to Recolonialization: Lessons of a Failure*. London: Harrap, 1973.

Moffitt, Michael. *The World's Money*. New York: Simon and Schuster, 1983.

Mosley, Paul. *Foreign Aid*. Lexington: University of Kentucky, 1982.

Nurske, Rangar. *Equilibrium and Growth in the World Economy*. Cambridge, MA: Harvard University Press, 1961.

Olsen, Mancur. *The Rise and Decline of Nations*. New Haven, CT: Yale University Press, 1982.

Pearce, Ivor F. *International Trade*. London: Macmillan, 1970.

Quigley, Carrol. *The Evolution of Civilizations*. New York: Macmillan, 1961.

Robbins, Sidney M., and Robert B. Stobauch. *Money in the Multinational Enterprise: A Study of Financial Policy.* New York: Basic Books, 1973.

Sampson, Anthony. *The Money Lenders.* New York: Penguin Books, 1983.

———. *The Sovereign State of IT&T.* New York: Stein and Day, 1973.

Stigler, George J. "History of Economic Thought." In *The Economist as Preacher,* ed. George J. Stigler, pp. 107–70. Chicago: Chicago University Press.

Solomon, Robert. *The International Monetary System, 1945–1981.* New York: Harper & Row, 1982.

Turner, Louis. *Invisible Empire.* New York: Harcourt Brace Jovanovich, 1970.

———. *Multinational Companies of the Third World.* New York: Hill and Wang, 1973.

Vernon, Raymond. *The Oil Crisis.* New York: W. W. Norton, 1976.

Weintraub, Sidney. *TIP: To Stop Inflation.* Bryn Mawr, PA, Frank M. Engle Lecture of the American College, 1978.

INDEX

ABOUT THE AUTHOR

DAVID Z. RICH serves as economic consultant to a number of business firms and international corporations. A resident of Israel since 1969, he is the author of *Contemporary Economics: A Unifying Approach* (Praeger, 1986), *The Dynamics of Knowledge: A Contemporary View* (Greenwood, 1988), and *The Economics of Welfare: A Contemporary Analysis* (Praeger, 1989).